W9-APH-565

Above and Beyond

Above and Beyond

From Soviet General
to
Ukrainian State Builder

Kostiantyn P. Morozov

Distributed by Harvard University Press
for the
Ukrainian Research Institute, Harvard University

Publication of this volume has been made possible in part by the generous support of Oleh and Irena Ciuk, in memory of Jaroslaw Ciuk.

CIP data available from the Library of Congress.

© 2000 by the President and Fellows of Harvard College
All rights reserved
ISBN 0-916458-77-6
Printed in Canada by Transcontinental Printing, Inc.

Jennie Bush, *jacket design;* Robert De Lossa, *interior design* and *maps,* pp. xii, 8, and 79; Adrian B. Hewryk, *maps;* pp. xii and 79. The map on p. 32 is taken from Harriet Fast Scott and William F. Scott, *The Armed Forces of the USSR,* 3rd ed. (Boulder, CO: Westview, 1984) and is reproduced with the permission of the authors.

Scholars interested in conducting research in the Kostiantyn Morozov Audio Archive at HURI (which includes thirty-five hours of taped interviews) or those wishing to send editorial correspondence, please write to: HURI Publications, 1583 Massachusetts Ave., Cambridge, MA 02138 USA, *E-mail:* huri@fas.harvard.edu.

The Ukrainian Research Institute was established in 1973 as an integral part of Harvard University. It supports research associates and visiting scholars who are engaged in projects concerned with all aspects of Ukrainian studies. The Institute also works in close cooperation with the Committee on Ukrainian Studies, which supervises and coordinates the teaching of Ukrainian history, language, and literature at Harvard University.

Contents

Above and Beyond

Photo Collections

Acknowledgments

This book had its genesis during my stay at Harvard University during the 1994–1995 academic year. I was a senior research fellow there, associated with the John F. Kennedy (JFK) School of Government and the Harvard Ukrainian Research Institute (HURI). I would like to thank the people who made that stay not only possible, but also intellectually stimulating: Professors George Grabowicz (the director then) and Roman Szporluk (the current director) of HURI, and Prof. Graham Allison (director of the Belfer Center for Science and International Affairs) and Dr. Fiona Hill of the JFK School of Government. Dr. Roman Procyk and Mr. Stephan Chemych, of the Ukrainian Studies Fund, contributed essential support for my stay. They also introduced me to the Ukrainian-American community across the United States, which provided me with indelible memories. I also thank Dr. Lubomyr Hajda of HURI for help that went beyond academic matters and eased my stay in a world very different from my own.

Certain scholars were critical to the process of seeing this book to its completion. Professors Ivan Jaworsky, Anna Procyk, and Teresa Rakowska-Harmstone conducted extensive interviews that gave me the basic materials from which to work and also, importantly, gave me a sense of how Western scholars viewed the times through which I had lived. To this group also belongs Professor Zenovia Sochor Parry, who died at all too young an age while this book was still in its early stages. Professor Sochor Parry not only impressed me greatly during our meetings at Harvard, but also opened up her home to me, which I still remember fondly. Professor Jaworsky continued for many years to work with me on this book and other projects. He provided critical insight for the present volume and a barrage of thoughtful questions that stimulated me to recall many things that I might otherwise have relegated to the farther reaches of my memory. Professor Roman Szporluk, whose work as a historian of Ukraine and Russia I greatly admire, provided the critical service of being my final reader and advisor.

On the technical side, Eugene Sloupsky, Ivan Jaworsky, and Robert De Lossa all translated portions of the text as it evolved from its original Ukrainian form. Oles Berezhny translated the documentary appendices. Ivan Jaworsky also helped me with the initial editing of the masses of Ukrainian text that I had generated. I would like especially to thank G. Patton Wright, my literary editor, for his fine work in assisting me in framing my story and for his excellent writer's eye that helped to make the English translation shine. Mention here should be made also of Professor Michael S. Flier, of HURI, who assisted Mr. Wright with Ukrainian-language issues as he edited the text. When I turned to Mr. De Lossa some years ago for help in recording my memoirs and organizing them into a volume, he responded quickly, overseeing the various steps that have brought *Above and Beyond* to light. He also first suggested the book's name and has—as a tough publisher should—consistently resisted my protestations that humility should give my story a less lofty title. Jennie Bush gave the book its fine dust jacket. Finally, I am grateful to Sherman Garnett for his past work with me, kind words and sharp insight, and, especially, his constancy in support of my country.

✳ ✳ ✳

While contemplating the dedication of this book, I found myself in a quandary. My wife, Raisa, and my mother, Kateryna—both of whom are so important to my story—were clear and heartfelt choices. While I discussed the dedication with Raisa, though, I found that she too felt the dilemma I faced. There were many good men who braved a dangerous world with me and neither of us wanted my story to overshadow them. I thus have dedicated this book to those true heroes who, with me, formed independent Ukraine's first Ministry of Defense. The steps taken to form that ministry were a declaration of belief in Ukraine's own future. And so, in a sense, I am dedicating this book not only to them, but to the future of my country, Ukraine.

These were the men of independent Ukraine's first Ministry of Defense. Risking all, they were true of heart, steadfast in cause, and patriots for their country and their people.

To them I dedicate this book

Lt. Gen. Ivan Bizhan
Lt. Gen. Heorhii Zhyvytsia
Maj. Gen. Heorhii Pankratov
Maj. Gen. Vadym Hrechanynov
Maj. Gen. Anatolii Palamarchuk
Maj. Gen. Grigorii Avdeev
Maj. Gen. Ivan Shtopenko
Maj. Gen. Yurii Prokofiev
Col. Volodymyr Muliava
Col. Ivan Kokoiko
Col. Vytalii Lazorkin
Col. Viktor Hura
Col. Oleksandr Skipalskyi
Col. Oleksandr Nikolskyi
Col. Pavlo Brahar
Col. Ivan Khaletskyi
Col. Vasyl Matyrka
Col. Valerii Pylypchuk
Lt. Col. Ihor Ischenko
Lt. Col. Heorhii Kuznetsov
Maj. Oleksandr Kluban
Maj. Hennadii Karasenkov
Maj. Yurii Iliuschenko
Maj. Serhii Bischuk
Maj. Oleksandr Fedorenko
Lt. Com. Ihor Teniukh
Capt. Yurii Ustinov
1st Lt. Ruslan Anufriiev
2nd Lt. Oleksandr Haidamaka
Chief WO Volodymyr Utenin
Chief WO Borys Dudka

Introduction

General Kostiantyn Morozov is one of those remarkable men who played a crucial role in the transition from empire to independence in the former Soviet Union. To the uninitiated he is less prominent than major Russian actors in the drama, such as Mikhail Gorbachev or Boris Yeltsin. He is less well known in the West than other Ukrainian actors, such as Leonid Kravchuk or Viacheslav Chornovil. Yet he is crucial to the story.

Morozov served as a key air force commander in Soviet Ukraine and later as independent Ukraine's first minister of defense. Though several years of Ukrainian economic and political stagnation have lessened both the hopes and fears that characterized Western observers during the last days of the Soviet Union, Morozov's memoirs remind us what was and still is at stake in Ukrainian independence. They recall the passion, promise, and uncertainty of the late Soviet period in Ukraine, when nothing was in fact certain, but independence no longer seemed like an unrealizable dream. They also record the courage of a man who risked everything for a new—and yet still unrealized—country.

I must confess at the outset my admiration for General Morozov. I first met him in November 1991—in the period described at the very end of this book. I worked in the Office of the Secretary of Defense and was in Ukraine with a delegation of American businessmen led by Deputy Secretary Don Atwood. My most vivid memory from that electrifying trip is not, however, Morozov. I remember how stiff and awkward he seemed at a reception hosted by the American Embassy. It was clear he was still working through the trepidations and responsibilities that his new position brought and which he describes so well in this book. Compared to the tectonic excitement that was felt everywhere we went, whether to see the student protestors in Independence Square or the headquarters of Rukh, it is not surprising that my first memory of Kostiantyn

Morozov is dwarfed by other larger-than-life personalities and events.

But Morozov quickly grew into his job—and I got to watch that growth. In August 1992 I was put in charge of the Pentagon office that was supposed to make some sense of the changes in the former USSR and to fashion new defense partnerships with Ukraine, Russia, and the other new states of the former USSR. In that capacity, I worked closely with Morozov and his senior staff until his resignation from the ministry in October 1993.

By the time of his resignation, Morozov had made a remarkable contribution to the creation of an independent Ukrainian armed forces and a Ministry of Defense. He achieved great progress in assuring the loyalty of the army, establishing Ukrainian administrative control over military installations on Ukrainian territory, and reducing the size of the military. He understood that he could not adopt a Baltic approach to reconfiguring the Ukrainian military. He could not start from scratch, given the size, importance and ethnic composition of Soviet forces in Ukraine. He had to give the opportunity for each and every military officer and enlisted man in Ukraine to remain in the new Ukrainian army if he wished. He had to facilitate a civilized reorganization of Soviet command, educational and training arrangements so that they would become Ukrainian ones. He did in fact give at least 10,000 officers their walking papers, but he managed to do this with no violence and no presumption of disloyalty.

Morozov also by that time had laid the foundations for a normalized security relationship with Russia, though his role consisted largely of necessary assertions of Ukraine's military independence in the face of Russian schemes for the integration of all defensive structures of the CIS countries. Later, more sweeping agreements were built on this foundation. Morozov also understood the importance of cooperation with the United States, Germany, other NATO countries, and Poland. He was the founder of regular consultations and cooperation with each of these countries and with the NATO alliance. He gave a crucial impetus to Ukrainian nuclear disarmament at a time when U.S.-Ukrainian relations were at a standstill over the issue. He did so even though he had doubts about the wisdom of nuclear disarmament in the absence of normal and stable relations with Russia.

My most vivid memory from this period is his visit to the United States in July 1993. He was the first minister of defense from any of the newly independent states of the former Soviet Union to come on an official visit to the Pentagon. During this trip, he pledged his support to further the process of nuclear disarmament in Ukraine. Though much remained to be done with both Russian and Ukrainian officials before this issue was resolved, Morozov's commitment was an important step toward what eventually became the Trilateral Agreement (of January 1994), assuring Ukraine's nuclear disarmament. Morozov's positive step did much to dispel the doubts many in the United States government held about Ukrainian intentions. His diplomatic efforts greatly facilitated the work of those of us who believed Ukraine ought to be an important American strategic partner.

The memoirs before you, however, describe an earlier and crucial period in the life of both Morozov and Ukraine. They begin with Morozov's childhood and early military career. There are many fine moments in this part of the text, including descriptions of the struggles of his mother to raise the family after his father's tragic death, reflections on the Soviet cadre system and its systemic russification, and Morozov's first attempts to understand his Ukrainian identity.

But the meat of the book is the account covering the days of the end of the USSR and the birth of Ukraine itself. In these chapters, Morozov provides a detailed reminiscence of the period from 1988 to early 1992, when he came to Ukraine as the commander of the Soviet 17th Air Army and ended up the first minister of defense of independent Ukraine.

There was nothing inevitable about this sequence of events. Any reader of the memoirs will see what those familiar with Morozov know very well: he is not a schemer or careerist. A careerist would never have put himself out of step with his commanders and the institution he had devoted his life to, while casting his lot with the uncertain enterprise of independence. But there he found himself, as the coup against Gorbachev unfolded and the Soviet Union was unraveling, one of the senior military commanders in Ukraine and a member of the Kyiv Military Council. He was no coup plotter or old guard Soviet officer, but as events began to unfold, he was also not part of the Ukrainian independence movement.

As political life in the late Soviet Union became more open, Morozov naturally followed events closely. His own ethnic background—which he had presumed to be half-Russian and half-Ukrainian (though this presumption later would change in a dramatic revelation)—made him more aware of the pressures exerted by the military to become Russian in behavior, irrespective of natal ethnicity. He had acted at times to promote men, including, but not exclusively, ethnic Ukrainians, who had little chance of reaching the higher levels of the Soviet military. He had even come close to "getting into hot water" over such attempts. But there is nothing in Morozov's early background that suggested how he would react as those epochal events in 1991 unfolded. Indeed, had there been, he never would have gotten so far in the Soviet military.

In the summer of 1990, the Ukrainian Supreme Soviet (*Verkhovna Rada*) passed a declaration of sovereignty. With hindsight, this action looks like the first in an inevitable chain that, along with other events in Lithuania, Russia, and elsewhere in the USSR, led to the break-up of the empire. Yet what would come next was far from clear. Gorbachev was continuing his attempt to fashion a new, more federal union. The voters in the Ukrainian SSR in fact approved such a plan in early 1991. In the aftermath of the sovereignty declaration, leaders of Rukh made the rounds to key political, military, and police figures to gauge their reaction. In that same vein, in August 1991, Ivan Drach came to visit General Morozov. Drach must have been pleasantly surprised to find that Morozov "absolutely accepted Ukrainian independence." Though sympathy for independence was more common among pockets of junior and field grade officers, it was rare at the senior command levels. Morozov, in fact, may have been a group of one at that point.

From then on, Morozov regularly demonstrated his willingness to think and act independently—something that we can appreciate more keenly from his earlier descriptions of the extreme conformism instilled by Soviet military culture. At the time, representatives of the Committee of Soldiers' Mothers were holding demonstrations in Kyiv and around military facilities. The group wanted better living conditions in the military and an end to hazing practices, but it also had a political agenda, insisting that Ukrainian soldiers serve only within the boundaries of Ukraine itself. Some of Morozov's subordinates, echoing no doubt a popular view throughout Soviet military circles in Ukraine, suggested firing a few shots to "teach the demonstrators a lesson." Morozov however issued orders that under no conditions was force to be used. Morozov's remarkable tolerance of change and dissent contrasts sharply with the Soviet military mentalité that he accurately describes as suspicious and hostile to outsiders.

It is during the August 1991 coup that Morozov truly demonstrated his mettle. His control of a major air command in Ukraine gave him a unique seat for observing the behind-the-scenes machinations of the coup. It gave him the possibility, if he so chose, to play a role to help or hinder the coup's success. The senior military officer in the region, General Viktor Chechevatov, commander of the Kyiv Military District, was a supporter of the coup. Chechevatov was helping to arrange the transport of senior military supporters of the coup down to Crimea to confront the vacationing Gorbachev. In doing so, he had to use airplanes and air crews from Morozov's command. Morozov thus early on was alerted to unusual goings-on at a very high level. He questioned Chechevatov about his unusual requests.

When the coup leaders issued orders for a state of emergency in the military, Morozov ordered his air army to remain at its usual status. He informed Marshal Shaposhnikov, then the commander of the Soviet air force, of his refusal to implement the state of emergency. Shaposhnikov, who himself was trying to maneuver through these politically troubled waters, took note of Morozov's actions but issued no supporting orders. Morozov thus found himself on his own—clearly a marked man if the coup succeeded. In the text,

Morozov makes clear his understanding that most of his deputies and the majority of senior officers in his command probably opposed him in his stance, but he proceeded to defy the state of alert and was confident that he would find "many who shared my views among the field grade officers."

In perhaps one of the most gripping episodes of those August days, Morozov learned that someone had ordered troops to be transferred from the Baltic states to Ukraine. He also discovered that these troops would fly into Boryspil Airport outside Kyiv. Ominously, they were ordered to overfly the city at low altitude on their way. Morozov ordered his ground control staff to forbid such an overflight, guessing correctly that it was intended to either provoke or intimidate the democratic opposition as well as ordinary citizens. His subordinates obeyed. The planes flew directly to the airport and were stranded there with their troops. Contrary to the coup plotters' intentions—and due to Morozov's intervention—these forces played no role in Ukrainian politics during this crucial period and Kyiv was spared a potentially destabilizing military threat.

As Morozov explains it, his main aim from August 20 on was to maintain control over his command and "to ensure that the personnel of the 17th Air Army would never be used against the democratic forces in Ukraine." Morozov ensured that his subordinates and others in Ukraine knew his intention, even calling Leonid Kravchuk, the Speaker of the Ukrainian Supreme Soviet, to inform him and to exchange views on the political situation. On August 22, Morozov called together his fellow officers and told them that the Communist Party's involvement in the armed forces was "anti-constitutional and anti-democratic." He later that day formally resigned from the Party himself.

* * *

As the memoirs make plain, Morozov became a more active player on the political scene during this time. He conferred regularly with members of the Supreme Soviet and the democratic opposition, even sanctioning a meeting between officers under his command

and Rukh. He held conversations with Drach and others on the likely composition of the Ukrainian armed forces. On August 24, the Supreme Soviet issued a declaration of independence (and became thereby Ukraine's Parliament). Three days later, Morozov took part in a meeting between Leonid Kravchuk and senior commanders of military units in Ukraine. He was the only one to support Kravchuk and talk about the development of the Ukrainian armed forces. On August 29, Kravchuk called to ask Morozov to become minister of defense. The Parliament soon confirmed the appointment on September 3, by a vote of 323 to 11.

The remainder of the story recounts Morozov's early dealings with Moscow and his first steps as minister. It turns out that Morozov was legally transferred to the Ukrainian military by Shaposhnikov, something that demonstrates Moscow's belief that the best thing to do was play along with new national militaries but steer them into an overarching, integrated structure. Morozov's first acts as minister focused on gathering trusted officers to occupy command and staff positions, ensure the loyalty and professionalism of the officer corps and begin the painful process of reducing the military at a time of economic chaos and collapse.

Morozov has subsequently gone on to serve in senior diplomatic positions in Brussels—where he was a Minister-Counselor and Deputy Head of the Ukrainian Mission to NATO—and now in Tehran—as Ukraine's Ambassador Extraordinary and Plenipotentiary. He was defeated in a race for the Ukrainian Parliament in 1994 in an election widely criticized for the other candidates' fraud. I frankly think the loss was a blessing in disguise, for Morozov is a very different personality from the dozens of Ukrainian parliamentarians I have met. He has always been military in bearing, impatient for action. In contrast, there have been many months when the Parliament has barely accomplished anything at all.

This books adds to the growing number of documentary collections, memoirs, and analyses that throw light on the end of the Soviet Union and the formation of independent states such as Ukraine. Memoirs such as these are especially important, particularly those by actors outside Moscow and outside Russia, for the end of the USSR cannot really be understood without taking account of events in Kyiv, Vilnius, Tallinn, St. Petersburg, Baku, Nagorno-Karabakh, Chişinău, and other important cities and regions. Moreover, the future strategic consequences of that end require coming to terms with the origin, possibilities, strengths, weaknesses and subsequent history of the states that have replaced the USSR.

Those without command of the various languages or access to what are frequently small press runs of books published in remote locations ought to be grateful to the Harvard Ukrainian Research Institute for helping Morozov, while he was a visiting senior fellow at the Institute and the Kennedy School of Government in 1994–95, to sit down and tell his story and for putting together such a fine translation of that account in English.

For me this book brings back quite vividly the anticipation and excitement of Kyiv in November 1991. During one of those days, I stole away from the official schedule to walk to Independence Square. There I spent a couple of hours talking with student activists, pensioners and working people. I asked each how they felt about the great changes and whether they thought independence would bring a better life. There were many responses, but all stressed the inevitability of change and most expressed optimism that the people of Ukraine could make something of themselves if given the chance. Kostiantyn Morozov's book describes both how that chance came about and gives, in his typically modest way, a model of someone determined to make the most of it.

Ukraine has become all too often mired in political squabbling and economic stagnation. Because of that, recalling what Ukraine's chance to wrest the future for itself meant—and seeing Morozov's model of the courage to take it—is perhaps even more important now than in those first heady days of independence.

Sherman W. Garnett
James Madison College
Michigan State University

Usage Note

All place-names are given in the language of the country of origin in modified Library of Congress (LC) transliteration. The only exceptions are those with long-standing English forms (e.g., Moscow, Warsaw). The form Kyiv, now recognized as the official English-language spelling of the capital of Ukraine by most governments, is used instead of the older English-language form Kiev. Primes for soft signs as well as the apostrophe (in Ukrainian) and double prime (in Russian) for the hard sign are not used. Transliteration of Ukrainian and Russian phrases also are made according to this modified LC system.

Transliteration of Ukrainian personal names defies such an easy solution. A fundamental problem is raised by the fact that the Ukrainian government enacted an official transliteration system in April 1996 that differed from the ones that had been generally used before. This system must be used by officials representing Ukraine's government in English-language environments. Therefore, officials that had an official spelling in one way in, say, 1994, may have an official spelling a different way in 1999 (for example, Pliushch or Plyushch in 1994, Pliusch in 1999).

In order to accommodate this and other issues of representing personal names, the editors have chosen the following rules:

1) For all Russian personal names (except as noted before), and Ukrainian personal names of individuals deceased before 1996 or not active since then (except as noted before), modified LC transliteration is used.

2) For Ukrainian personal names of individuals active after 1996, the new transliteration system adopted by the Ukrainian government is used.

3) Where a preference in usage of a Ukrainian or Russian name form can be discerned for a given individual, the form of preference

is used. In those cases where a preference is not clear, a Ukrainian form is used.

4) For individuals with common English-language forms in the Western press, those forms are used: for example, Yeltsin and Yevgeny Shaposhnikov, instead of Eltsin and Evgenii Shaposhnikov; and Hryniov and Kendzior, instead of Hrynov and Kendzor (remembering in three of these cases that soft signs are *not* marked).

In the translations of the documentary appendices, name forms are given according to the language of the original.

In all cases, variant transliterations are given in the index in order to aid the reader in referencing individuals or places in other sources.

The Ukrainian term *Verkhovna Rada* translates literally as 'Supreme Council,' but is usually translated as 'Supreme Soviet' for the period before independence. After the act of independence, the common translation (also used by the Verkhovna Rada itself), is 'Parliament.' This distinction—"Supreme Soviet" referring to the period before August 24, 1991 and "Parliament" for reference thereafter—is followed herein.

Above and Beyond

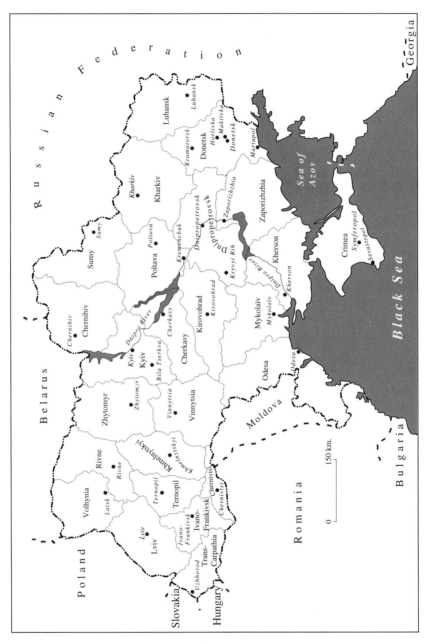

Ukraine
(including oblast borders and larger cities)

1 "So, You Are Ukrainian?"

Marshal Yevgeny Shaposhnikov* and I always had a healthy regard for each other. We both were pilots and had worked together for years. Yevgeny Ivanovich had graduated from the Gritsevets Kharkiv Higher Military Aviation School, as had I. We had similar career paths and temperaments. He was the one who had nominated me for my post as commander of the 17th Air Army and had personally flown to Kyiv to present me to the troops in my new command. Most of all, we respected and trusted each other—and that respect and trust had helped see us through the recent coup attempt against Mikhail Gorbachev.

But all this faded away and now it was my attitude toward the USSR that concerned him at this crucial juncture of political and military uncertainties. The abortive coup attempt against Gorbachev on August 19, 1991, had called into question the Soviet Union's political and military stability. Deputies in the Ukrainian Parliament had declared Ukraine an independent, sovereign nation, no longer a part of the USSR. The Soviet Union itself was falling apart.

Appointed minister of defense for the USSR, Shaposhnikov was a resolute man staunchly devoted to the idea of a single military under central, Russian control—the traditional Soviet ideal. He had no use for those who stood in the way of his mission, and the idea must have occurred to him that I, once his protégé, now stood in his way. He was confronted with the fact that the Parliament of Ukraine—our Verkhovna Rada—had recently approved my appointment as Ukraine's first minister of defense. I could imagine his irritation, perhaps his shock. After all, he knew what was all over the

---

* Explanatory notes are marked with an asterisk and found at the back of the volume, starting on p. 265.

newspapers as soon as I was appointed minister of defense: Kostiantyn Morozov is half-Russian, half-Ukrainian. Although he was a reformer and had quit the Communist Party immediately after the putsch—as I had—he still believed firmly in the USSR, first and foremost. For Shaposhnikov and anyone with that old Soviet outlook on the world, being half-Russian meant being all Russian, and that was supposed to "inoculate" me against the Ukrainian patriotism that had so consumed many of my countrymen.

In the fall of 1991, after my appointment as minister of defense of Ukraine, I was still working closely with (and, theoretically, still under) the USSR Ministry of Defense. Shaposhnikov confronted me there. He fixed his gaze on me and with a look of dismay asked a question to which he already knew the answer:

"So, Konstantin Petrovich, it turns out that you're Ukrainian?"*

That question had heavy implications for me: had Shaposhnikov and other senior general officers known earlier that being part Ukrainian might have mattered to me, the Soviet military establishment would have treated me quite differently. I would not have commanded a division or been sent to the Voroshilov Academy of the General Staff of the Armed Forces of the USSR. After twenty-one years of commended military service, I certainly would not have been appointed commander of the 17th Air Army in Ukraine in 1990. Had the military brass known that I deeply respected the work and political views of many democrats in my homeland, I would have been relieved of my duties altogether. But that did not happen, and now my life and military career had once more taken a turn I could never have predicted.

"Yes, I am Ukrainian," I replied. I forced a small joke: "It looks as if they made a mistake on my documents, Yevgeny Ivanovich."

Shaposhnikov was stunned and simply repeated the question to me, "So, it turns out you're a Ukrainian?!"

I answered honestly what I knew—that I was half-Russian, half-Ukrainian, born and raised in Ukraine.

It speaks volumes about the confusion and turmoil of the time that even at that high level our Soviet comrades were shocked upon finding out that colleagues whom they had assumed to be "safe"

Russians were actually "dangerous" Ukrainians determined to gain independence. But it was not so easy for the Soviet mind to bend itself around the idea that a successful man could want to be anything but a Soviet. And at its core that meant "Russian." So how could it turn out that a general officer—Shaposhnikov's own man!—was a Ukrainian, when his passport said "Russian"?

Shaposhnikov tried one more time. "But…but, how come?"

Ethnicity and Destiny

Just how that came about is, in part, the story of the first forty-seven years of my life. I had always assumed that I was Ukrainian on my mother's side and Russian on my father's. I grew up in the heavily russified Donbas region of eastern Ukraine, home to over four million Russians and completely russified Ukrainians, a large proportion of the total population. In my family we spoke Russian, only occasionally Ukrainian, in spite of the fact that my mother taught both languages at the local school. Moreover, my Russian patrilineage was guaranteed—or so I thought—by virtue of the fact that my father's name was Morozov, the Russian variant of a surname based on the East Slavic root *moroz* meaning "frost." My Soviet internal passport, which had no place for "hyphenated ethnicity," said simply that I was Russian.

As far as I could determine through the meager records my family kept, my father's family had settled many years earlier in the Donbas region, a vast area rich in minerals. I was a product, if you will, of the great ethnic mix that today comprises Ukrainians and those who came in search of work or were relocated from every direction in successive waves during the tsarist and Soviet periods.

In my case, no less so than in thousands of others in the Soviet military, it can truly be said that ethnicity is destiny.

Exactly where my ancestral roots lie is a question I cannot answer, given how sketchy our family records are. Even as a child, I knew that my mother's ancestors were Cossacks named Semenchuk from the area near Chernihiv on Ukraine's northern border with Belarus and Russia. In the 1920s her father moved the family to the Donbas region in hopes of building up his small business for the

3

manufacture of household items, footwear, and harnesses. Demonstrating an entrepreneurial spirit remarkable for the times, he even hired a few workers to help with the production and turn a small profit on which he and his family survived.

After a brief period of economic liberalization in the 1920s, however, the Communists sought to destroy the small-business class in Ukraine and elsewhere in the USSR. Capitalism and self-sufficiency they saw as incompatible with the interests of the state and its values of economic integrity and communal ownership. My grandfather exemplified precisely those characteristics and values that the Soviet regime hoped to stifle—initiative and self-reliance. He thus distinguished himself in the region as a "businessman," a designation that in our family history is unparalleled among our acquaintances, my school friends, or their parents. At his death, he left behind a cache of tools and equipment that became something of a celebrated subject in the stories our family told.

In the years following World War I, the Donbas region promised a better life than anything the people had known: jobs were plentiful, at least in the coal mines, pig iron factories, and metallurgical centers. Four successive five-year plans implemented by Stalin from the late 1920s to 1950 helped turn the region—already extensively developed as an industrial center during tsarist times—into the most heavily industrialized region in all of the USSR. Given the enormous environmental consequences we now have there, it has been a mixed blessing for the people who call this area home. During World War II, as the German army was about to invade this region, Stalin ordered the coal mines closed and flooded. In the years following the war, the mines were reopened and repaired, and millions of Russian immigrants and refugees moved there, some looking for better-paying jobs and some forced to relocate from the other republics of the Soviet Union.

We were all "Soviets," but all citizens had to declare their "nationality." This meant something like "ethnicity," but was complicated by the existence of constituent "national" republics within the USSR. Thus, Soviet citizens had in their internal passports—which we used for official identification and carried at all times—their *natsional'nost'*, which was typically identified with the republic of their birth or the nationality of their parents. The nationality of parents trumped the place of birth. (Russians in Uzbekistan would *never* have "Uzbek" in their passports.) If parents were of different nationalities and one was Russian, then that trumped the other and it became a blatant "abnormality" to put the non-Russian nationality into the child's birth certificate. It was also often possible for non-Russian Slavs who spoke Russian as their mother tongue to finesse the situation, either by simply declaring Russian nationality or by bribing the appropriate officials. Recognizing the benefits of membership in the most powerful ethnic group in the country, many native Ukrainians thus answered "Russian" when queried for the census or had it put in their passports. I personally know Ukrainian families in the Donbas who officially registered as Russians because they did not want to be considered second-class citizens or associated with a politically disenfranchised ethnic group. Political expediency often took precedence over familial legacy in such matters.

My father's family settled in a small village in the Donbas area where my paternal grandfather, by virtue of the fact that he owned a horse and a carriage, managed to avoid working underground in the mines. Instead, he was employed at a huge construction site for a new "palace of culture," helping to transport the tons of stone that came from the Luhansk region* some 80 kilometers (about 65 miles) away. Stalin was particularly fond of such massive architectural edifices that proclaimed the cultural and political dominance of the Soviet Union. Focal points in the urban landscape from Minsk to Vladivostok, these buildings housed auditoriums, exhibition halls, and performance centers. From just about any vantage point in or around the city, it was impossible not to see the towering palace of culture.

My father Petro Morozov was born in 1915. When he was just nineteen years old, he was called up for military service and assigned to a unit located in the Baltic Military District. Here he took part in the 1939 campaign that the Soviet Union waged against Poland, Finland, and the Baltic states. (He took part in the Finnish campaign.) When German forces overran all of Ukraine and western Russia, reaching almost to Leningrad and Moscow, my father served as a

5

regular conscript (the equivalent of a GI in the U.S.) until he was captured by the Germans in 1942. I remember his telling my brother, sister, and me terrifying tales of how he and his friends were surrounded by the enemy. He would roll up his trousers to display two enormous scars above his knees, the result of wounds he had suffered in combat. Held in a POW camp, he received hardly any medical attention for his wounds, but in the spring of 1943, an Allied bombing raid destroyed that part of the camp where the prisoners were housed, and in the confusion my father and his friends managed to escape.

Most of his comrades were from the area around Donetsk in the heart of Ukraine's industrial region. After an arduous journey, they crossed the front lines—by 1943, the Donbas region had already been freed from the Germans—and my father returned to the house that he had left as a teenager. He registered with the local military commissariat and spent the next several months recovering from his injuries.

In response to the German invasion of Ukraine, Stalin had ordered that during the retreat all valuable property—whatever the Soviets could not rescue during the evacuations—should be demolished. Determined that if he could not save it, he would destroy it, Stalin instituted a "scorched earth" policy, leaving much of that part of Ukraine in shambles, as well as hindering the advancing German army.

After the war ended, there was plenty of work for people to do to recover from such widespread destruction. For my father, a young electrician, the new opportunities took him deep into the mines that had to be rebuilt and opened for production. With perseverance and a strong sense of duty, he worked his way up to become the foreman of an electricians' brigade assigned to install and repair electrical equipment and elevators in the mine shafts. But the work was terribly dangerous and casualty figures were high. Suffice it to say that to this day hundreds of miners continue to die every year in the coal mines of the Donbas.

The first of three children, I was born on June 3, 1944, in Brianka, a small coal-mining village in Luhansk Oblast. Whether my father took an active role in rearing me and in seeing to my education I cannot recall. Once or twice he took me to the mines where he worked, and I remember that my ears hurt from all the noise of the machinery. It seemed that everyone, each worker nameless to me, knew my father and would call out to us and wave as we passed by. I saw that he was a popular man with his coworkers, highly respected for his skills and his devotion to his family, and I felt proud to be with him. For me that was the best and most rewarding memory from those early years in Brianka.

Rewriting History

Another set of memories centers on the events of 1953. That was the year Stalin died. I was only nine years old at the time and obviously did not have an overwhelming interest in politics, but with the announcement of the leader's death, I sensed a major change in the political atmosphere of the Soviet Union. For a while the only news my family heard was the official line given out over the radio. Report after report focused attention on the emotional and political turmoil that the entire Soviet Union was experiencing.

More disturbing—and even then it raised in me a sense of injustice—was the official line on the rewriting of our Ukrainian history. Names were crossed out of registers, and pages torn out of our textbooks. As students we were forbidden to take earlier editions of some books out of the library, instructed instead to read those books that had been "corrected" and updated. New information, based on the results of recent Communist Party congresses, was woven into the fabric of Soviet culture in which we were wrapped. Official reports turned our attention to the activities of the new Soviet leaders, who I now know were trying to drum up public support in their struggles with each other. In an epiphany of sorts, I came to realize that the entire historical period that had constituted such an important part of our lives had been drastically "reevaluated" and sanitized—and we were to accept it without questioning. How was it possible, I wondered, that what people once believed was right, what they once were willing to give their lives to protect and defend, now turned out to be so wrong?

7

The death of Stalin also marked an important shift from the tight-lipped and fearful conditions of the past to a somewhat greater degree of social and personal freedom throughout the Soviet republics. Although still extremely cautious, my parents began speaking more freely and openly, enjoying a sense of personal freedom they really had never known before. From family discussions with my parents and grandparents I learned that under Stalin people had been afraid to reveal matters of family origin or history. They feared that the information might be recorded and used against them in the government's explicit efforts at suppressing ethnic and national identities. Most people had not even wanted to say what kind of work

The Donbas Region
(see full map of Ukraine, p. xxiv)

they or their parents were in. This climate helped explain, of course, why the Morozov family records were so sparse.

Taking on New Responsibilities

In the early 1950s, my father was promoted from foreman to manager of a unit that installed and repaired electrical equipment in the mines. Soon thereafter—in 1954, at the age of only thirty-nine—he was fatally injured in a workplace accident. I don't remember many of the details. I was only ten years old at the time. But I know that he never regained consciousness and died at the hospital.

When my father died, my mother was instantly thrust into the role of head of household with three children to support on an elementary schoolteacher's salary. Having graduated at age sixteen from the local workers' community college, she had embarked on a teaching career that had seen only minor changes over a period of twenty or more years: she had moved from one school to another as the administrative divisions in the Donbas had been redrawn, but she always worked in that same region, since we never moved. Everyone in our little town knew Kateryna Morozova, not only because they had had her as a teacher, but also because their children—in some cases, even their grandchildren—were now in her classes. By the time I was an adult, three generations in my hometown knew our family.

The three of us children—my brother Yevhen, my sister Valentyna, and I—were students at the school in which my mother taught. Her visibility put a special burden on us children because we felt the pressure to safeguard her reputation and authority as a teacher. Even as young children, we became aware that everyone was watching us, judging our mother by our actions.

Extremely popular and well known, my mother was named a "People's Teacher," a special honor granted in the Soviet Union which meant for her a slight increase in her pension. In addition to the prestige and additional responsibility, this designation also increased the social pressure and responsibility for all of us. She made it absolutely clear to us that she had always had the respect and trust of the people around her. If one of us did something wrong, even the slightest transgression, our actions would reflect on her and people would know that it was *her* children who had erred. Perhaps it was because I was the oldest of three children and had to play the role not only of elder brother but also of father; perhaps it was my sense that our financial standing was so uncertain; or maybe it was my awareness that my mother, widowed early in her life, was so utterly vulnerable. Whatever the cause, as I now look back over these events, I believe that my need to protect her and her position in our community greatly influenced my career and helped me develop that deep sense of duty, honor, and responsibility that has served me so well in later years.

Mother was an immensely courageous and principled woman who always had a strong religious faith, even in a society that officially had no use for such "excesses." Like her parents she was baptized in an Orthodox service, and despite the prevailing ideology against religion, she risked both her job and her family when she insisted that the three of us children should also undergo the Orthodox sacrament of baptism. Had what she had done been discovered, she could have been fired from her teaching post and banned from all contacts with us children. For our spiritual well-being, however, she considered this risk to be absolutely necessary. Afterwards, when asked whether her children had been baptized, she had to tell the truth, since God was her constant witness and it was inconceivable for her to lie on that matter.

Even when my mother did not directly instruct us in those positive character traits she considered important, we learned by simply observing the modesty and grace of her behavior. After my father's death, we lived an increasingly frugal existence. Like her father, Mother was very good with her hands, and throughout her life used a hand-operated sewing machine to make and repair our clothes. In addition, she did some embroidery and often painted. Rather than ordering special teaching devices, my mother would cut materials out of paper and fabrics, gluing or stitching them together to construct some inventive teaching aid to help her students, including us, learn new concepts and skills. Until I entered the tenth grade, the last grade of our high school, I had only one shirt to my name, which I had worn since the seventh grade and which I had long outgrown. We knew exactly what we could or could not ask our mother to buy. And knowing how difficult her situation was, we rarely asked for anything. She herself decided what we needed, what she could buy for us, or, more likely, what she could make with her own hands and ingenuity.

Many Ukrainians—most of our neighbors, in fact—suffered for years trying to make ends meet on a standard of living which, like ours, was well below average. My friends lived no better than we did, even though they came from families who had not experienced the loss of a father. My mother, however, was determined that we not look less well-off than others in our vicinity; thus, she worked very hard to look after our needs. Rarely could we afford to invite guests to eat with us or stay at our home. Holidays, at least those officially recognized by the Soviet government, were marked as special occasions by my mother's buying or making something for us—underwear, a shirt, a pair of shoes—to put us in a festive mood.

Learning and Relearning Ukrainian

As I was growing up in the Donbas region I knew at some level that Ukraine was my homeland, but I had almost no concept of Ukraine as a nation defined by a common culture, language, and internationally recognized geographical boundaries. The Soviet "system" as it had developed under forty years of Communist rule promoted the image of the USSR as a monolithic society, an entity comprising all sorts of people who had exchanged their various ethnic affiliations, willingly or not, for a single new identity as "Soviet people." For all practical purposes, as everyone knew, all Soviet citizens were not created equal. Most Russians, in fact, had a deep distrust of ethnic minorities in the USSR—Ukrainians, Belarusians, Lithuanians, Uzbeks, Turkmens, for instance—and the feeling was mutual. As a child, however, I rarely heard anyone talk about the Ukrainian people's struggle for independence; indeed, to do so at that time was practically unthinkable. Instead, all the media—film, radio and television, books, and so forth—presented an image of several republics seamlessly welded together with an ironclad social psychology promulgated by Communist ideology and propaganda.

It was impossible, however, to live in this republic and not see that the ideologues were bent on making Ukraine look less and less Ukrainian. Throughout all the republics the political propaganda machine attempted to demonstrate that the all-Union or Soviet (i.e., Russian) culture took precedence over other cultures. Government officials, for instance, ordered that only Russian was to be used in libraries, schools, and education systems, and those few schools in the Donbas that remained Ukrainian had to be strictly regulated. I learned to read and speak Ukrainian because my mother was Ukrainian and taught the language. Whenever we were out and about, I heard her speaking Ukrainian to people she knew well, and it was not long before I had a substantial, if not fluent, knowledge of the language. I received excellent marks in a Ukrainian literature course that I later took.

Twenty-two years spent in the armed forces in various remote regions of the Soviet Union where only Russian was spoken so completely separated me from my native language, however, that when I returned to Ukraine in 1988, I had to relearn the language. I immersed myself in Ukrainian texts and worked with special tutors who could help me with pronunciation and intonation. Within a few months, perhaps four at most, I had regained much of my fluency, although even today much of my speech is unconsciously filled with russisms. It is not so easy to eliminate these words and phrases from everyday speech, especially after so many years of using only that language. As I quickly learned, though, the Ukrainian language is as grammatically sophisticated—if not more so—than Russian. This was a great surprise to me, considering the pervasive (but often unspoken) Soviet stereotype of Ukrainian as a simple, rustic, "ethnic" language, not a modern, literate one.

As a young boy growing up in the Luhansk region, I also had an opportunity to see and read Ukrainian in spite of the official policy that favored Russian. Inscriptions written in Ukrainian appeared throughout the area and were only gradually replaced with Russian

12

ones. I read Ukrainian books—particularly science fiction—but as I grew older, that genre had less and less appeal for me. As a teen, I began reading the classics and important authors such as the nineteenth-century novelist Panas Myrnyi and the poet Lesia Ukraïnka. I cannot claim to have read all of Taras Shevchenko's poems, but at least those titles recommended for school held my interest for some time, and I found them especially challenging.

Many of these classics, however, highlighted for me themes of Ukrainian identity and freedom from Russian oppression, and I continued to read and reread them up until the age of nineteen when I entered military college and my career in the armed forces obliged me to turn my attention elsewhere. As a young student, I also looked forward to the school time that was devoted to reading newspapers with a guided discussion of current political events. I am delighted today to see my own daughter enjoying these same activities, quite uncharacteristic of young people nowadays. Everyone in the family says that my daughter likes to do the kinds of things I used to do.

Life without a Father

In 1963, when I entered the Gritsevets Kharkiv Higher Military Aviation School, my brother Yevhen, who is three years younger than I, was just beginning the seventh grade. Valentyna, who is seven years younger than I, was still in primary school. Much later, after her retirement from teaching, my mother lived for a while in her own home, but as she grew older, we recognized that she would one day be unable to care for herself. As so often happens in families nowadays in Ukraine, the day-to-day care for an aging parent falls to a daughter, and so it was that Valentyna, having completed her training as a nurse, took charge of watching after our aging mother. The two of them decided to exchange apartments: Mother then had her own apartment, the smaller one, that was not far from my sister and her family. They, in turn, moved into the place where we all had grown up.

Yevhen finished high school while I was still enrolled at the military school. He wanted to become a pilot like me and enter a military college, an ambition I tried to help him realize by having him study the proper subjects in school and prepare himself physically. He enrolled in a kind of correspondence course for a while. During my third year of cadet training, I helped Yevhen to prepare his formal application to military school. He did not, however, pass the rigorous medical examination required for the institution he had chosen.

Because all young men at the time were eligible for conscription into the military and Yevhen still had two or three years before his eligibility, he decided to enter the Donbas State Mechanical Engineering Academy in Kramatorsk and study for an engineering degree. After graduating, he spent several years in the Far East where he worked as a chief engineer and later as manager of a plant. Eventually promoted to deputy director of an industrial corporation, Yevhen married and lived for several years in Russia.

Once I left Ukraine in 1967, I did not return for twenty-one years, time enough to lose facility in the language, lose track of old friends, and lose touch with the cultural heritage of my country. I returned in 1988 to continue my military service, hardly expecting that a new Ukraine, fully independent and sovereign, would become a reality in 1991.

In 1992, I persuaded Yevhen to return to Ukraine, despite the immediate hardship of finding an apartment. Housing was a perpetual problem, and there were large numbers of young couples recently married who went on local housing lists, eager to live away from their parents and begin their own families. What is more, the newly independent Ukraine had not yet developed a policy to compensate people for pensions they had earned while working in Russia but had to give up upon moving back to Ukraine. Under the Soviet system such pensions had been transferable no matter which republic one worked in. No doubt many people assumed that because I held a high position in the Ukrainian military I could simply pull the right strings in order to help Yevhen and his wife secure an apartment wherever they wanted. After all, most well-placed bureaucrats exercised such perks of their office. In 1992, property in Ukraine had not yet been privatized, and the government owned practically all of it. Yevhen and his wife, however, never entertained any thought that I

14

would use my official position to help them find an apartment. Accordingly, they lived for a time in Kolomyia in western Ukraine, waiting patiently for their names to come up on the list there. At last, in 1995, they moved to Donetsk, back to the Donbas.

Although my mother enjoyed good health all through her seventies—another sign of her Cossack origins—she grew gravely ill and died in 1997. Her death was a terrible blow to all of us, but it is gratifying to know that she lived long enough to see all of her children back in their native land.

Like all families, my brother, sister, and I have had to learn to adapt and maintain a close relationship that becomes increasingly complex the more it is grounded in truth and honesty. Indeed, when we were faced with decisions based on moral principles such as human dignity, justice, and responsibility, the three of us have almost always been of one mind. Both of my siblings openly state that they consider me an example to emulate. Being the oldest of three children who too early lost their father made that elevation an inevitability perhaps, but there were years of my military experience that reinforced the trust and respect that my brother and sister have for me.

Close to forty years after my father's death, I was looking through the family papers for biographical information. Among some scattered letters and registration forms, I found my birth certificate, officially listing the place and date of my birth, as well as important information about my mother and father, including their ethnic identity. Reading quickly through some familiar data, I stopped abruptly at the line giving the details about my father's ethnic background. There on the document was the name Petr Morozov, officially registered as Ukrainian! He was not Russian, as I had always assumed. Rather than sharing ethnic identities, I was fully Ukrainian. This was the first inkling I had of my true ethnic roots, and the revelation left me speechless.

To my knowledge, no evidence exists as to why I was kept in the dark about my ethnic heritage. There was no intentional cover-up, no attempt to deceive me or make me into something that I wasn't. Perhaps my parents simply assumed that all the while I knew, but more likely they understood the political realities of the Donbas region at that time in our history. Whatever the case, the introduction of this new information caught me by surprise and caused me to reevaluate my family life, my loyalties, and my military career—in essence, the core values of my being. This book flows from the fact that during a critical period in the early 1990s I had to set new priorities and reassess the principles that have been with me, I believe, since my earliest experiences.

Back in that fall day when I stood across from Marshal Shaposhnikov I was at the middle point of my new journey. I did not know then that my "Ukrainianness" was not only spiritual and psychological, bound up with my love of my country and sense of duty toward it, but that I was ethnically Ukrainian on both sides of my family. Irrespective of the family details, the process of my "re-ukrainianization" had taken deep hold and I was well aware of it. With a broader and deeper understanding, I could now look across the table directly into the eyes of Marshal Shaposhnikov and say to him, as an equal, "Yes, I am Ukrainian."

2 The Touchstones of Character

In spring 1964, when I was only nineteen years old—about the age that most college students in the U.S. are beginning to decide what their major will be—I piloted my first airplane. Captain Volodymyr Lavryk instructed me in the cockpit. As a father teaches his young son to take first steps and begin walking, so Captain Lavryk taught me how to fly a plane. Long before that initial flight I spent many hours in the classroom, of course, learning the principles of aviation and the details of instrumentation. But there comes a time in the training process when the student has to take the controls. He must take time to develop the necessary respect for the vehicle and to experience the intimate relationship between pilot and plane. That is what Captain Lavryk taught me.

I'm sure I must have been half blinded by the perspiration dripping from my forehead when I first gripped the flight accelerator and adjusted the flight pattern as he instructed. With paternal benevolence Captain Lavryk guided and praised my actions—albeit inexperienced and unconfident—so long as they were the correct ones. That is, he understood a fundamental difference: a child's first steps are always uncertain, but if the mechanics of the action itself are correct, a patient teacher can help even the clumsiest toddler learn to run. No teacher can supply the talent that enables that child to become a superb athlete—only nature can nurture that ability—but the really good teachers, by trusting their students, make it possible for them to develop those talents they have.

That is a principle my mother knew and one of the things for which she was named a People's Teacher. Captain Lavryk knew it too, and I like to think that over the years I have developed some of the same qualities. Like all students I have had plenty of examples to the contrary—teachers who berate their students or express disappointment and frustration because their students can never do the task as well as they can. They define the ideal and move the bar ever higher, knowing full well that they themselves could never jump that high. I was fortunate to study under Captain Lavryk who knew not only what to praise and how much, but how to correct and guide in ways that built up my confidence and ultimately my independence.

He was but one in a number of fine teachers and educational experiences—some good, some bad—that I had in my career.

Choosing a Military Career

When the cosmonauts in the USSR space program needed special training, they attended the higher military aviation school for fighter pilots in either Chernihiv or Kharkiv.* Famous for the rigorous training of future pilots, these two institutions maintained the highest standards and the richest traditions, as illustrated by the number of its graduates who received the order of Hero of the Soviet Union. Becoming a fighter pilot was a dream of mine from the earliest age I can remember. Early on, I set my sights on a military career as the best way of developing those skills and traits of character that would serve me all my life. The first step toward realizing this goal was to gain admission to the illustrious Sergei Ivanovich Gritsevets Kharkiv Higher Military Aviation School for Pilots.

I applied for admission immediately after completing high school in 1961. It was not difficult for me to decide what direction my future education should take. I had been deeply interested in a military career since my childhood. To put it mildly, my mother was not enthusiastic about my choice. The family's financial situation, however, helped me to win her over to my side. We all knew that the family budget would hardly allow me to study at a university or technical school, either of which would require funds we did not have. Since I had both a deep interest in the military and the option of going to a military school (where our out-of-pocket expenses would be much lower than they would have been at a civilian school), my decision to apply to the military aviation school in Kharkiv made imminent practical sense, since it left our family budget intact and allowed me to help my mother provide for my brother and sister.

Although my family's economic condition was a factor in my choosing to pursue a military education and career, it was by no means the only thing prompting me to apply to this institution. I knew that I had "the right stuff," as it's called in America, to fly a Soviet MiG fighter jet—or any other plane, for that matter. I also believed that a life spent in the military offered career benefits not to be found elsewhere, and I was eager to undergo the discipline and learn the necessary aviation skills to become a pilot. I wasted no time, therefore, in applying to this school of cosmonauts and military heroes.

Then came a major setback: I was rejected by the admissions panel because I failed the vertigo test. This news was disappointing, of course, but I vowed not to be utterly devastated by it and to reapply as soon as I was able. For the next two years, I worked as a civilian, all the while learning from my experiences and marshaling those inner forces I needed to resubmit my application to the military academy. Returning home, I worked for a year as a laboratory assistant at my high school. Then for another year I worked on a locomotive with my uncle, my father's brother, through whose help I had been able to find the job. That work was extremely difficult and I was not particularly well suited for it, but I stuck it out for a year because it paid good money and allowed me to make my contribution to the family budget.

And how did I overcome the vertigo test? At first I used a swing at our house and a carousel at the local children's playground to master the ability of not becoming dizzy while swinging or revolving at high speed. Eventually I rigged up a special swing and carousel device at our house and spent hours on them. While I was working on the locomotive, I would try to fulfill all my work requirements as quickly as possible and then simply sit and choose a point on the ground as my "fixed horizon" until, finally, I was able to stare at it, unflinching, for thirty minutes without losing my sense of balance or peripheral perception of my surroundings. I had no problem with the vertigo test when I took it the next time.

In 1963, I reapplied to the Gritsevets Kharkiv Higher Military Aviation School and this time was admitted. From that moment just about everything else in my life became secondary to my military education and service.

For four years I lived in military barracks under the same restrictions established for enlisted soldiers. Unlike students at the university, I could not simply return home for vacations or take a holiday or visit relatives and friends whenever I wished. Practically every moment of my life was regulated, as it was for my fellow students at the academy: we ate the same food in the same *idalnia* or "mess hall" as the soldiers used; we obeyed the same rules and answered to the same chain of command as ordinary conscripts did. The only difference between my life and that of an enlisted soldier was that for a good part of the day I was obligated to attend classes in aviation technology, military strategy, combat preparedness, and leadership training. In addition, I had to prepare lessons and study for examinations. Free time was scarce in this demanding environment, and when it did come, I spent it sharpening my skills as a pilot and trying to master some technique or other that might be useful to me. Occasionally I took time out to write some poetry, usually about the exhilaration of flying or about my feelings for Raisa, which were even more intense. Raisa and I were already engaged when I became a cadet and we married during my second year at the school, so that she truly has shared my entire military life with me.

Candidates for military aviation assignments have always faced more stringent requirements than their land-based colleagues, and the job of piloting an aircraft, military or civilian, belongs to those few who make it through a strict selection process and health evaluation set by the air force. This statement will no doubt raise objections from colleagues who command ground troops, and a word needs to be inserted even at this early stage regarding the tension between ground-based forces and the air force. There was frequently an element of condescension from senior ground troop officers who viewed the air force as primarily a support function: it was the task of air force pilots, they reasoned, to ensure that ground forces could carry out their missions. Disagreements frequently arose over training and planning, and mistakes were widely interpreted as resulting from deficiencies in the air force—for example, insufficient training, careless attitudes, and a lack of respect on the part of air force personnel toward their counterparts on the ground. At times the disagreements became insulting and brutal, even in the presence of subordinates. I personally experienced such a situation more than once, extending over the time that I was a student at the military aviation school until I became commander of the 17th Air Army. Fortunately, as Ukraine's minister of defense, I did not feel that I was held in any disrespect simply because I was a pilot. My authority was based on the strong support I received from the majority of deputies in Ukraine's Parliament and from the president of Ukraine.

But back to the air force training process as I experienced it. First, one needs an appropriate education in order to master the complicated modern aviation and navigation technology and weapons systems. Second, candidates for aviation training have to be certified as having outstandingly good health, eyesight, hearing, and other physical capabilities that will conceivably allow them to enjoy long and robust careers as pilots. In other words, not only do young recruits have to be in the prime of health when they apply, but they also have to receive a positive prognosis that they will, barring an accident, continue to have good health for perhaps another twenty or thirty years. While there are, of course, no guarantees that one will continue that long in good health, the air force does not want to go to the trouble and expense of training young people only to lose them to health problems in five years or so.

Another important factor was the different nature in which the operational mission of our aircraft was approached. The human factor was always important in Soviet designs—the ability of the pilot to achieve certain things and to be able to perform certain actions was taken for granted in those designs. The operational standards for performance overall would be similar to a comparable Western aircraft, the difference being that part of the Soviet design include the pilot and his training. (This is much less the case in Western aircraft where operational standards, it seems to me, are achieved mainly through mechanical means.) Thus, for a Soviet aircraft to perform to its design, the pilot had to be in excellent shape, physically and mentally.

Because of these facts, the requirements set by the air force are probably the highest among the military professions. To be admitted to the Gritsevets Kharkiv Higher Military Aviation School, I had to pass the most thoroughgoing medical examinations and become something of a medical expert in the daily monitoring of my own health. As if I were enrolled in a medical school and studying for a degree in internal medicine, I had to develop a specialist's knowledge of my circulatory, endocrinal, digestive, and nervous systems, among other things. Even more demanding, I had to define the limits of my psychological preparedness, learn what it means to take risks and demonstrate courage. The human body has peculiar and unpredictable responses, for example, to flying at Mach speed, cruising upside down at 40,000 feet, or ejecting while a jet is tumbling through the sky at several hundred miles an hour. One has to know one's physical limits and be aware of the multifaceted interdependence of the body's various functions.

My day-to-day activities at the aviation school, therefore, were informed by my medical condition. Every day that I piloted an airplane I went through some type of medical examination—from my heart rate to my psychological stability. If anything looked out of place or raised the least suspicion, it meant being grounded for the day at the very least. Not only did we pilots have to satisfy these stringent requirements, but those who were directly responsible for the operation of our jets, in the air and on the ground, had to meet similarly strict standards.

Nothing so thoroughly tests character as piloting a military jet. Flying at a speed faster than sound makes a crash or death an ever-present possibility. The pilot and his family have to understand this fact of military life. In 1966, when I was just a third-year student at the aviation school, I flew a MiG-15 jet in a convoy of planes piloted by fellow classmates and a number of military personnel. On one flight assignment, through no fault of my own, another jet collided in midair with my plane. Shaking violently from the sudden shock of the collision, my plane was unnavigable because of severe damage to its wing structure and jet engine. I must have been in a state of shock because the whole event took on the semblance of a film in slow motion. Seconds seemed like minutes. Yet it was clear that I had no time to ponder what to do or to consult an aviation manual: I had to size up the situation immediately and act according to my best judgment.

Had my plane experienced engine failure at a high altitude, I no doubt would have responded quite differently—for example, dropping several thousand feet and attempting to restart the engine, so long as there was no fire on board and little chance of an explosion. Dangerous situations like these can arise in an instant, and when they do, a pilot has to be prepared to take responsibility, evaluate the danger and the various options, and act immediately. Verifying that the plane could not be controlled and that there was no heavily congested population center below, I pushed the ejection button. Exploded out of the plane, I thought my body would be crushed by the force of the ejection. As I tumbled through the air, I felt completely disoriented, but fortunately was able to regain my composure and parachute to earth, a bit dazed but otherwise uninjured.

For several days after the crash, all military flights associated with the military aviation school in Kharkiv were postponed while a special commission investigated the incident. The specialists needed time to analyze the wreckage for any mechanical failures and interview all the participants and witnesses. Upon completing its task, the commission judged that my decision to eject was absolutely the right thing to have done, since even a one-second delay could have proven disastrous. Had I been flying over a heavily populated area, for instance, this accident could have caused widespread damage and resulted in great loss of life.

The psychological pressures one feels at every moment of flight, in every maneuver, can make or break even the best of pilots. Flying a military jet requires a lot of courage and a tremendous amount of confidence in the one's ability to make the right judgment in a split second. Every landing, usually the most dangerous maneuver, is different, depending on weather conditions, the time of day, the tactical changes at the landing site, the weight, speed, and type of aircraft, for instance. One can learn only so much in the classroom; the real knowledge and the growth of certainty come from years of experience, each landing a lesson in how the plane and the human beings who fly it function together.

My years as a pilot and a military leader have convinced me that human character—the unique composition of morals and values, judgment, bravery, perseverance, attitude—is forged out of life's experiences—not taught in a classroom, not observed in the mirror of society and merely copied. While there are obviously steps one can take to change one's life—for example, by an exercise of willpower— the foundation on which those steps are taken is laid early in life. I have always had the greatest respect for those who have a long and distinguished record of service in the air force, flying fighter planes and carrying out missions with the highest degree of professionalism. It is not just a matter of age: both young and old can demonstrate the kind of intuitive decision making I'm talking about. Air force pilots are special people, combining robust physical training, moral judgment, and analytical skills, all of which render them models of courage and true leadership.

This line of thinking must have inspired the serious and systematic effort in the Soviet Union to use stringent physical and psychological testing to identify those individuals best suited for carrying out the responsibilities of a military pilot. Later, under my watch as minister of defense for Ukraine, we established a similar set of tests, which involved the screening of candidates by various medical commissions, as well as a battery of psychological profiles. The results were carefully processed and measured against the most demanding criteria before any candidate for flight school was selected.

As I look back on my schooling, I cannot say that I actively set out to imitate the behavior of certain adults—teachers, professors, political leaders, even members of my immediate family—although I admired many of them for their perseverance, courage, and joy in life despite the economic hardships under which they lived. No doubt each one of these people somehow influenced the development of my character and helped turn my life in new directions, but I never consciously sought to change anything specific in my character to make me more like some ideal they had constructed for me. In this way, I believe, I have acted in accordance with the assumptions I have stated about the development of character.

I am not talking, of course, about the kind of imitation that a student goes through in observing and following the actions of a master craftsman or an expert with some technical skill. Whether it's playing a musical instrument or flying a jet airplane, every neophyte needs to practice the kind of close observation and imitation that he will need to perform intricate maneuvers later. But I believe that the elements of character must essentially be in place from the outset, or else all the skills in the world will not make a person turn out as a great artist or fighter pilot.

Political Ideology and the Education System

At the same time that we were mastering the technical challenges of becoming fighter pilots, we were being "enlightened" on the irreproachable role of the Communist Party in Soviet society. Not only the humanities but even the highly technical subjects thoroughly absorbed and presented the Party's ideology and its view of history. All textbooks contained an ideological component, especially those that covered the history of the USSR or modern European history and social science. Even technical books had to include introductions or acknowledgments to the Communist Party for attending to the needs of this or that branch of industry or science, as well as a statement to the effect that the book owed its very existence to the diligent Party members working in their congresses or plenary meetings. The authors of these textbooks—the scientists or teachers who had devoted their careers to research and truth—had to begin with this sort of concession, else their books would never appear in print and they would find even greater obstacles to their scholarship.

The entire education system, in fact, was permeated by Soviet propaganda and Communist ideology, which students from the primary schools all the way up through the higher grades absorbed like sponges. Even in the military colleges, where future pilots and engineers devoted most of their time to developing aviation skills and studying how to operate and repair planes, even here the ideology was considered to be in the mainstream of the curriculum. An enormous amount of time was dedicated to the study of subjects such as the history of the Communist Party, the political economy, and the philosophy of Karl Marx and V. I. Lenin. In the educational institutes that trained specialists in ideology or Party functionaries, including political officers for the armed forces, the study of these subjects consumed most of the instruction time.

My education continued later, in 1972, after a five-year stint in northern Poland. Raisa and I moved to Moscow, where I attended the Gagarin Military Air Academy, graduating in 1975 with my second diploma. Even in a military college, where future pilots and engineers devoted their time to developing their professional skills and to learning about the operation and maintenance of planes, we were bombarded with political ideology and the study of Communist Party history. At times the academy seemed more interested in preparing specialists in ideology or Party functionaries, including political officers for the armed forces, than in training military specialists.

It was clear to me then that no part of the system was free of ideological interference in a soldier's professional pursuits—neither at his entry into the system, nor later during his professional advancement. No subject could be dealt with if one did not fully acknowledge the central role of the Communist Party in our history and interpret the rest of history and the world through the lens of the Party's ideology. Like all the other students at the Gagarin Military Air Academy, I was expected to master that history as it was presented, regardless of its relationship to reality. In all other subjects my work was considered excellent, and I had hopes of being included in the top of my class. During one of the exams, however, I did not describe certain historical events in the way that the Party would want, so to speak. Accordingly, I received a very low mark and was excluded from top honors.

I again undertook the study of history, including military history, with its ideological bias. I mastered the lessons as they were prescribed, but my fellow students and I still were extremely curious to learn about other points of view and evaluations of important events in that military history. Given the power of propaganda, however, our desires continued to be frustrated even at the very highest levels of the educational system. In all branches of the educational system and at every level, ideology seemed always to win out over the ideal of historical accuracy. My experience at the Voroshilov Military Academy of the General Staff of the Armed Forces of the USSR (later, in Moscow, in 1984–1986), where I received my third diploma in higher studies at the strategic level, did nothing to dispel that sense.

Thus, I was educated in accordance with the principles of this ideological system—in a spirit of total devotion to the Communist Party. Whenever the issue of a promotion came up, my loyalty to the Party was one of the first things to be scrutinized. Not only did the Party provide the ideological basis for the state, as was stressed in all documents, but also the Soviet constitution of 1977 stated unequivocally that the Party was the guiding force of society. I think that a majority of people, those who had at least a high school education, understood that this was complete rubbish, for the Party itself defined its exceptional role in society, and the state simply confirmed that role. There was little to differentiate party from state, and all this rhetoric was designed to create the impression of the unity of the Communist Party and the people. It was very useful for the Party to identify itself with the people, for in speaking of the wisdom, greatness, and elemental strength of the people, the Party appropriated those characteristics for itself. Of course people everywhere saw through this ruse, but the Party hypocritically continued to assume for itself more and more of the best features and qualities of the people it was supposed to serve.

A general atmosphere of distrust and suspicion prevailed even during the period of so-called perestroika.* Such distrust always had rather dire consequences. I'm not referring to the notorious repressions and the search for enemies of the state, which have characterized much of Soviet history. Even then one's fate often depended on the whims and personal impressions of a rank-and-file KGB bureaucrat. Rather, those in managerial or command posts of any kind received special scrutiny. Most were constantly aware of this "attention," and their activities always embodied a certain level of hypocrisy or a kind of split personality. Although they never provoked any suspicions, many of my friends knew exactly how they had to act and under what circumstances. They learned to follow one set of rules in order to survive and get all they could out of life, but quite another set of principles that allowed them to remain human beings and act in accordance with their principles.

During my studies and military service I normally had no direct access to the so-called subversive literature. In the 1960s, however, first at home and then in the military, I managed to listen to some of Solzhenitsyn's works being read on the radio. My friends and I were of course doing something that was strictly forbidden, but we were starved for more information than we could find in the newspapers. At night we would listen to Radio Liberty or the BBC broadcasts of entire chapters from *August 1914, The First Circle,* and *The Gulag Archipelago,* even though we knew that we could not discuss what we had heard. Had one of our colleagues reported our actions to the authorities, we would have been in deep trouble. No doubt that would have spelled the end of my military career.

Each of us reacted in his own personal way to this new information, keeping it as a kind of personal secret. I was struck not by the discrepancy between the actual contents of these books and their critical evaluation in the Soviet press—for example, *One Day in the Life of Ivan Denisovich* was described as second-rate literature—but by the analysis of circumstances surrounding the political situation.

Throughout my military service I lived in closed garrisons. I always occupied command positions: first, at the low level; later at progressively higher levels, and eventually at the most senior levels in the army. Thus, I had no access to literature and other materials considered politically dangerous in the Soviet Union. The radio broadcasts convinced me that the Soviet media were distributing disinformation for mass consumption. The deeper the conflict, the greater our need for other sources of information, whether Western or independent, something to be expected in any country in the free world. I wanted to have that kind of access too.

Prevailing ideological norms also dictated the official position on religious belief. In Soviet society, for example, it was impossible to hold anything like strict religious beliefs and be considered a loyal state citizen or military man at the same time. Obviously, I was not going to church on Sundays or using Biblical phrases in my conversations with colleagues—and I cannot say how deep my faith at that time might have been in other circumstances—but I know that my attitude during those years was one of respect for spiritual belief as among the deepest and most profoundly personal feelings that a person can have.

My life flying planes—which by its very nature involved a high degree of risk—seemed particularly susceptible to questions related to the spirit. I was not free to discuss them, however, in the conditions under which I served. Whether out of prejudice or not, it was always understood that such topics were not for public discussion. Not only was there a social stigma attached to sharing religious views in public but also a psychological one. That is why all such feelings and attitudes were kept strictly personal. It took me some time to even consider discussing such matters openly.

This new attitude I owe to friends who, despite severe restrictions on the practice of their religious beliefs, followed the prescriptions of their faith throughout their lives. But even more I owe to my wife and daughter, who began discussing religious issues at home. Like me, they showed a deep respect for spiritual issues from a variety of religious traditions, and they cultivated a world view that values human dignity and tradition. Today they observe the feasts and holy days of the Orthodox calendar. The circle of our friends who have benefited from more opportunities to demonstrate their religious convictions seems to have grown wider over the last several years, especially as we have come to see that we share a common point of view with them. All of us—my wife, my daughter, and I—were baptized in the Orthodox sacrament soon after birth. Like our parents, Raisa and I ignored the prevailing Soviet taboos and, without drawing attention to ourselves, quietly observed religious holidays. And I should add that it is a most welcome fact that when our grandson, George, was baptized this year—the year 2000—it was already an open, joyful, *natural* family affair for his grandparents and parents, my daughter Eva and son-in-law Valerij Sigaev.

An Assessment of Higher Education

The single-minded emphasis on political and social ideology was not the only deficiency of the military educational system. In all the professional schools—engineering, aviation, or other higher military studies—little attention was devoted to learning foreign languages. Only now I am trying to muster my resources to learn English, but I truly regret that I did not make better use of the time I spent studying in three different educational establishments. It is an embarrassment to admit that a person with a diploma from a Soviet university does not necessarily have even a minimal knowledge for speaking or writing a foreign language.

In my view the system of higher education, especially in military institutions, did have many positive aspects. I had plenty of opportunity to study, for example, various philosophies and world views that I had not known before. At my disposal were well-stocked libraries for pursuing individual interests, which I could do during special hours allocated in the schedule of studies. I could study anything within the scope of my interests and educate myself, with the help of highly qualified instructors, even if the topic involved some theoretical aspect of literature, art, or culture. Students who wanted to raise the level of their cultural awareness or general education had plenty of opportunities for doing so.

I keep in touch with old friends with whom I studied or served in the military, including both commanders and subordinates. We remain friends today just as we were when we were beginning our careers. Among them are Oleksii Netai, who was born in the Kharkiv region, and Volodymyr Antonets from the Poltava region, the commander of the 14th Air Army, as well as others who served in aviation from a very young age. Recruited from Ukraine, they always seized the opportunity to return to their homeland whenever possible.

When I look back at the way my colleagues and I were trained, I am very pleased with the professionalism and high standards we were asked to meet. Whether one was working to become a jet pilot, a flight engineer, or a member of the ground crew, the training was rigorous and disciplined. Years later, after I became Ukraine's minister of defense, I had several opportunities to observe Western aviation technology in such advanced aircraft as the F-16, the FA-18, the Mirage 2000, and the Tornado—some of the best modern fighter planes. On visits to the United States, France, and Great Britain, for example, I was permitted to check out this technology in person, a great thrill for me because as a student and later as an instructor, I knew these planes only on the basis of what I had read in textbooks or viewed in training films. As a specialist in this field, who had flown in the latest models of Soviet MiG fighters, I felt fully qualified to compare this aviation technology with our own planes. The Western technology rated very high indeed.

This direct experience, however, only further increased my respect for the skills of our own flight personnel, who had to repair and fly planes in which operational imperatives were considered more important than personal needs and comfort. In spite of these difficult circumstances our pilots achieved results which were in no way inferior—and in some respects they were superior—to those of pilots using more advanced equipment. This achievement resulted from their excellent physical condition and endurance, their psychological preparation, and the level of their training. Although our electronics, guidance systems, and information systems may have been inferior, our overall performance was not. Indeed, I believe that our military schools in Ukraine could stand shoulder to shoulder with the best training schools in the West in preparing young recruits for a career in aviation.

Political realities determined where my military career took me. Although I was born in Ukraine and graduated from the Gritsevets Kharkiv Higher Military Aviation School, it was a fact of life that I would not be permitted to continue my military service in my homeland. That was how the Soviet system worked. Though there were no explicit laws or correspondent requirements, all Ukrainian nationals whenever they were planned for promotion had to be appointed to the positions outside of Ukraine on the territories of other republics. There was, I learned, a heavy price to pay for a career in the military.

Military Districts, Fleets, and Air Defense Districts

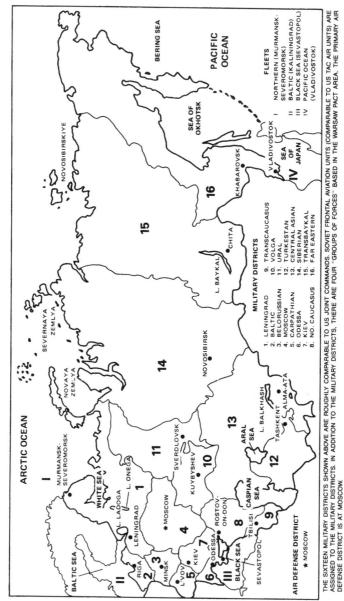

THE SIXTEEN MILITARY DISTRICTS SHOWN ABOVE ARE ROUGHLY COMPARABLE TO US JOINT COMMANDS. SOVIET FRONTAL AVIATION UNITS (COMPARABLE TO US TAC AIR UNITS) ARE ASSIGNED TO THE MILITARY DISTRICTS. IN ADDITION TO THE MILITARY DISTRICTS, THERE ARE FOUR "GROUPS OF FORCES" BASED IN THE WARSAW PACT AREA. THE PRIMARY AIR DEFENSE DISTRICT IS AT MOSCOW.

SOURCE: *AIR FORCE MAGAZINE*, MARCH 1975. COMPILED BY HARRIET FAST SCOTT.

MILITARY DISTRICTS
1. LENINGRAD
2. BALTIC
3. BELORUSSIAN
4. MOSCOW
5. CARPATHIAN
6. ODESSA
7. KIEV
8. NO. CAUCASUS
9. TRANSCAUCASUS
10. VOLGA
11. URAL
12. TURKESTAN
13. CENTRAL ASIAN
14. SIBERIAN
15. TRANSBAYKAL
16. FAR EASTERN

FLEETS
I NORTHERN (MURMANSK-SEVEROMORSK)
II BALTIC (KALININGRAD)
III BLACK SEA (SEVASTOPOL)
IV PACIFIC OCEAN (VLADIVOSTOK)

AIR DEFENSE DISTRICT
★ MOSCOW

Soviet Military Districts

(*From:* Harriet Fast Scott and William F. Scott, *The Armed Forces of the USSR*, 3rd ed.
Boulder, CO: Westview, 1984, p. 184. Reproduced with permission.)

3 The Price of Advancement

The year 1967 was a major turning point in my life: I graduated from the Gritsevets Kharkiv Military Aviation School and thus began my military career in earnest. Raisa and I had been married in 1964, but at the time she and I both had only the dimmest notion of the implications my military training in Ukraine would have for our life together. I was about to undertake a career in the Soviet Union's armed forces, but where this career would take us we could not say.

About one thing, however, we had no illusions: very few Ukrainian-born military personnel ever secured an assignment in their home republic; rather, as a matter of policy, the central command in Moscow saw to it that nearly all of us were transferred out of Ukraine to other regions of the Soviet Union, while Russian-born personnel were assigned to the bases in Ukraine and the other republics. With no uncertainty, we knew that we would spend the next several years on the move. How many years and how far the moves would take us from Ukraine remained a source of no little anxiety.

In Soviet military service lay both difficulty and opportunity. Assignments in remote regions typically placed great strains on family life, which not all military personnel could withstand. Wives and children of military men had to leave friends and relatives, adjust to new climates and cultures, and for years cope with material deprivations and loneliness. Servicemen worked under less than optimal conditions, having to deal with the stress of daily life in a strange place. Always there was the sense of being an outsider, even though we all lived under the umbrella of the *sovetskii narod:* we were all Soviet men and women.

At the same time, the opportunities could be very appealing, even compensating for the drawbacks. Not only did the military life afford the chance to see other parts of the world, learn about different cultures, and meet new people, but assignments to distant outposts, if completed with distinction, could often result in career advancements. It was the price to pay, and, fortunately for me, I had Raisa's support and encouragement all the while.

Life Abroad in the Military

My first opportunity to serve abroad came soon after my graduation, when I was assigned to an air force regiment of the Soviet Union's Northwestern Group. I was based in Chojna, near Szczecin, in the northwestern corner of Poland and not far from the border with East Germany. Here the standard of living seemed much higher than it was in Ukraine and other parts of the USSR. Stores in Poland, for instance, were full of consumer goods we rarely saw in our stores. Public services—transportation, utilities, and medical care—were, comparatively speaking, much better developed and more widely available. Small, private businesses, although still limited, operated throughout the cities and in many towns. Law enforcement agencies seemed more efficient and orderly, at least to the passing observer, and whether accurate or not, it seemed to us that everything in Poland was created to improve the lives of the people themselves. Driving through Polish cities, I observed how people lived, the conditions of their housing and their communities, which looked significantly higher than those of Soviet citizens. Under conditions that seemed the most prosperous we had observed in years, Raisa and I secured an apartment in Poland and took advantage of the higher standard of living.

In the Soviet Union, Poland was never considered to be exemplary in its achievements in building Communism. On the contrary, by its own prerogative the USSR was alone elevated to the status of the Communist utopia. Geographically and in many ways culturally closer to the West, Poland demonstrated the extent to which access to modern Western technologies and cooperation with Western Europe contributed to a more progressive development of society.

Perhaps that is why I found it so very strange to witness the

34

social protests that took place in 1969 and in 1970 in cities such as Gdańsk and Gdynia. In organized demonstrations Polish workers marched through the streets, indignant at unfair working conditions and price increases in staples. They demanded redress from the government but were met by a violent backlash from the authorities in which many protesters were killed. At first I was mystified by these demonstrators' motives: Why were they protesting? What was their political motivation? Later it became apparent that all these events were inspired by the Prague Spring, which had culminated in 1968 with the entry of Soviet troops into Czechoslovakia. I believe that from their perspective ordinary citizens could see the need for change better than those in authority—not just changes in the Soviet Union but in all of the countries of the Warsaw Pact.

As a military man I had witnessed the actual intrusion of the coalition troops into Czechoslovak territory. The ideological brainwashing and absence of truthful information were components of a well-prepared campaign. We simply had not known the real truth. We had no prior accurate political information about events in Czechoslovakia in the late 1960s, and we had not known what the people's political motives or demands were. All information regarding protests of Czechoslovak dissidents against the intrusion of troops, as well as similar demonstrations by young radicals in the Soviet Union, had been severely suppressed from public scrutiny, and especially from personnel in the Soviet army. The army's own political organs, as well as the KGB itself, saw to it that no information leaked through. If any discussion did take place, the authorities had to be informed of all participants and the points of view they expressed. This information was collected and thoroughly analyzed in order to keep control of any situation that might arise. The propaganda machine at the time explained the need to send the coalition military forces into Czechoslovakia by saying these measures were taken in direct response to the appeal of Czechoslovak people and their progressive democratic government. In reality, however, this operation was undertaken in order to preserve the existing borders of the Soviet bloc and to ensure the absolute control of Eastern Europe under the USSR leadership. By defending its parts, the system acted to guarantee its own stability in the face of potential new political demands of the people.

In 1981, thirteen years after these events, I served in the garrisons that the Soviet troops had actually occupied during the Prague Spring. At this time it was, as they say, "business as usual," no different from that experienced by military personnel in other Soviet garrisons. In this span of only thirteen years, the USSR armed forces had managed to overcome hostilities and build good relations with the national army of Czechoslovakia. We even held joint training sessions for air force personnel in the use of new Soviet aviation technology. Working closely with the commanders and staff of the Czechoslovak air force in the various military districts, we frequently conducted joint military exercises.

Hypocrisy was evident everywhere: in false slogans, in false reports, and in constant reminders about the unity of the Party and the people. The greatest hypocrisy was the duality of truth, the difference between the dominant, official truth and the truth that most people personally accepted. This duality was also evident in the degree to which people could remain principled and honest with themselves and others, but still not fall under suspicion of those who were called on to ensure the purity of the Party's intentions. The overbearing nature of the entire ideological machine became starkly clear there.

The irony of our situation was that we clearly were not the same as our Czech or Slovak brothers. They had our socialist ideology, but they also had their own country. Reflecting on my own "Soviet people," it was clear that there were "Soviets" who had languages and customs much more different from mine than were the Czech and Slovak ones. Still, the Party line told us that we Soviets were a monolithic people who should not be divided along the lines of national, cultural, or religious differences. The ideology insinuated to us, "Why would the representatives of various nationalities in the Soviet Union ever need to refer to their national culture or the history of their ancestors?" But then why should the Czechs and Slovaks need their national culture or history. Why were they *allowed it*? Nothing could hide that double standard.

Turkmenistan

This ideology permeated even the remotest regions of the Soviet Union, as I was soon to observe firsthand. Near the end of 1979, I was serving in the city of Lipetsk, about 350 kilometers (220 miles) southeast of Moscow, when I received an offer to become commander of the air force base and chief of the military garrison in Mary (Merv), Turkmenistan. My wife, daughter, and I would be posted to the Central Asia, thousands of kilometers from our homeland and even farther from the culture we were accustomed to.

Preferring to work independently and looking for new adventures, however, I agreed. My fears had been eased by the fact that I had learned about the peculiarities of this position earlier when I had had a chance to visit this base with a group of officers undergoing part of their training before being promoted to higher positions. In a few days we packed our belongings and moved out of our apartment in Lipetsk. My wife, daughter, and I flew to Moscow on a raw, cold November day, when the thermometer had trouble getting above –20° Celsius (about -5° Farenheit). There we transferred to a plane bound for Tashkent, the capital of Uzbekistan, where the summer was still on and the temperature a much more pleasant +15° (60° F).

I had to spend a few days in Tashkent getting to know the military district's air force staff, with whom I would be working. The region was impressive for the grandeur of its ancient culture, and I was particularly struck by the Central Asian monumental art and architecture. The Tashkent area had experienced a devastating earthquake in 1966, which left parts of the city in ruins.* The local population had made great efforts to preserve their cultural legacy and undertake repairs both here and in other locations in Uzbekistan, such as Samarkand and Bukhara. The situation was similar in the Turkmen city of Ashkhabad after a heavy earthquake there in 1948.

Here at the junction of great empires, I observed numerous problems threatening to overwhelm the people. In terms both of geography and of domestic policies, Uzbekistan and Turkmenistan were truly on the periphery. The Soviet Union intended to keep these regions under its central control and always within the Soviet orbit.

As a visible sign of that intention, the military had located in these regions a large number of garrisons, including air force units—practically one for every large city.

I saw firsthand the impoverished living conditions of both servicemen and officers whom fate—and the Moscow central command—had chosen to serve in these distant outposts. Many Ukrainians were stationed here, men who had graduated from the higher military schools in Kharkiv, Kyiv, or other cities back home. As in my case, they were not allowed to serve in their own republic, but could prove their loyalty and military skills by serving in Central Asia or in regions as distant as the far eastern reaches of the Soviet Union or the Trans-Baikal region on the border with China. Service in these outposts typically held out better prospects for career advancement. These servicemen could think about satisfying their personal interests after they retired from active duty, but this outcome depended on their successfully climbing up a long ladder of incremental promotions while the local authorities, year by year, handed out living quarters to military pensioners. This fate awaited all the junior and senior officers living in Central Asia at the time.

I remember one case, that of Lieutenant Colonel Yatsun, who was born and reared in Ukraine, studied there, yet spent over twenty years of his adult life outside his home republic, serving in various military garrisons where the living conditions were extremely difficult. Most of his postings were in Central Asia, in remote places such as Mary and Kizyl-Arvat (in Turkmenistan), and Kokaity (in Uzbekistan). Water supplies in these garrisons were very poor; in fact, little had changed in the course of the half century during which Soviet forces had been stationed here.* Living conditions were very poor not only for their families, but even for servicemen themselves.

As chief commander of the air force base in Mary, I got exactly what I bargained for. The town itself was located in the southeastern portion of Turkmenistan, at the crux of a huge "V" formed by the main rail line (and road, which on occasion might disappear entirely) that cuts across the republic. Up the northwest branch from Mary lie most of the major towns and cities of Turkmenistan: the capital Ashkhabad (Ashgabat), Kizyl-Arvat (Gyzylarbat), and ultimately Krasnovodsk (Türkmenbashi) on the Caspian Sea. Up the northeast branch the population thins out, centered primarily in the towns of Bairam-Ali and Chardzhou on the Amu Darya River, which runs along the border with Uzbekistan and finally flows into the Aral Sea.* Mary sits among the northern tributaries of the Morghab (Murgab) River, which flows south into Afghanistan. The border with Iran lies only about 150 kilometers (about 95 miles) to the west.

The facility I commanded was actually an air force target range, subordinated neither to the Turkestan Military District nor to any military unit. Nominally an air force garrison was subordinated within its territory to the head commander of the military district, but in this case, I reported to the central office in Moscow responsible for the military training of air force personnel. This line of command was one aspect I found appealing: I have always preferred carrying out my duties where I am responsible for solving problems and developing relations with subordinates and commanders. In practice my activities as leader of an air force unit with two squadrons of modern fighter planes were regulated only by the existing organizational documents for the air force in general. Thus, I could design my own methods for the implementation of these regulations and establish contacts with other institutions involved in the military training of air force personnel.

(I must mention as an aside that years later, when I was minister of defense of Ukraine, I was invited by U.S. Secretary of Defense Dick Cheney to visit Ellis Air Force Base near Las Vegas, Nevada. I was deeply struck by how physically similar it seemed to the base I commanded near Mary.)

Even in this periphery, Party literature and slogans were evident everywhere. The portraits of Party leaders appeared on walls and buildings. Speeches, whether political or military, always began with the phrase "under the leadership of the Communist Party." In my work a heavy emphasis fell on the writing of lengthy, tedious reports. Much of the political rhetoric stressed the importance of bringing in a good cotton crop, the Turkmens' most important agricultural product. Various provinces within the republic competed with each other to see which could report the largest harvests of cotton—all produced for the glory of the state, of course. Corruption was rampant, and with Rashidov and Gapurov reigning as the top Party officials of these Central Asian republics,* the manipulation of harvest statistics was not out of the ordinary. These leaders maintained their authority through coercion and drew support from the political machine whose ideology they controlled. All in all, it was not hard to see through this charade, which reeked of falsehood and Potemkin villages.

Both the Turkmen and Uzbek republics were within the Turkestan Military District, which in its totality covered an area roughly the size of France and Germany. Although I was stationed in southern Turkmenistan, I frequently participated in meetings or conferences in Tashkent, Uzbekistan. Thus, I had many opportunities to meet with the people of those regions. Since it was considered the duty of senior officials like me to stand for election to local councils, I was nominated and elected a deputy of the Mary (Turkmenistan) Oblast council, in which capacity I represented the local electoral district outside the garrison. The majority of my constituents were local civilians, ordinary workers employed by an industrial conglomerate involved in building and maintaining irrigation systems in and around Mary.

Although I took part in the oblast council's sessions and in meetings of the Party group of deputies, my role was little more than a formality. In fact, I saw little sense in it. My hands were tied by a long tradition of Party bureaucracy. About all I could do was fulfill my duties—meeting with my constituents to inform them about the political situation in the republic, Party decisions affecting their lives, and the progress made in meeting goals set by the central government. Genuine political discussion of controversial issues—even in the mild form this assumed later during Gorbachev's restructuring efforts—was simply out of the question. No one could imagine engaging in this kind of behavior.

Despite the restrictions, I was able to help some of the local people in cases of blatant injustice. Whenever possible, I intervened on their behalf, assisted them in filling out forms, helped them gain access to senior officials, or met with those officials myself. While I

(con't on p. 53)

40

Photo Collection I

1. Morozov at age 18, after graduation from high school.

This was taken in 1962, a year after I had graduated from high school. At the time of this photo, I was working as a lab assistant, having failed the vertigo portion of the medical test during my first attempt to enter the Gritsevets Kharkiv Higher Military Aviation School. This is the first photo that I gave to my future wife, Raisa. At that same time she gave me one of her and we now have them together in our family photo album. We were married two years after this photograph was taken.

2. Morozov as a cadet at the Gritsevets Kharkiv Higher Military Aviation School in fall 1963.

My first year as a cadet. Between this picture and the last, there is a world of difference. This was taken when the first-year cadets had made their first parachute jump. (Note my parachutist's pin.) The jumps were made from an An-2 light transport. About eight of us would make the jumps at a time. I remember that the jump instructor was a lieutenant colonel, whose name I now do not recall. I do recall that each one of us had great trepidation about how our first jump would go, so we tried to make the jumps as quickly as possible. This was our first real experience in the environment of the air—the first time when we were not merely soldiers, but "attached to the air."

Чугуев. 1966 г.

3. Morozov as a cadet at Chuhuïv, near Kharkiv, in 1966, flying a MiG-17.

This is in the summer 1966 during one of my first flights after the accident (see p. 22). Note that this is a fighter without an instructor's seat; it was based at a true air force base—not an academy field. The flight is significant. After my accident, I could have chosen to leave the military with an honorable discharge and fulfilled my constitutional obligation for military service—saying that the psychological stress of the accident made it impossible for me to continue. I would have been discharged with no negative repercussions and could then have entered a civilian university as a second-year student, without having to take the requisite entrance exams. My superiors asked me directly, "Will you continue?" I unhesitatingly answered in the affirmative. This picture is important because it was precisely at this point that I had begun to get my flying rhythm back and was entrusted piloting jet fighter aircraft on my own.

4. Morozov as a cadet at the Gritsevets Kharkiv Higher Military Aviation School in spring 1967.

We had begun to fly the MiG-21—this was taken right after my first super-sonic flight. Experiencing the exhilaration of breaking the sound barrier, which is a completely different phenomenon than subsonic flight, made us feel like cosmonauts. My "look toward the heavens" is meant to convey that. This was at the Kupiansk Air Base in the Kharkiv region, during my last year at the Gritsevets Military Aviation School. I felt that I soon would be a true officer, and not long after that I flew all of the modifications of the MiG-21 (there were many modified versions of that particular fighter plane).

5. At the Yuri Gagarin Air Force Academy of Higher Military Studies in 1975. The commandant of the Academy, Gen. Nikolai Skomorokhov, with Morozov and other students.

I was finishing up at the Yuri Gagarin Air Force Academy of Higher Military Studies and was getting ready to be appointed as a commander of an air army squadron. The fellow next to me is Alexander [Oleksandr] Netai. Speaking to me is Col. Gen. Nikolai M. Skomorokhov, who was a well-known pilot in the Soviet Union, a veteran of the Second World War (he was an ace with forty-six kills) and much decorated (he received the order of the "Hero of the Soviet Union" twice). I was a captain at the time.

45

6. At the "Penki" park in Moscow in 1975, during a Gagarin Academy picnic.

This was shortly before the end of our course at the Gagarin Academy, when we knew that we soon would be dispersing to various parts of the Soviet Union. So we tried to get out into the fresh air, into the green places, as much as possible. Maybe a little beer, a little wine. And to be honest, I wasn't very good on the guitar, but I always wanted to play it, so I grabbed one every chance I got. The people that I was with at the Academy were good men and I enjoyed their company.

7. At a divisional air force sports competition in Milovice, Czechoslovakia in 1982.

I was the deputy commander of a division. As one of my responsibilities, I coordinated the sports events for the division. This was a series of competitions between pilots and flight crews of different regiments within the division. On the weekends, many of the pilots and other air personnel would come together for these events, with their families in the stands as spectators. Here, I am giving an award to one of the participants.

47

КШУ. КП чад. 1983г.

8. A Command and Staff emergency training exercise, Hungary, October 10, 1983.

This was 1983 when I was the commander of the 11th Guards Fighter Division in the Soviet Southern Strategic Command (of the Southern Group of Forces) in Hungary. My command post was located outside of Budapest. This photo was taken during a command and staff training exercise. I received a message at my home before dawn that I was to come quickly to my command post. I contacted my subordinates by radio phone from the car on the way to the post and we had to send out three separate fighter groups to converge on a predetermined location that had been decided by the central military command. The fellow standing behind me is my subordinate, the chief of staff, Col. Barannikov.

9. Following the October 10, 1983 Command and Staff exercise, with Marshal Aleksandr Yefimov.

This photograph was taken at the successful conclusion of the command and staff training exercise shown in the previous picture. I went out to meet one of the fighter pilots who had returned from the mission. With me (and slightly in front of me just to my left) is Marshal Aleksandr N. Yefimov (the commander in chief of the Soviet air force). Marshal Yefimov had come to the divisional command to monitor the exercise. Like Skomorokhov he also received the order of the "Hero of the Soviet Union" twice. The plane in the background is a MiG-23.

49

10. Raisa, Kostiantyn, and Eva Morozov, 1986.

This is my family in 1986 in Smolensk. The portrait was taken after my graduation from the Kliment Voroshilov Academy of the General Staff of the Armed Forces of the USSR (in Moscow). I was given the position of chief of staff and first deputy commander of the 46th Air Army in Smolensk.

11. In Smolensk in 1987. Kateryna, Kostiantyn, and Raisa Morozov.

This was in Smolensk, in 1987, when my mother, Kateryna, came to visit us. I had been at a local governmental meeting as a deputy of the Smolensk Oblast Council (which explains my civilian clothing). After the meeting, I called home for my wife and mother to meet me for a walk to the park. My tour of duty in Smolensk marked the second time I had been elected to an oblast council (the first was in Mary, in the Turkmen SSR). An oblast is similar in size and governmental function to an American state or a Canadian province.

(con't from p. 40)

know this intervention was appreciated, I had to limit my involvement in order to carry out my military duties as garrison commander. Besides, the military personnel who served under my command faced many problems of their own, particularly in dealing with the poor housing conditions in what seemed at times a foreign country. Living on the periphery, my family and I came to share with many staff members a sense of estrangement, particularly at a time when we could see through the sham of political propagandists all around us.

A Return to Eastern Europe

In 1981, Raisa, Eva, and I returned to Eastern Europe where I accepted a military command in Czechoslovakia. Needless to say, the contrast to the republics of Central Asia was overwhelming, and it took us a long time to readjust to a much higher standard of living. (Sometimes it is as hard to go from deprivation to relative plenty as it is to experience the opposite.) Not only did the Czechoslovak people enjoy better living conditions, but their exercise of human rights and their sense of security were substantially greater than what we had experienced elsewhere. Indeed, I saw the political and social condition of Czechoslovakia in much the same way that I had seen Poland several years earlier. Largely because of their proximity to the West and their access to Western technology and consumer goods, the countries of Eastern Europe had introduced many changes to improve the standard of living, changes which had never made their way to the Soviet Union.

I observed the same situation in Hungary, where I served as a division commander after my one year of service in Czechoslovakia. I had earned two university-level diplomas and had studied both social and political sciences, as well as philosophy and history; moreover, I had read a great deal of literature, which no doubt contributed to my impressions about the quality of life in the Soviet Union; but I was still at a loss as to why the peoples of Eastern Europe had been able so quickly to rebuild their economies in the post-war period and to make steady improvements in their standard of living. Why had the Soviet Union become a leader only in political sloganeering? How was it that the Soviet Union had been so successful in spreading the Communist ideology and establishing, even on scientific grounds, a program of rigid behavior and control? How had the countries we helped rebuild after the Second World War managed to surpass us in the quality of life they now provided to their citizens?

Such questions rarely have simple answers. Throughout Eastern Europe democratic principles had long ago taken hold of the people's imaginations and their vision for a better society, as evidenced by the protests and demonstrations from the Prague Spring to the '90s. Despite the dominance of the Communist Party, the multi-party system was a political reality in most of these countries. Furthermore, the experience of the Western democracies had become something of a beacon to the peoples of Eastern Europe, its light refracted by the prism of their having lived under Communist control for so many years. Although the Soviet Union's rigid control was an undeniable fact of life, the Poles, Czechoslovaks, and Hungarians had their own statehood and could determine their relations with the West, if not absolutely independently, then at least in the direction prompted by their own interests.

The Return to Ukraine

In 1988, over twenty years from the time Raisa and I first left our homeland, we moved again—this time to Kyiv. To be near our relatives, to be once more in our motherland, to live at a time when political and social change was about to flood into our lives—this was the most exciting and promising move of my entire career, up to that point in my life. My daughter completed her studies and took a job in Kyiv.

In 1990, roughly two years later, it was suggested to me by my superiors that I could be transferred from my post in Kyiv and take an equivalent position (or perhaps one with even more responsibility) in the Far East of the Soviet Union. The responsibility and authority of such a position would be even greater than what I had in Ukraine, but I felt a discomfort I cannot articulate. Indeed, I suspected that there were other reasons for my superiors to suggest my transfer from Ukraine.

Raisa was unequivocally against the idea. In her view there was no reason to accept it either as a promotion to a higher position or as an expression of reliance. "We did not move back to our Ukraine," she said, "in order to move again to some other place, to the Far East." Despite the argument that the family had already given years of sacrifice, she recognized that I was the one that would have to make the decision: after all, a refusal would have serious consequences for my military career and service, to which all our family affairs had been subordinated for the past twenty-three years. In the end it was a decision I did not have to make, because the transfer order was never officially put through and I was able simply to avoid responding to the proposition. I must say, looking back on it, as a military officer I would have found it impossible to have turned down the transfer if it had been officially put through rather than unofficially suggested to me as a possibility. I know of no case in which an officer refused a transfer, once it was officially presented to him. I'm sure that had they handed me the transfer as a fait accompli and I had refused, my career in the military would have been over and remaining as an officer in Ukraine would have been moot.

The real point, though, is that they expected me to jump at their suggestion without them having to openly push the issue of getting me out of Ukraine. The system of the Soviet military was constructed to inculcate into a person, especially someone in an administrative position, a sense of devotion to the state. That man's obligations—his sense of duty to his society, his country, as well as to his position—held the primary importance for him. Any facts in his individual biography or on his résumé, particularly anything denoting personal qualities and family relationships, for example, were considered secondary if not irrelevant. I always took note of how high-ranking officials in democratic societies are not shy at official receptions or in public gatherings to speak openly about their families, to identify their spouses and parents, or to speak of deep friendships and recall some incident in their formative years. All of these "facts" cast a light on the man, illuminating personal features that help us understand his human qualities.

In Soviet society, however, to speak about family matters or to reveal personal feelings was considered inappropriate. The entire system operated under the motto "Think about your motherland first and yourself afterward." One's individual interests—in life, work, or fantasy—were strictly personal, not to be discussed in public or in any professional context. Even a question regarding a problem connected with, say, a new appointment or a new place of work was appropriately posed only to those administrators directly related to one's duties and responsibilities. To ask a question about some personal interest, for instance, or the conditions of life at a new location, or the progress one's children were making at school was taboo.

Reconciling the demands of professional life with those of one's family—including the desire to maintain close contacts with parents, children, brothers, and sisters—has always been a challenge for me, but an issue in which I have a great interest and concern. I always found time to share my thoughts, to talk with Raisa, to take part in some family activity. When away from home, I missed my family a lot, and I always considered a return home as a kind of holiday that restored me and renewed the family's daily routines. No doubt those feelings are universal among people in the armed forces, even though they were rarely given free voice in the Soviet military. In contrast to the apparently free expression of personal feelings that one finds among military people in democratic countries, this interdiction seems to me unnatural and damaging.

Ideally, a man's feelings—his attitudes toward his family life, his life at home, as well as the way he conducts his business—should directly express his character. I always considered it a means of observing and learning important details about this or that man's character. Call it a window through which we see his inner being, what defines him and his values. For a man in a position of authority, it provides essential evidence his subordinates can use to predict the character of his business relations; it allows them to put a human face on their leader. Anyone who would command others must develop such personal qualities, for these create not only the authority of the position itself but also the authority of the person who holds it. Developing these qualities was one of the most important tasks of my life, and without them I never would have progressed so far as I did. The support and understanding of people around me—whether those who served under my command, or my closest friends, or the members of my family—enabled me to achieve what I did. And of all of them, I owe the greatest debt of gratitude to Raisa.

She always knew when I, as an active pilot, was supposed to come home, when a flight was completed safely, or when bad weather conditions postponed an exercise. From the first days of our life together, Raisa's support of me and my career decisions showed her willingness to put her own interests in second place. Not even the prospect of making a life together in Central Asia, far from our native land, deterred her or softened her resolve to devote herself to her family. My challenge was to try to live up to the level of trust she put in me.

No one in Raisa's family had been involved in the armed forces, and there was no particular reason why anyone should have expected her to be so supportive of me as a military man. That is, there were no soldiers in her family background, as there were in mine. We did, however, share many other experiences. Like me, she had also lost her father early in life. Her mother, a worker in the Donbas mines, supported her children, much as my mother had supported me and my brother and sister. Our families lived close by, and the two of us met at school when I was fifteen and she was fourteen. We have rarely been apart since.

In the times I had to be away—when, for instance, I went to work before being accepted to the Gritsevets Kharkiv Higher Military Aviation School and when later I studied at the school to be an air force pilot—we continued to see each other whenever possible, during vacation periods or when my work brought me back to the Donbas region. Although it meant time apart, Raisa fully supported me in my decision to study at the higher military aviation school. It was during this time that we began to build a set of common values, a commitment to honesty, decency, kindness, and sincerity. Raisa is very sensitive to anything false or artificial in human relations, and it is not in her nature to be hypocritical or to hide her true feelings. She never hesitated to speak her mind or to criticize me when I deserved it. Our life together has been built on a system of mutual support, a complementarity that characterizes the best and most successful marriages.

Moreover, Raisa never took the position that she would wait at our old home in Ukraine and leave investigating the conditions of the next assignment up to me. (In one case, I did have to serve abroad and had to leave her behind in order to arrange for her invitation to join me later.) Instead, she plunged right in with me, accepting the transfer as a "fact of life," and looking upon it as an opportunity to gain new experience and perspectives. It was not merely a sense of adventure that she was after, or willing to endure; rather, it was a deep respect for our growth together under each new set of circumstances that elevated her above the hassles and disappointments of daily life. She never once set any preconditions that might affect my decision to accept or reject a transfer—except in the case of the proposed transfer in 1990 from Ukraine. Only then did she object. Upon reflection I agreed that we should stay where we were.

My military assignments to some of the remotest bases in the USSR played havoc with Raisa's plans to study and her desire to become a historian. These outposts offered little in the way of professional work for her. (My daughter Eva, too, found the military life difficult, having to change five or six schools in ten years, for example.) Raisa's commitment to her family, however, took precedence over all else. Her resolve, I am convinced, has exerted a deep and positive influence on me, particularly as I began making my own commitment to the democratic movement in Ukraine.

4 The Cadre Policy in the Soviet Military

For the fourth consecutive time, Lieutenant Colonel Liubomyr Petriv had failed to be appointed commander of the 14th Fighter Regiment in the 11th Division, which I commanded. He had been only a deputy regimental commander for more than four years, a position in which he served with distinction. On previous occasions when his name had unsuccessfully been put forward for a promotion (which would come with his appointment as a regimental commander), he was told that a regimental commander had to be an active pilot. Of course, this requirement only served to raise his hopes of eventual success because, after all, he *did* fly military aircraft on a regular basis. Moreover, he had amassed a great deal of experience in his position of deputy commander. And so he continued serving in his subordinate position, trying ever so bravely to put forward the best face possible even after so many disappointments.

Since taking over as division commander, I myself had twice recommended Petriv for promotion. In each instance an "outside" candidate had suddenly arrived on the scene and beat him out of the position for which he had applied. One young graduate of a military academy came in bearing papers that required me to find some assignment for him because he had a degree signifying his "higher" education. In fact, Petriv had also graduated from the same academy—albeit by taking correspondence courses rather than matriculating as a full-time student—yet his accomplishment was ignored when it came time to evaluate the candidates. That Petriv had not attended the academy as a regular student was actually held against him.

On his fourth rejection, I invited Petriv into my office to give him a chance to vent his frustration and anger. I needed to calm him down, but first I had to hear him out. In this instance, I wanted to avoid playing the patronizing father figure. I did not want to utter anything insincere or string out clichés that would surely alienate him. Nor as his commander did I want to become his confessor, although he certainly bared his soul in a cry of anguish. In all likelihood I was trying to assuage my own conscience, hoping to find some way of explaining the situation to Petriv. Finding the right words was excruciating: his primary deficiency—which was no fault of his own, but which in his case was enough to ruin forever his chances of promotion—was merely that he was from western Ukraine.

The Question of Nationality

Although western Ukraine was by all accounts a Slavic area and we were all purportedly equal in the eyes of the Soviet state, some of our Slavic brothers in the USSR were "more equal than others." That is because russocentrism permeated all aspects of society, not just the officer ranks of the military. Whenever I read about "the Russians in space" or "the great artists of the Russian ballet," I always perceived such references as an injustice and an inherent discrimination against the people of non-Russian backgrounds. After all, how can one speak only of Russians when referring to the accomplishments of all the people in a multinational country consisting of fifteen republics and over a hundred different nationalities?

The same slight is evident in any study of the long traditions in the military. The Soviet armed forces comprised personnel representing all fifteen republics of the USSR, but propaganda materials such as books, movies, posters, and music show that Russian history, cultural traditions, and military ethos were used by the Communist Party to promote Soviet patriotism in the armed forces. Certainly, official ideology acknowledged that the armed forces represented and served the interests of the fifteen Soviet republics. All we heard, however, was that the Soviet military ethos had its roots in the Russian military, which achieved its great glory thanks to brilliant Russian strategists. Naturally, then, this glorification of Russian military traditions meant that there was no room for discussion of the military traditions of other peoples of the Soviet Union.*

This was true even in the case of Ukraine, although there are many fascinating examples, from the Cossack period and later, of the courageous defense of Ukraine's soil against foreign incursions. In particular, if these non-Russian traditions in any way contradicted the stereotypical portrayal in official ideology of the "friendship of peoples" and the leading role of the Russian "elder brother," they were mentioned only in a negative context. A related problem for Ukrainian military history was the presence of Ukrainians in the pre-revolutionary Tsarist army. In the early history of the Soviet military there were several well-known figures of Ukrainian background. Many of them, however, such as Marshal Semen Tymoshenko (S. K. Timoshenko), had earlier served in the Tsarist army, which was a Russian army. The traditions they fostered in the Soviet military were Russian ones; thus, they were Ukrainians in name only, and no one ever spoke of them as representatives of the Ukrainian people or as having any specific Ukrainian qualities. In spite of all the rhetoric one heard about the "Soviet people," in the armed forces it was Russian military tradition that prevailed and excluded other military traditions. In the end, this meant that our job, effectively, was to continue to prepare Soviet soldiers to defend what was considered Russian soil.

I first became aware of the nationality litmus test during my studies at the Gritsevets Kharkiv Higher Military Aviation School. Simply stated, the criterion of ethnicity was used to discriminate against certain recruits and to reward others in terms of military assignments and promotions. Among the students ethnic Russians were the majority, with ethnic Ukrainians not far behind. When it came to preferred treatment, however, there was no contest: ethnic Russians always came out on top. Many of my fellow students who had lived in Ukraine before they were admitted to the military schools were destined after graduation to serve for lengthy periods in remote regions of the USSR. This discrimination was evident in all institutions of higher education, particularly those that prepared students for the military.

Moreover, as the number of non-Slavic students in military schools grew smaller with every passing year, various attempts were made to bolster their numbers. Eventually, quotas for the Caucasian and Central Asian republics were established, and local military commissars were expected to fill them by whatever means necessary. Whether because of insufficient propaganda or because the schools themselves were located primarily in the Slavic regions of the Soviet Union, very few students from these distant republics wanted to enroll. I remember not more than five among the 150 students who graduated in my class.

When as a chief of staff I became more involved in the military higher education system, I received directives to recruit natives of various republics so that their proportion among the student body could be artificially raised. The non-Russian students, however, were made to understand that Russians, solely by virtue of their ethnicity, were considered more trustworthy, more capable, more skillful. This unwritten assumption became all too evident when the non-Russians finished their studies but were given job assignments in undesirable locations. They felt the impact of discrimination throughout their careers. Ukrainians were less likely to suffer from the discrimination than Uzbeks or Turkmens, but even they felt the ill effects of such a policy. Lieutenant Colonel Petriv certainly did.

The Central Committee of the Communist Party of the Soviet Union was the final arbiter of personnel decisions. Before the USSR minister of defense signed promotion papers, a candidate was scrutinized by military councils and commanders at all levels—initially the military council of the unit in which the officer served, and later by the council of the appropriate military district and the central council of the military services branch. If they were appointing a senior officer, administrative types of the Central Committee also studied the candidate's personnel file, taking into account nationality, class origin, parental information, previous training, political views, social behavior, and of course, participation in Communist Party affairs. If the candidate received the Central Committee's approval, the minister of defense was given a go-ahead to order the candidate's appointment to the appropriate position.

"Cadres Decide Everything"

No Communist Party administrator or military personnel, of course, would ever admit that nationality played such a determining role in an appointment. In official statements no attempt to differentiate among officers on the basis of ethnic background, especially at the senior level, was made. There were always "more serious" deficiencies in a candidate to be found in order to turn down a request for transfer or deny a promotion. Still, no one doubted that issues of nationality had a major impact on one's career path. Colleagues once told me that they had seen resolutions specifying the percentages of various nationalities to be appointed to senior positions. Ukraine figured prominently on this list, though far behind the percentage for Russia, for in the inner circles of the military the representation of Ukrainians in senior positions was taken seriously.

As part of what was called "cadre policy," the criteria for moving up the ranks were clearly specified and widely known (but not to everyone). Through cadre policy the political element was introduced into the selection and preparation of senior officer personnel—that is, the commanders who shaped the outlook of junior officers and thereby influenced the entire education, moral and otherwise, of everyone in the military. In firm control of cadre policy, the Communist Party—which held uninterrupted power and, according to the constitution of 1977, played the leading role in society—ensured its ability to shape the consciousness of the military's personnel. "Cadres decide everything" was the old Stalinist slogan. Although it later came under criticism, it was never thoroughly rejected. Indeed, a network of Party operatives ensured that all section chiefs, especially those holding senior rank, considered themselves to be direct representatives of the Party's Central Committee.

In theory one's political awareness was not related in any way to ethnicity or region of origin, and no attempt was made to distinguish among officers on the basis of nationality. Officers themselves did not underline this aspect of their personal background, and they were intentionally downplayed by the military's leadership. According to the standard line, the "Soviet people"—a phrase that gained widespread popularity in the last years of the Brezhnev period—constituted a new entity in which all nationalities of the Soviet Union were eventually to be merged, all separate national identities and ethnicities supposedly subsumed under the Soviet ideal.

Should one ask, "Are there any Ukrainians in the Soviet armed forces?" one might be thought to be speaking nonsense. Of course, at one level it was obvious that Ukrainians constituted a huge percentage of Soviet military personnel, just as they were found in all state institutions. No official data on this issue existed, however, and one dared not even bring up the possibility of conducting research on the question. One could only try to analyze a given situation or reflect upon the case of an individual whom one had met or with whom one had served in various garrisons or regions. It's my impression that Ukrainians in the military were found among the conscripts, rank-and-file servicemen, and deputy commanders, but rarely in the top echelon of leaders.

The System Works

I frequently heard it said that conscripts from Ukraine, Belarus, and the Baltic republics were far better prepared for military service, both in physical conditioning and in educational background. They knew Russian better than conscripts from other republics, especially those from Central Asia. According to the prevailing prejudice, they were more trustworthy (although not so much as Russian conscripts). From the moment when they were first screened by the military commissars who made decisions about the professions these young men would follow or to which branch of the military they would be assigned, this supposed ethnic trait of trustworthiness insured that the Slavic conscripts would be assigned to work in areas demanding a strong sense of responsibility.

In the garrisons where I served, many of the aviation mechanics were Ukrainian. It's not that Ukrainians are, by nature, better mechanics or that there is an ethnic trait that ensures someone from Ukraine always takes a meticulous, conscientious approach to his duties. Rather it was assumed that conscripts from the Ukrainian

SSR distinguished themselves from other conscripts and could be trusted with such work. These technicians did not need to be monitored at every moment. Similarly many of my Ukrainian friends who were pilots or officers in other service branches were highly regarded because of their sense of duty and devotion to their work.

No doubt, some long-standing historical traditions are at work here in support of cadre policy.* Ukrainians, or so it was widely believed, have a certain disposition to serve admirably in the military, albeit at the junior level in the officer corps. Curiously, most of the officers in the Academy of the General Staff who had Ukrainian backgrounds *did not* have Ukrainian surnames, and Ukrainian surnames were even rarer among the most senior commanders. More than once, in conversation with military personnel involved in cadre work, I heard people say, "He's a fine fellow. But if only his last name were not *Bahlai,* but rather *Baglaev,*" or something similar.* How offensive that they thought me sufficiently enmeshed in cadre policy to share that prejudice!

I spent the better part of my military career under the assumption that I was not a "pure" ethnic Ukrainian. My father was Russian, or so I thought, and I had been born in Luhansk Oblast, in the russified Donbas of eastern Ukraine. After completing my studies in Kharkiv and receiving my diploma as a pilot-engineer in 1967, I spent twenty-one years serving outside of Ukraine. My case, I am sure, is hardly unique in this regard. Indeed, many of my friends who were born and reared in Ukraine, even if they were of mixed ethnic background or had Russian surnames, served everywhere imaginable, but not in Ukraine. The same could be said for those of other nationalities such as the peoples of the Caucasus, the Baltic states, and Belarus. The similarities were too numerous to be attributed merely to coincidence or fate.

I knew many Ukrainian officers like Lieutenant Colonel Petriv who served as deputy commanders of regiments or divisions, but were consistently denied promotion to senior officer rank. Likewise, I knew of Ukrainians who served in positions of great responsibility as advisors to staff members or other administrators in the Warsaw Pact armies. But I am hard pressed to name a Ukrainian candidate who made it to the top—without benefit, as in my own case, of a presumed Russian ethnicity. Ukrainian candidates always encountered a "glass ceiling" as they were denied the senior posts always for seemingly legitimate reasons. Cadre operatives involved in the review and accreditation procedure, had clear directives or instructions to guide their work.*

According to cadre policy, it was convenient to have young, new Ukrainian recruits in the position of deputy commanders, conscientiously and reliably fulfilling their duties. These individuals did not even need to be given assignments; they knew what had to be done and what results were expected. Cadre policy worked in such a way that these military personnel were assured of being kept indefinitely in deputy command posts. After a long tenure, their age could be used as an argument to deny them further promotions: they would be too old to take on a senior post. Often it was hard to deny the accomplishments of a Ukrainian deputy commander who could easily and perhaps better have fulfilled the duties of his superior. Such an officer might be given the post of advisor or assigned to travel abroad where he might earn some cash. The cynical view among cadres was that there is nothing like hard currency to pacify a soldier or soften the blow of his being passed over for a promotion.

Cadre policy was sophisticated and carefully controlled by the political and security organs. Every commander had the right to his own opinion on personnel issues, but he was not supposed to insist on it if other considerations came into play. On several occasions as a division commander, I resubmitted promotion documents of worthy subordinates even after my superiors had rejected them. When the documents were again refused, I was warned that if I did not cease my efforts, I could end up in very hot water. By regulation, my colleagues and I had the right to make such promotion decisions. As division commanders we could recommend officers for appointment as regimental commanders, to be confirmed by the division's review and accreditation commission. In reality, however, the real promotion decisions were made at a different level where another set of rules, administered by cadre or party-political organs, came into play. These rules were never stated explicitly to us, although we understood them and could see quite clearly their effect. So long as everything appeared to be done by the book, in "fairness," the cadre system flourished. Few people fully understood how or why the system worked so well. It was known rather by its effects, as individuals such as Lieutenant Colonel Petriv, who personally suffered through the frustrations and disappointments, can attest.

Victims of this policy reacted in various ways. Most continued to hold out hope that they would someday see justice done. Personal dignity did not allow them to show how upset they were at blatant discrimination. I know of no one who became so frustrated that he quit the military and turned to drink. As a badge of honor, officers simply did not talk about their disappointments. They might show their dissatisfaction if denied an opportunity to continue their studies and improve themselves, but never did they show envy or take a "sour grapes" attitude. To admit that one had served for four years as a deputy commander and never received a promotion, whereas someone else had been in a similar position for only one year and had already been promoted—this was inconceivable. Officers considered such talk idle and undignified.

The life of Ukrainian and other non-Russian officers who felt an attachment to their cultural heritage was further complicated because of the difficulties they faced in maintaining ties with their homeland. For example, it was very difficult for Ukrainians, who served in the most distant regions of the Soviet Union, to receive transfers to Ukraine to continue their service near their hometowns. At the same time Russian officers with no roots in Ukraine typically had no difficulty getting such transfers. Even near the end of their service, many officers from Ukraine couldn't find apartments in Ukraine so that they could retire quietly and have some guarantee of security in their old age. Thus, they retired outside of Ukraine, putting themselves on municipal waiting lists for apartments in Ukraine. After being led by the nose for years, few of them managed to settle in their homeland.

A System Failure or a Momentary Lapse?

The purpose of cadre policy was to weed out potentially untrustworthy individuals. Individuals like me. Believing that I had a Russian father and had been reared in a Russian environment in eastern Ukraine, Marshal Shaposhnikov was shocked to discover that he was only half right. I am sure that when he later discovered that my parents were both ethnic Ukrainians, he must have been equally shocked to learn that the old system had not always worked. The corollary of his comment was simple: if the system had worked more effectively, then someone like me would not have made so successful and advanced a career in the military.

A system that purports to control so many people and institutions usually suffers lapses or failure of will somewhere along the line. Cadres, in this regard, were no different. Any officer appointed to a command post, for example, was strictly monitored as to his family, his interests, the people with whom he associated, his behavior, his presentations at military and Party meetings, and so forth. Nothing seemed to escape the critical eye of cadre policy. Every commander—and I was no exception—was constantly aware of this supervision, even though it was supposed to be conducted in secret.

Secrecy was essential. When the person under surveillance knows what is expected of him, only so much can be learned in an official setting. When a person relaxes, it is much easier to learn what makes him tick. The individuals monitoring my activities wanted to be among my friends, to visit me at home, even to exchange family visits. As diplomats, foreign visitors, and military personnel everywhere have observed, it is not unusual for those responsible for the surveillance to cross a social line and even become good friends with the people they are supposed to keep an eye on. My case was no different—I often had good relations with some of the individuals whose job it was to watch me. No matter how friendly we became, the rules never changed, official duties prevailed, and everyone had to be controlled.

One thing the monitors did not like to see was an officer so immersed in his work that he never had a social life. The reason is not hard to fathom. A newly appointed commander beginning his service in a garrison often devotes himself to his duties and pays little attention to making new friends or entertainment. I was a prime example of such behavior. Individuals like me had to be monitored with special care, not only because it was difficult to get to know and thus control us, but also because the sense of newly gained powers might go to our heads. The authorities found it convenient when we became involved with a circle of friends who spent their free time together and who might occasionally "break the rules," so to speak, taking off on a drinking binge or leaving for an off-limits location where the fishing was especially good.

In the same boat with his colleagues out for a good time, the officer was more likely to consider himself one of the guys. When the system worked, a sense of mutual trust was created, thereby enabling the authorities to control the officer more easily. Of course, the officer had to take care not to step over a certain dividing line in these relations, a particularly difficult assignment given that the system, when it worked, worked so well that some people lost their awareness of it entirely. The sensitive individual, however, never dropped his guard. If he was promoted and assigned to the post of commander of a division (or higher) or became head of a political department, he had to know that his behavior was constantly monitored, especially if that position was on the *nomenklatura* lists of the Party's Central Committee.*

A political officer was, formally speaking, a deputy of a commander, but both of their appointments were controlled by the administrative organs of the Central Committee. Both officers, therefore, could be regarded as the Central Committee's representatives in the armed forces. These officers, in conjunction with the chief of the security section, comprised a team—united in all respects, equal in stature, and sharing "one mind"—which worked to gain the absolute trust of the Central Committee. Cadre policy focused primarily on such appointments and tolerated no secrets or arguments among the three members. If one became a good "team player," there were really no problems. One could even complain out loud about conditions, violate regulations, or even abuse a position of authority—within limits, of course. All would be forgiven. But woe to the commander who stood up for some principle or moral obligation, against the wishes of his team players. Then he was considered the odd man out. His behavior was deemed unacceptable, and he became the object of criticism, distrust, and rumor.

Sometimes I would ask myself, "Why am I having problems with my superiors? Everyone around me treats me in such a friendly way." In fact, however, each of my "colleagues" had an obligation to monitor me and enable the system to exert control over me. They would never be so gauche as to say, "Well, we've got a job to do on you, and we'll use this red phone to Moscow to do it." Instead, they just tightened the screws. Here or there a "problem" for the commander would arise, then another, then another. Sooner or later, the commander who had bucked the system would be brought under control and corralled.

All my life I had observed this *modus operandi*. If a man has a strong moral compass and insists on standing on principle, he can never expect even the most minor of his flaws to be forgiven. Each of his minor missteps can be used as the pretext for discriminating against him: perhaps he is reassigned to a distant base or sent off to study a "situation." Reputation, like rumor, flies ahead and often arrives before the man himself. Thus, he comes to be known immediately at the new posting, and he is hard pressed to say who knows him better, he himself or the authorities. The higher his position, the more information the authorities have.

Once, when I arrived as division commander of a garrison completely unknown to me, my predecessor had already left for other parts. I recognized no one from my earlier studies or service, no one who could give me a detailed history of the garrison and its problems. This I had to get on my own. Moreover, even if the commander enjoys the authority inherent in the position, he is still responsible for establishing a level of moral authority, for both are essential if subordinates are to do anything more than simply offer lip service to the officer. In the case where the authority of the position is high but the moral authority is at zero, people take notice of every action the commander takes to raise it. Likewise, they note when the commander's level of moral authority approaches the level of his command authority. The object before the commander is to establish an image of himself in the minds of his troops that he is just and fair and that he means business. They will then be able to say (and believe), "He is a just person and has won the moral right to lead us and be our commander. We are obliged to be subordinated to him."

So, there I was at my new post, analyzing the situation and working at all hours of the day or week—nights, Saturdays, Sundays, holidays—handling documents, people, more documents, more people. After some months of this behavior, the monitors began issuing reports to the Special Department, and the rumors flew fast:

"Morozov is at the headquarters all the time. I twice invited him to go on a fishing trip. But he never went."

"I invited him twice to the bathhouse, where we could enjoy cognac and liquor. But he did not go."*

"He no longer goes to the bathhouse with me, his own deputy. Why doesn't he want to go? Either he is so stupid that he doesn't understand what the good life is, or he thinks that we should not go there ourselves and booze it up."

"If the commander would just once go there with us and enjoy himself, then he'd never raise an eyebrow. If he doesn't go, he'll always be after us, saying, 'Come now, comrades, what kind of behavior is that?'"

Sooner or later, the chatter turns to conspiracy:

"He's putting on airs with all this work at HQ. We have to find some way to rein him in."

"Does he drink?"

"No."

"His wife, what about her?"

"She's a nice lady, and their daughter too. Always supportive."

"Well, what shall we do then?"

"Let's invite him to a celebration…no, make it a wedding. We'll watch him in action there. But make sure that he's alone and that a pretty girl sits next to him so that he could, you know…We need something compromising."

"If not that, dig into his background materials. As a young lieutenant he was studying for a course with some friends and the friends took him off to get drunk."

"But did the commander get drunk?"

"Well, maybe not, but his friends boozed it up."

"Okay, then, we'll have to settle for that."

That's part of how the system worked. A lot of people never understood it and they suffered because of it and because of their naiveté—not physically, but psychologically, when careers suddenly came to a halt or pilots suddenly discovered that they could no longer fly planes because of some fabricated reason. To succeed in the military, one had to be loyal, polite, share the established and accepted viewpoints, and take an active social role. Nonconformity, open dissent, and protests against authority were anathema. Under such conditions, a strong sense of justice and fairness could eat away at the soul like acid. The day when Lieutenant Colonel Petriv stood in my office and railed against the system that denied him a promotion for the fourth time was one of the most painful examples I witnessed.

Years later, when we announced our intention to create an independent Ukrainian military, I remembered Petriv and tracked him down. By that time he had become a colonel, in charge of an operational unit in Ukraine, but he had never been promoted to the level of a commander of a division or garrison. In my view, this was a clear injustice, given his talents and sense of duty. I acted to rectify that situation, promoting him to major general.

5 My Ukrainianization

An army should be representative of the people it defends, knowledgeable about their history and culture, and sympathetic to their experiences and values, particularly their sense of justice. Of course, an army should remain independent of politics, although it has to be subject to democratically elected civilians or government appointees, much as we see in Western democracies.

Civil-military relations in the Soviet Union, however, never even came close to achieving this ideal. The political process was totally dominated by the authoritarian Communist Party, which did everything possible to control all meaningful links between the military and society. This isolation from society at large was most keenly felt by non-Russians in the armed forces, for although the military was supposed to promote pro-*Soviet, Communist* values, the military was dominated by the *Russian* language, by *Russian* military customs, and by *Russian* traditions. Those of Russian background felt perfectly at home in this institution. A certain distrust of non-Russians was also reflected in a cadre policy that rarely permitted senior officers of non-Russian background to serve in their ethnic homelands.

For decades, moreover, the central authorities rewrote or expunged the history of every subordinate group in favor of an all-Soviet, often russocentric interpretation. Essentially denied the very possibility of studying and understanding their own culture and history, Ukrainians came to expect that no high-ranking officer in the army could possibly hold a sympathetic view toward the emergence of a full-fledged Ukrainian national movement in 1989 and 1990, events that ultimately led to Ukraine's declaration of independence.

Like other members of the armed forces, I had been assigned to posts far removed from my homeland. The long stint in

Turkmenistan and the years spent in Eastern Europe—Poland, Czechoslovakia, and Hungary—afforded me a great opportunity to witness the vast differences between extremely poor parts of the Soviet Union and relatively well-to-do parts of the Warsaw Bloc, and later to contrast these with conditions in Ukraine when I finally returned in 1988 after my twenty-one-year absence. My military career prior to 1988 meant not only that I was cut off from Ukraine, but also that I found myself in an environment in which everything possible was done to promote very specific and rigid views of Soviet history, culture, and society. My contacts with individuals such as General Dudayev, however, helped open my eyes to the difficulties which officers from certain ethnic groups faced in the armed forces.

Dudayev's Dance

The case of General Dzhokhar Dudayev illustrated to me the injustice and short-sightedness of the Soviet bias against non-Russian military leaders with strong ethnic ties. His homeland declared its independence from the Russian Federation in 1991. It was no accident that Dudayev was proclaimed president of Chechnya when at that time the National Congress of the Chechen People (or Chechen All-National Congress) organized elections to achieve a popular mandate after its seizure of power. Dudayev was well known and greatly respected. A bomber pilot and Chechnya's first Soviet air force general, he embodied several positive personal traits and had a great deal of charisma. Not only did he combine the official authority of his position with a great self-confidence in his natural "right" to command people, but he also carried an aura of moral authority. For his honesty and decency, for his self-discipline and devotion to duty, for all those features that we officers call in Russian *voennaia kostochka*—real military backbone—I have a deep respect. If ever there was a case of a man born to command, that would have to be Dzhokhar Dudayev.

I first met Dudayev after my graduation from the Kliment Voroshilov Military Academy of the General Staff of the Armed Forces of the USSR in 1986. I had recently been appointed chief of headquarters for the 46th Air Army covering the territory that stretches from the Baltic Sea to southern Ukraine. Dudayev, then a colonel, was the chief of division headquarters and was assigned to the army garrison in Poltava. All the headquarters work in the army fell under my jurisdiction, and during the first weeks of my tenure, I first met Dudayev when I visited the garrison.

He impressed me as an experienced headquarters commander, as a professional who quickly gained people's respect and support. And he felt that people believed him to be a just and fair man. They acknowledged this sense of justice and equanimity not merely with the respect due an officer, but with a heartfelt affection for him as their leader. Perhaps he recognized some of these same qualities in me, for almost immediately we established a relationship of mutual trust and respect that far exceeded what commanders find expedient for conducting military affairs.

It was painful to watch what happened to Dudayev when his positive traits of character came into direct conflict with Soviet policy. As we have all come to expect, it is policy that wins. Dudayev's case showed me how a member of an ethnic minority—despite working many years as the deputy division commander and as that division commander's right-hand man—could be shunted aside and not promoted when a suitable position became available. As a member of the military council, I strongly recommended Colonel Dudayev for the post of division commander, which would ensure him promotion to major general. As the chief of the air army's headquarters, I personally took part in the preparation of his review board, which issued an extremely positive evaluation of his performance. Although the review was written by his division commander, I took it upon myself to present it to the military council and spoke as eloquently as I could to confirm my complete agreement with its assessment.

Dudayev, however, found that many barriers had been erected to keep him from the deserved promotion. The central authorities in Moscow even created a special commission that traveled to Poltava to verify the quality of the staff work being carried out at the garrison. That was an extraordinary, unprecedented move.

After scrutinizing Dudayev's work, the members of this commission had no choice but to submit a positive evaluation. They could find no dirt on him, no information that might compromise his promotion. But they watched him closely, even as they were promoting him. And, of course, their observation had an unstated, but nonetheless specific aim—namely, to mark any expression of "nationalism" that he might unintentionally let slip out.

Dudayev was at the airport when he heard the news about his promotion. He was absolutely ecstatic, carried away by his emotions, which probably got the better of him. Right there on the tarmac he danced the *lezginka,* a traditional folk dance of Chechnya and much of the Caucasus region. Hardly had the music in his mind stopped playing before the official report of this display of nationalism was winging its way to Moscow. It came back to me this way: "You see, he has just been appointed and he has already danced the *lezginka.*" I am struck still by the irony of these words, as well as saddened by the attitudes and biases lying behind the need to watch his every move until, inevitably, he would make a "mistake."

Regardless of what the review board saw as negative information about his candidacy, Dudayev was promoted to general. His appointment suggests that he was surrounded by decent people who refused to make a political issue out of his love for the history and culture of his people. Had it been otherwise, such information would have been used to torpedo the promotion for sure. There is no question of that. I even heard people advise him to keep quiet about the whole matter, but he remained convinced that what he was doing to inspire his people to celebrate their national heritage was right and just. He understood, however, that at that particular moment in our history it was impossible for a top military man to speak out in defense of one's national identity. That moment would come, all in due time, but for the moment he simply danced the *lezginka.*

Very well, I might add.

After his promotion, Dudayev was assigned as the commander of a heavy bomber division based in Tartu, Estonia. By the way, that is the garrison that was often mentioned while he was president of Chechnya, the garrison where he established a good relationship and close ties with the local population.* I met him there several times because his division was assigned to our air army.

After my 1988 return to Kyiv, sometime in 1990, I heard that Dudayev was preparing to leave the armed forces because Chechnya had declared its sovereignty. I was told that the people had laid their hopes on electing him chairman of the Chechen-Ingush Supreme Soviet or something along those lines. (At the time I wasn't exactly sure.)* I felt that it was a just cause, that if the Chechens wanted to find a conscientious, well-prepared leader, he was an excellent choice. He knew the history of his people very well—not that such knowledge would have ever been construed as a positive quality by the military commission in Moscow or would have scored points for him in his bid to be promoted to general. Indeed, in light of the conditions of the time, his interest in Chechnya's culture and history was not considered by the military's top brass to be a positive trait at all.

Dudayev's personal inquiry into the history of his people—about such issues as the deportation and resettlement of the Chechens, for example—raised his consciousness about his national heritage and the suppression to the point of near obliteration suffered by that national spirit. As chief of headquarters in the region, I received reports even about Dudayev's collecting newspaper articles and information about what had happened to his people. From what I could determine, his knowledge of the plight of his people was enormous and, even more important, that knowledge carried over into his emotional ties with the people he served.

After Dudayev became president of Chechnya, I did not meet him again. But I continue to admire him for the honest and decent man I knew him to be. He was a gifted officer and a man who deserved to be the leader of his people.

A Search for Roots

Although I (and many others with similar backgrounds) had a deeply sentimental attachment to Ukraine, I was reared in such a way that I knew very little about this country's culture, traditions, and history.

Before my return to Ukraine, I devoted most of my reading to political and social developments in Russia. I had no access to Ukrainian or other samizdat* literature in the closed military garrisons in which I served, and I did not have the kind of family ties that might have provided me with links to nonconformist circles.

Thus, when I arrived in Ukraine, I must admit that I knew very little about its history and its current political situation. I was largely ignorant, for example, of this republic's distinctive historical traditions and the brutal fashion in which western Ukraine had been incorporated into the Soviet Union during World War II.* I knew even less about the dissidents who were playing an increasingly important role in Ukraine's politics and about new leaders such as Ivan Drach, the Ukrainian poet whose work had been censored during the cultural purges of the 1970s, and Dmytro Pavlychko, who headed the Taras Shevchenko Ukrainian Language Society (*Tovarystvo Ukraïns'koï Movy*).* After 1986, Gorbachev's policy of glasnost opened up the media and allowed much previously forbidden literature to be published, but no one—least of all myself—was prepared for the revelations accompanying the 1990 elections and the public appearances and speeches of numerous outspoken political candidates. Only then did I undertake a rather formal, albeit self-directed, process of educating myself and learning about the abuses my fellow citizens had suffered in the past.

A Close-Up View of Ukraine

In the context of these turbulent political developments of the late 1980s, I began to develop my own strong views on various controversial issues in Ukraine. In 1989, after assuming command of the 17th Air Army, I visited numerous military bases in the regions under my jurisdiction, such as the garrisons located in Chernihiv Oblast in the north, Luhansk and Donetsk in the east, and Crimea Oblast, where the Black Sea Fleet was located. In the early 1990s I was traveling almost every day, flying on military transport planes and visiting various regiments four or five days each week. This rigorous schedule gave me an excellent opportunity to observe the country and to

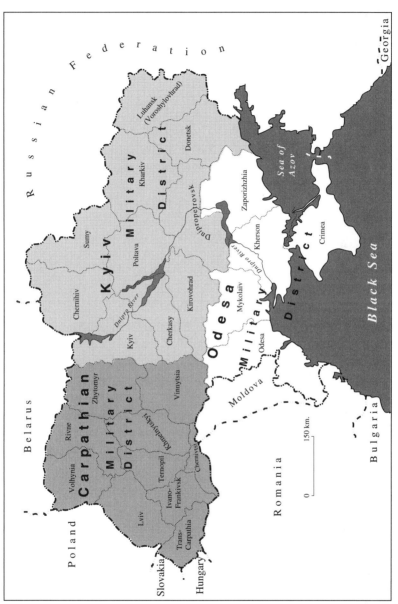

Military Districts in Ukraine

(including oblast borders; Soviet period and independent Ukrainian military districts are the same)

witness the changes that occurred between visits, often no more than a few weeks apart.

These military units were greatly influenced by events in the civilian settings in which they found themselves. On many occasions, after meeting with local government officials and members of the Communist Party, I gained a deeper understanding of local political and social issues such as the housing deficit and the relationship between a particular army base and the local community where it was located. Military personnel always, it seemed, had difficulties finding suitable housing that was affordable and livable. As I mentioned earlier, even my own brother had experienced the frustration and anxiety of not having an acceptable standard of living and place to live.

I saw it as my obligation to study each situation in which a military unit or school found itself and to help the military commanders and local government officials resolve problems. It was not just a matter of satisfying my curiosity, of traveling around the country like a tourist on a holiday. Rather, as a senior commander and member of the military council of the Kyiv Military District, I was able to bring no small amount of authority, which often proved useful in resolving disputes.

As someone who was born and reared in the heavily russified Donbas, I had rarely heard my parents or relatives talking about Ukraine's history and the repression of the Soviet period. After the second world war, many Ukrainians from the extremely nationalist western regions came to the Donbas to help put the mining industry back on its feet, but they usually kept silent about the wide-scale repression visited upon western Ukraine. In the Donbas, as in many other regions, people were afraid to speak out.

The Voices of Dissidents

The military is one of the last places one would expect to find open dissent and expressions of nonconformity, but from time to time it did occur. Over the years such voices of protest grew louder and more numerous, and their cumulative effect was to send shock waves through all levels of the army and the public at large. One of the rare but early cases of dissent within the military was that of General Petr Grigorenko (Petro Hryhorenko), who helped found the Ukrainian Helsinki Group in 1976.* Although I never met General Grigorenko and it would be too much to say that he was a major role model for me, I would stress the cumulative effect that his example of dissidence and that of others like him had on me. I began to see more and more clearly just how destructive the system was to the individual, how unjust it was, and how it perpetuated itself through lies and suppression.

Let me give an example. When I graduated from military college, there were only about 115 graduates in my class, a relatively small number when compared with the large number who had begun their military studies with me. After we began our service, every week or month the incomplete and tantalizing news filtered in to us: so-and-so had resigned; this person had been dishonorably discharged; that one had had a psychological breakdown. No wonder that the number of my fellow graduates who continued in their military careers and now have thirty years or more of service in the army is extremely small. Whatever the official reason given for their departure, I am convinced that the system was to blame in most cases.

The system I speak of permeated all of Soviet society, but the army was one of its most fertile areas. Conservative in its very nature, the army tolerates almost no deviations from its strict rules and regulations. For this reason the case of General Hryhorenko was so shocking. Equally shocking was that of Valerii Sablin, the Soviet naval officer who led a mutiny in November 1975 on the missile frigate *Storozhevoi*.* The system stamped out the individual—both in the sense of suppressing individual thought and in the sense of producing like-minded people whose political views were predictable and intolerant.

Given my rank in the military, I had many opportunities to observe its impact on so many lives. It tested people. History knows very few examples when, let's say, a Sablin or Grigorenko steps out of the faceless crowd and criticizes the system, thus making himself a target of suspicion and repression.

81

Uncovering the Past

The elections in March 1990 opened my eyes even more to Ukraine's history and the brutality it suffered in the 1930s and later. Although held under relatively liberal conditions, the elections were by no means fully fair (in some regions the political elite used old-style Soviet practices to ensure their victory at the polls), but these elections were distinct from previous ones in that for the first time the voters had a genuine choice among various candidates eager to state their views on Ukraine's political and economic future.

I was particularly struck by the appearance of a new brand of politician, ready to speak before enormous crowds about the abuses and crimes committed against Ukrainians during the Stalin years. Even four years of glasnost had done little to bring to the public a full disclosure of these abuses, but many candidates for public office in 1990 had either themselves suffered through those events or had learned of them from relatives. Now they were speaking out. They included former political prisoners such as Viacheslav Chornovil, Levko Lukianenko, and Mykhailo Horyn, who had served long terms of imprisonment for their nonconformist views; poets such as Ivan Drach and Dmytro Pavlychko, who had maintained an uneasy relationship with the power brokers in the official Union of Writers, but who had come to play an important, positive role in Ukraine's political life in the late 1980s; and younger figures, such as Serhii Holovatyi, who were greatly influenced by the example of the former dissidents. The official media had branded the dissidents and their supporters as narrow-minded nationalist extremists, preoccupied with the past, who would plunge Ukraine into civil war. It soon became clear, however, that they were political moderates who were concerned not only with the state of the Ukrainian language and culture, as well as the distortions of the country's history, but also with the disastrous ecological problems facing the country, the horrendous legacy of the command economy, and the pervasive cynicism of the Communist Party elite.

The political drama unfolding in Ukraine before my eyes did not end when the ballots were counted. A number of former dissidents and other anti-communists (at the time they were lumped together under the name of "democrats") were elected to the Supreme Soviet, and they often set the tone for its proceedings. In fact, their influence spread far beyond the walls of the Supreme Soviet, for its sessions were transmitted live and then rebroadcast in the evening.

Because of my military duties, I had little free time to follow all these debates, but what time I did have I devoted to tracking current events, even if it meant staying up late at night to hear the broadcasts of the day's parliamentary proceedings. I was one of the millions of Ukrainians, blue-collar workers as well as intellectuals, who patiently sat by the radio to hear our deputies discuss issues that would affect our future. Again, I felt strongly that it was part of my duty, my responsibility as a citizen of this country, to be open to all opinions, to hear all sides of the public debate about the prospect of independence for Ukraine, and to weigh the possible consequences of such a momentous decision.

When I had free time, I would attend a session of the Supreme Soviet, listening to the debates and seeing people fully committed to their causes defending their positions. For the first time, I heard the live speeches of former dissidents and political prisoners. These were men and women whose very existence, according to the propaganda message of the past, had been denied in the Soviet Union, which supposedly had no political prisoners. I listened carefully to their opinions and arguments, and I soon came to know these deputies as individuals, learning their names, surnames, and even their patronymics. The mainstream press called them "nationalists," charging them with infiltrating the Supreme Soviet and threatening the Soviet Union and the new union treaty, which Gorbachev was trying to negotiate between the center and the republics. However, I was greatly impressed by their words and their commitment to Ukraine's freedom. I instinctively understood that the authorities, and society at large, had done them and their cause a great injustice.

The debates in the Supreme Soviet were often heated, and much of what I heard was new to me. For example, I remember the debates on the language law and the vivid descriptions of the blows the Ukrainian language had suffered during the Soviet period. A thoughtful person who carefully considered such issues could not help but sympathize with the arguments of the democrats. I am sure that many officers at the time shared my opinions, for it was impossible to deny the truth of what democrats such as Ivan Drach, Dmytro Pavlychko, Volodymyr Yavorivskyi, or Ivan Zaiets said about the fate of the Ukrainian culture and people. Representatives of western Ukraine such as Ihor Yukhnovskyi, Mykhailo Kosiv, Yaroslav Kendzior, and Larysa Skoryk also had a great influence on shaping the public mood and changing our perceptions of the society in which we lived.

Some of the issues raised by deputies from western Ukraine, such as the rehabilitation of members of the OUN-UPA [Organization of Ukrainian Nationalists–Ukrainian Insurgent Army], found little resonance outside this region because of the extent to which Soviet propaganda had slandered these nationalist organizations and succeeded in demonizing them. What was necessary in such cases was a balanced assessment of *all* of Ukraine's history—not from an ideological point of view, but objectively, with an open mind, and with honest convictions. The Soviet system did not allow us to do that and as a result there were certain subjects, like the OUN-UPA, that some people would never want to revisit, even in freer times. Whatever the view on something like OUN-UPA, however, all who were truly attached to their homeland of Ukraine, including many who were not of ethnic Ukrainian background, could not help but be concerned about the state of the Ukrainian language, and that became an important rallying point.

Although Russians were a minority in all of Ukraine's regions except for Crimea, imperial tsarist and Soviet policies had provided them with a full range of Russian-language schools and other institutions to satisfy their cultural, educational, and other needs. Ukrainian, in contrast, came to be treated as a rural, peasant language, and over time this image of the supposed inferiority of the Ukrainian language and culture had been accepted by many ethnic Ukrainians, especially in Ukraine's eastern and southern regions.

This inferiority complex was similar to that found in many other colonial-type situations. As a result, many residents of Ukraine, including ethnic Ukrainians, had only a weak knowledge of the Ukrainian language. By the late 1980s in some regions of the republic only a small number of newspapers, journals, and books were published in Ukrainian. In many places in Ukraine it was almost impossible for children to learn the language of their forefathers, and Russian had become the overwhelmingly dominant language of all official transactions.

Gorbachev's policy of glasnost, however, allowed all Soviet citizens, including those living in Ukraine, to challenge old stereotypes and question the so-called official version of history that the authorities had imposed upon us and our children. Every thoughtful person had to come to terms with the way in which his or her views of the world had been seriously distorted by the deliberate lies fed to us, over decades, by a very powerful propaganda machine. I experienced this dilemma firsthand and saw it take a toll on my wife Raisa.

Educated and trained professionally as a historian, Raisa had taught at the university level for many years, but as we moved from one military base to another, she could not always find a suitable job and her professional career consequently had suffered.

But her dedication to searching for the truth was never diminished, and her search in many ways came to be mine as well. After 1986, for instance, when the true history of Ukraine started to come to light, she was forcibly struck by discrepancies with the official interpretation of past events. On the one hand, there were the various historical documents and eyewitness accounts published in the press, which enjoyed a respite from censorship—at least as it had been practiced in earlier decades. On the other, there were the official versions of these events as published in textbooks.

At this point Raisa decided to leave her job so that she could digest this newly revealed information and come up with a new perspective on Soviet history and particularly the history of the Communist Party—the subjects of her academic specialization. She kept waiting for new methodological guidelines to be published, but they did not appear. The usual delays—so characteristic of the period of perestroika—kept them out of reach and out of sight. After we moved to Kyiv in 1988, she decided to stop her research in this particular field of history.

The study of history and other ideologically sensitive subjects—and in particular, the teaching of these subjects—was regulated by a set of norms and instructions elaborated ad nauseam by so-called leading scholars whose interpretations were widely regarded as reliable. They prepared such publications as textbooks, curriculum guides, and handbooks, which provided a strict methodological base for other scholars and instructors. The study of history, especially the history of the Communist Party, was subject to rigid strictures. These largely evaporated during the late glasnost period.

No longer working for the government, Raisa today studies documentary materials that for years have been concealed from the general public. She focuses her attention primarily on the history of Ukraine, its political literature, and the works of Ukrainian writers and essayists. No doubt the current availability of this material has led my wife and many others to revise their views of Ukrainian history—and the revision begun by professional historians like Raisa has gradually begun to filter down to the rest of society. In fact, we have all had to look at our own history with fresh eyes and open minds, taking into account the new information derived from independent political studies such as those Raisa and others have conducted. For me those revisions have been necessitated not only by my close relationship with my wife, but also by my deeper understanding of and sympathy for the viewpoints of some of our leading political activists.

Rukh

During the first years of Gorbachev's period in power, Ukraine became known as a backwater of the Soviet Union, where reform policies were promoted with great reluctance. In addition, with the exception of western Ukraine, popular attitudes concerning the possibility of independence were much more restrained than, say, in the Baltic republics. This restraint was reflected in the official title of a major political movement that emerged during this period. The "People's Movement in Support of Perestroika in Ukraine"—better known as Rukh (the Ukrainian word for 'movement')—was a "popular front" organization that sought to unite all the democratic forces in Ukraine.

Rukh quickly became an enormous organization, an umbrella group not only for those Ukrainians who were often labeled "nationalists," but for all those concerned with the present state of affairs as well as extremists and radicals. In addition, Rukh membership included many of the intelligentsia, those who could no longer keep silence in view of the recently uncovered lies and open distortions of reality which prevailed in the Communist Party.

In my opinion, Rukh represented the will of the Ukrainian people to defend their right to their own culture and traditions, to revive their language, to create their own system for governing society and the economy. Regarding this cause as just, I supported Rukh and the democrats. I frequently use the term "just" when talking about the democrats, for I believe that justice was on their side and on the side of all those who had fought for Ukraine's freedom.

Rukh held its first congress in 1989, but at that time hardly anyone used the word "independence." Instead, Rukh members referred to perestroika. Their reticence is not surprising, for it was difficult to challenge the Communist Party so openly and come out in support of independence. Moreover, the first order of business was to build a consensus among a large number of people with varying degrees of commitment to an independent Ukraine. Ivan Drach, the well-known poet, was elected the first leader of Rukh—an excellent choice, it seemed to me. And Drach succeeded where many others, less skillful, might have failed.

As one might have expected, Rukh was plagued by many internal disputes and divisions.* Drach and other moderates, who had taken a more pragmatic attitude toward the political realties of the day, openly debated with Viacheslav Chornovil, Levko Lukianenko, Mykhailo Horyn, Bohdan Horyn, and other former dissidents. Some Rukh members pressed for radical, almost revolutionary change in the political and socio-economic spheres (remember that advocating immediate and outright Ukrainian independence and embracing a capitalist market economy were "radical positions" even up to August 1991), whereas others called for gradual, evolutionary reforms. There were heated discussions on the nature and tempo of policies needed to reverse the impact of many years of russification, on Ukraine's future relations with its neighbors (especially Russia) and with the West, and on the best ways of building a strong national identity while accommodating Ukraine's regional diversity and ethnic minorities. I saw these initial disagreements as "growing pains" and concluded that the radical democrats were acting more as a point of orientation so that moderate politicians, often more sensitive to public opinion, could address the gap between the current state of Ukrainian society and the ambitious goals proposed by idealists. For example, much of Ukraine's population, especially in the east and south, was convinced that Ukraine's economy had to remain very tightly integrated with that of its Russian neighbor, and that anything more than a symbolic form of political or economic autonomy for Ukraine was unrealistic. This gulf made it necessary to mold public opinion gradually and to help people see the need of putting forward such demands. Over time, issues once raised by the human rights activists of the Ukrainian Helsinki Group* and by the political activists and prisoners of the 1960s and 1970s began to re-emerge.

I further believed that it was my responsibility as a senior military officer in the armed forces and as a resident of Ukraine to study carefully these issues and debates, as well as to develop an opinion about them, independent of the propaganda and rumors that flowed freely at the time. The leaders of Ukraine's Communist Party, for instance, warned that Rukh was a zealous, xenophobic, and radical organization that could lead society to catastrophe. True, it was radical—perhaps too radical on some issues—but its members were willing to address and find compromise solutions for social and political problems that were very real and of significance to many ordinary Ukrainians. Thus, many observers were surprised when Rukh strongly condemned all expressions of extreme nationalism, including anti-Semitism, supported the efforts of the Crimean Tatars, who had been deported by Stalin, to return to their homeland, and called for an inclusive citizenship policy which would allow all residents of

Ukraine, without regard to their ethnicity, automatically to gain Ukrainian citizenship.

Paradoxically, Rukh served as a kind of compass that Communist Party members could use, if they so desired, to gauge the mind of the public. Leonid Kravchuk, the senior Communist Party official who later became Ukraine's first president, for example, criticized Rukh during its first congress and defended the Party's platform, which of course he had been assigned to do. Later, however, he expressed great interest in Rukh's position on many issues and eventually incorporated many of Rukh's policy proposals into his own electoral platform in 1991. Kravchuk's attempt to understand Rukh's positions, coupled with his own doubts about the feasibility of preserving the old system, led to fundamental changes in his thinking. He wanted to encourage a gradual and peaceful transformation of society so that at first a few people would change their views and behaviors, and in turn influence a broader group of people to make the same changes. Over time this process would lead to broader and more solid changes in Ukrainian society. Even when he could not openly express his support for the democratic movement in Ukraine, Kravchuk was firmly convinced that it was taking the correct path. He was only waiting to find a mechanism that would allow him to change his position and bring others along with him.

Most senior military officers in Ukraine did not have close relations with the local civilian population. They were under the influence of official military and other publications, published both locally and in Moscow, which invariably painted Rukh in very negative colors. If they did not closely follow the local media and take a strong interest in the local political scene, they could not help but have a rather distorted view of political developments in Ukraine. Thus, even when Kravchuk began using some of Rukh's rhetoric, these officers viewed Kravchuk as a fairly moderate-to-conservative figure who represented continuity with the past, as opposed to unpredictable "radicals" such as Chornovil and Lukianenko.

The Nationalism Question—Again

During all the negotiations and debates, the question that kept coming up for me was this: Why could one not work on solutions for any of the age-old problems of the Ukrainian people—namely, independence, statehood, or equal representation of the Ukrainian people at the all-Union level—without being called a "nationalist"? Many of my military colleagues and I, those of us who took a more liberal attitude toward this question, considered that the official response was an absolute injustice. Ukraine was denied its rightful identity, not because its borders were erased on the maps (nobody spoke about borders at that time), but because it was refused for so many years the right to represent its own culture and history justly in the framework of all-Soviet history and culture.

I have asserted that the army was and is outside politics, but people in the army, particularly officers, are not mannequins. We have families and feelings of pride in our national heritage, including even the darkest times that our homelands have experienced. Many army officers in the late 1980s and early 1990s, like me, began to question the justice of the official position on nationalism and to listen to the voices for democratic reforms. Our attitudes were influenced greatly by the reactions that the leaders in Moscow and in the Ukrainian military districts showed toward an inevitable tidal wave of events that swept over the republics in the early 1990s.

Ukraine, like its fellow republics, had taken the road to sovereignty and independence, and there was no turning back.

6 I Take a Stand: The Coup Attempt of August 1991

Early in 1991, when external and internal forces exerted enormous pressures on the Soviet Union, I began to think that Ukraine could actually become a separate state. Struggling to keep the Soviet bloc unified, Mikhail Gorbachev and other officials of the Communist Party had become increasingly concerned about the rise of nationalist-democratic forces in Ukraine and elsewhere. In the Novo-Ogarevo negotiations, for instance, the leaders of the Soviet republics considered reforming the federal structure of the USSR to achieve greater decentralization.*

At the same time that these negotiations were taking place, the central military authorities in Moscow were drawing up contingency plans to transfer some of the most valuable military property—particularly nuclear weapons—from Ukraine to Russia in the event that Moscow continued to lose control over the situation in Ukraine. So long as the Soviet Union existed as a formal federation of republics, all military units in Ukraine, large and small, were directly subordinated to Moscow. Thus, at the time, Ukraine's leaders had neither direct access to the personnel in these units nor any real control over military property in Ukraine.

Several republics, Ukraine among them, already had held relatively open elections. Leonid Kravchuk and a number of others emerged as new leaders who could genuinely be said to represent their parliaments. Gorbachev had to take them seriously and negotiate with them in good faith, a position that differed radically from the prior pattern of relations between Moscow and the "periphery."

Kravchuk's Stand

President Kravchuk, however, was not the kind of leader Gorbachev and others were used to dealing with. His behavior clearly differed from that of most other republican leaders, and he showed great determination in defending Ukraine's interests. In his discussions with the central Soviet authorities, for instance, he faced a serious dilemma: as the speaker of Ukraine's Supreme Soviet, he did not feel that he could act decisively on his own, yet he had to negotiate from a position of power and control. Kravchuk now examined every contentious issue Gorbachev put forward, not from the perspective of a committed Communist Party activist (a perspective that had dominated most of his career), but from that of the most prominent representative of the Ukrainian Supreme Soviet and thus the people of Ukraine.

The stance taken by Kravchuk represented, in my opinion, a brilliant strategy, one that allowed him to neutralize Gorbachev's argumentative tactics by saying to him, in effect, "The position I'm taking is not necessarily my personal belief. I am simply the speaker of Ukraine's Supreme Soviet. If you don't like what I'm saying, go to Kyiv, make an appearance before our deputies, ask that they discuss each issue and put it to a vote. Then you'll find out what they want."

The negotiations in Moscow required that Kravchuk have the support of the democrats back home, for they increasingly set the tone for the parliamentary debates in Ukraine's Supreme Soviet. No important issue could be resolved without their approval. One could say that there was even a tacit agreement between the democrats and Kravchuk, a recognition that they needed each other. Eschewing an authoritarian role for himself, Kravchuk argued that only Ukraine's Supreme Soviet could speak for the country, for it was a representative body to which each deputy had been elected in relatively free elections by his or her constituents. Whatever his personal point of view, Kravchuk could not simply arrive in Moscow and agree with Gorbachev's proposals; nor could he speak as if his were the only voice for Ukraine. No doubt his position annoyed Gorbachev greatly, but I fully supported Kravchuk and considered his stance to be courageous, honest, and realistic. Who else at the time could have so effectively represented our interests in Moscow?

Everyone watched as Kravchuk again and again disagreed with his Russian counterpart. It was a pleasure to see him take a hard, well-grounded stance, which was genuinely supported by most of Ukraine's parliamentarians. It seemed that we were more united in those days.

Although my interest in politics in Ukraine grew steadily throughout the period 1990–1991, as did my sympathy for the democrats who were so keen to change the political situation in this republic, I had not yet been forced to make any difficult choices and show my political colors. That would change quickly as a result of the attempted coup against Gorbachev in August, 1991. But for the first part of that year, I simply continued to fulfill my regular duties as commander of the 17th Air Army.

The turbulent events of this period actually had little impact on the role and behavior of the military, but various efforts were made nonetheless to shield its personnel from the influence of the new political forces emerging in Ukraine. In spite of these protections, a number of officers in the armed forces were honest, principled individuals who were aware of the latest political developments and prepared to accept the harsh truth about the past. If I strictly followed the directives and orders that we were receiving at the time, I would have monitored the activities and interests of the officers and checked to see who was falling under "inappropriate" influences and had been infected by the so-called viruses of democracy and nationalism. There were many such officers, but I could not condemn them, for I shared their sentiments. Of course, we could not openly discuss many of the topics raised in public debates, but over time there was a definite change of tone during our conversations on political issues. Because I occupied such a senior position at the time, I had to conduct myself very carefully, but my subordinates could tell that I favored the democratic trends in society.

The Committee of Soldiers' Mothers

I was quite sympathetic, for example, toward the Committee of Soldiers' Mothers, an unofficial organization that tried to influence the conditions of service in the military. In the spring of 1991, various attempts were made to help military personnel from Ukraine facing the prospect of extended service in far-off "hot spots" of domestic conflict, such as Karabakh and Sumgait in Azerbaijan or Tbilisi in Georgia. These prospects were very real: many residents of Ukraine served in the airborne troops and in units of the Ministry of the Interior, which were often used in efforts to restore order in such conflict zones.

Supported by other democratic forces, the Committee of Soldiers' Mothers launched a number of protest actions. In the early spring of 1991, this Committee organized a major protest outside the headquarters of the Kyiv Military District. The organizers prepared appropriate slogans* and drew up a list of demands in order to attract the attention of the district's commanders as well as the press, but there was absolutely no threat of force being used during the picketing. The Committee simply wanted to demonstrate that times had changed.

And the times had truly changed! A year or two earlier it would have been impossible to hold such a protest in public, but now people felt that they had the right to voice their demands openly. The democratization of society had created an atmosphere where this kind of protest was bound to occur, and those who were inclined to sympathize with democratic positions accepted the justice of the Committee's demands. After all, the safety and lives of their loved ones were at stake, and public protests elsewhere had given people a new sense of what could be achieved by asserting human rights. The Committee of Soldiers' Mothers wielded much influence, although a great deal depended on whom they were trying to influence.

Anticipating a large crowd of demonstrators and the possibility of violence, we began making preparations for this event at a furious pace. We placed on duty a large number of military personnel in case the protestors stormed the building or physical violence erupted.

Contingency plans were put in place to deal with any situation: the Kyiv garrison organized watches, installed a communications system, and stationed armed soldiers in the headquarters in case the situation changed and administrative offices were seized, but the ultimate responsibility rested with those individuals who supervised all of these activities.

Many of my peers, those at the level of deputy commander, said they should just fire a few shots...to "teach the demonstrators a lesson." There was nothing to be gained, they said, merely by closing doors and increasing the number of guards. I issued an order, however, that under no conditions should lower-ranking officers resort to the use of force. Confident that I would never have to issue an order for weapons to be used, I made it clear to my subordinates that only my personal orders were to be followed.

It is easy to understand what motivated these officers to wave their weapons and challenge anyone who attempted to interfere with military business and traditions. After all, the army was such a closed system that entire generations of soldiers were educated to believe that military affairs were their domain. Many senior military officers were faithful defenders of the status quo and hostile to democratic ideals. Although they rarely had roots in Ukraine or family ties here, ironically it was they who were irritated and indignant that "outsiders" were trying to interfere with their sphere of influence.

Let me clarify what I mean by the word "outsider." Senior leaders of the Communist Party, who were technically not military personnel and thus might be considered "outsiders," often intervened in military affairs. They were members of all senior-level military councils, and no secrets could be kept from them. At the same time, all senior military officers were invariably Party members, and usually a good relationship existed between the two institutions. It was a symbiotic rather than hostile relationship.

Any attempt by members of unofficial organizations—true "outsiders" in the eyes of many of my colleagues—to influence the military was another matter entirely. This was seen as a threat, immediately to be repulsed. Some military personnel simply looked upon the activists as noisy, frivolous individuals who had no concrete propositions and with whom one couldn't even have a serious conversation. They were seen as disruptive forces, blocking traffic outside the military headquarters buildings, chanting their protests, and calling upon the military to observe human rights. Others, however, considered the Committee of Soldiers' Mothers a thoroughly negative force guided by principles of nationalism that would inevitably undermine Ukraine's position in the constellation of Soviet republics. The Committee's slogans emphasized the important strategic mission of the armed forces and the unshakable principles on which the country's defense was based. Both Party members and military officers, however, accused the Committee and other unofficial organizations of weakening the defense system of the Soviet Union, conspiring with capitalist imperialists and even assisting in the reconnaissance work conducted by American satellites.

All their efforts to oppose the Committee and other such organizations represented a vain attempt to seal the cracks through which democratic ideas were beginning to infiltrate the army. The existing system protected the army from any criticism and prevented any attempt to expose the true state of affairs. It also stressed the absolute necessity of maintaining a huge military budget, which was then used by the military as it best saw fit, with no accountability to ensure the effective use of these funds. These were all considered to be internal issues, of no concern to the public at large.

The Committee, however, persisted in its work, providing shelter to conscripts who abandoned their units because of the vicious abuse they had suffered. Most important, its members defended human rights. Young conscripts were powerless to defend their own rights, and the system in which they found themselves repressed them so harshly that their only alternatives were to escape or commit suicide.* Since both desertion and suicide were considered crimes, the commanders who opposed the democratic trends within the military accused the Committee of assisting criminals. This charge, however, was related to the much broader issue of human rights in general in the Soviet Union and the total lack of civil control over the military.

Neither this particular protest nor any of the others staged by the Committee resulted in notable violence, injuries, deaths, or property damage. Document checks at headquarters buildings were made more rigorous, and special armed units were assigned to the headquarters buildings themselves to guard the premises and repel any intruders. In such situations, ammunition was to be issued to those standing guard only on the basis of a separate set of instructions. However, all these preparations introduced a sense of great unpredictability into the daily rhythm of our duties. There were some arrests, of course, but the purpose of the demonstration was to present a united front and build recognition for the rights of military personnel. Three days after these protests began, the demonstrators transferred their attention to other buildings in Kyiv and eventually ended their protest peacefully.

Given the vast changes that I had seen already in Soviet society in the period 1990–1991, as well as those in my own political thinking, I believe that my attempt to ensure that force would not be used during this confrontation was both responsible and justified. My position generated support throughout the ranks of the military, and I was both gratified and relieved to find it so strong. The event was but one of several that were harbingers of my growing sympathy with the democratic forces in Ukraine. I was relieved and gratified to discover that my position, which reflected my growing sympathy with the democratic forces in Ukraine, met with a fairly high level of support throughout the ranks of the military.

Challenges to My Ideals: The Events of August, 1991

In spite of the great turmoil, such as the vociferous and public protests staged by the Committee of Soldiers' Mothers in the early months of 1991, the actual coup attempt in August of that year came as a great surprise to all of us. When I look back on this period, I see that my preoccupation with day-to-day administrative affairs prevented me from immediately understanding what was taking place. On Sunday, August 18, we celebrated Aviation Day, a holiday also known as Air Force Day, and as a member of the Kyiv Military Council, I was directly involved in the celebrations leading up to this holiday.* In connection with the festivities I had been designated to deliver a major speech to military personnel and the public at large on Friday, August 16.

The speech went off uneventfully, and most of my colleagues went home for a rest over the holiday weekend. My duties, however, kept me on the move. I was responsible for overseeing all the air force garrisons in my jurisdiction, which covered an enormous geographical area, stretching from the northern part of Chernihiv Oblast all the way to Belarus and to Zhdanov (Mariupol), south of Donetsk, as well as to the Baherove Air Force Base in Crimea. Because this huge territory had to be monitored daily, I returned on Saturday to my command post to maintain contact with garrison commanders and to oversee the implementation of our aviation transportation plans.

The air army under my command was not an integral part of the Kyiv Military District. Rather, it was subordinate to the USSR's central headquarters in Moscow, with Marshal Shaposhnikov as commander in chief.* Contacts with the headquarters of the Kyiv Military District were usually limited to dealing with operational issues such as the organization of our daily program, military discipline, combat readiness, and preparations for mobilizing forces. Thus, although I was a member of the district's military council, I was quite surprised when suddenly I received a call from the chief of staff of the Kyiv Military District.

Naively I thought that the chief of staff had simply remembered that Sunday was Aviation Day and that he wanted to congratulate the aviation personnel of this district. I did not at all expect what I got instead—his instructions to prepare a plane for General Viktor S. Chechevatov, the military district's commander, who was on vacation in Crimea and who had to be brought to Kyiv. I was led to believe that the flight was necessary so that Chechevatov could return to his regular duties the following week.

This was an unorthodox request, and I was opposed to unwarranted interference with established procedure. Our flight schedule had been confirmed on Thursday and sent to the proper authorities, including Moscow, and it did not allow for personal travel plans for any military officer. Besides, all flights had to be monitored by the air defense forces, and any change in the schedule would have to be carefully negotiated and coordinated with many other officers. It was dangerous for those on duty in various command posts—in both the air force itself and the air defense forces—to have to deal with surprise changes. Occasionally an exception could be made, but it had to be directly confirmed by the appropriate senior commanding officers. I was also perturbed by this call since this flight was to take place not just on any Sunday but on a holiday weekend, which I had hoped my personnel could use for a well-deserved rest.

I am the first to acknowledge that I am a man who likes order and dislikes surprises: I strictly keep to existing schedules. True, the air force has to be constantly prepared to carry out new assignments on short notice, and certain flight teams are always kept on reserve to look after such contingencies; however, in this case the plane assigned to satisfy the travel requirements of the senior personnel of the Kyiv Military District—and, in particular, its commander—was constantly in the air. The plane's crew, all of whom lived in Kyiv, did not know more than a day in advance what demands would be placed on them. Now they had to be found, summoned, brought to the airfield, and given time to prepare themselves. I did not believe that a whimsical change in the district commander's travel plans warranted this degree of disruption in our schedule. If it was very important for him to get back to work on Monday, he should have made the necessary arrangements well in advance, instead of at the last minute.

Thus, I specifically asked whether it was clear to Chechevatov that this was a holiday weekend and that the existing schedule had not foreseen the need for this flight. The answer came back: This was an essential flight and it had to take place without delay. Nonetheless, I replied that I would not violate the schedule. If it really were all that important for the flight to take place, I advised that the Kyiv Military District headquarters contact the appropriate officials in Moscow and set a new schedule. My caller agreed to call the General Staff headquarters and told me that I would also receive a call from General Chechevatov to confirm the importance of this flight.

I knew that we would end up fulfilling his request, but I was irritated and frustrated. I wanted the Military District Council to understand that I favored clear lines of authority as well as strict adherence to existing schedules. This change in plans represented a violation of our regulations.

A short time later, General Chechevatov called me from his residence in Crimea to say that he unexpectedly had to be in Kyiv on Sunday, August 18, to attend an event with the minister of defense, Marshal Dmitrii Yazov.* This was news to me, for information about such events involving individuals at the level of deputy minister or higher were made public only a few hours before they actually took place. When I asked what kind of event was being planned and where it would be held, I was told that it involved the final phase of ground force division exercises held at the Pryluky garrison in Chernihiv Oblast and that it would involve the final phase of exercises conducted by a ground force division. Because Marshal Yazov was to be present, General Chechevatov advised me that it was, of course, only appropriate that the commander of the Kyiv Military District be present as well. When I asked him when the plane should be ready, so that the flight team wouldn't waste time at the airport, he told me simply to start making plans and that he would call back to settle the details.

Afterwards, I told the local commander to inform the central command post in Moscow about this new requirement and to inform the authorities that there would have to be a change in the flight schedule. I decided to let my decision about what to do in this matter be determined by Moscow's reaction.

Soon I received a second call from General Chechevatov. He reported that he had just spoken with the commander of the ground forces, Deputy Defense Minister General Valentin Varennikov, who confirmed that the minister of defense and he would participate in the exercises in Pryluky and that the commanders of the various military districts were to attend. I was surprised to learn that my presence was also required, since the air army under my command was not included in the combat structure of the military district and there were no plans for the air force to play any role in these ground

(con't on p. 113)

Photo Collection II
My Command in Kyiv, Profound Changes for My Country, and the New Ukrainian Armed Forces

12. As the commander of the 17th Air Army, spring 1990.

Here you see me in full parade uniform, taking part in the graduation ceremony for young officers and technical engineers from the Vasylkiv Military Aviation-Technical School in Kyiv Oblast. In that year, in that one institution (only one of the eight institutions in our command), we had approximately eight hundred graduates.

13. With Marshal Yevgeny Shaposhnikov, July 1991.

This was taken during the graduation of the Gritsevets Kharkiv Higher Military Aviation School cadets. Marshal Shaposhnikov took part in the graduation along with me. We met with the young officers, the instructors, and other staff. It was the eve of major changes in both of our lives. After this meeting, Shaposhnikov and I had a number of very important and difficult telephone conversations, but we did not meet again face-to-face until we both were defense ministers—of different countries.

14. Reviewing a division (*photo by M. Sunika*).

This was a review near the end of the training year of the preparations of an armored division. The division commander issues commands to his troops as I look on.

15. As minister of defense, 1992, during a meeting with the staff of *Narodna Armiia.*

This photograph was taken during my meeting with the staff of the military newspaper Narodna Armiia. *We spoke about the creation of a "Ukrainian" atmosphere in the Ukrainian armed forces. The editor of the newspaper was Col. Vasyl Bilan. The newspaper, with the support of the Parliamentary Commission on Defense and National Security, was founded in the first days of independence on the basis of the previous newspaper of the Kyiv Military District.* Narodna Armiia *played an inestimable role in the formation of officers' attitudes toward the creation of an independent armed forces in Ukraine and their readiness to take the Oath of Loyalty in the spring of 1992.*

16. With Leonid Kuchma, then director of the Pivdenmash Factory Complex, in Dnipropetrovsk, May Day, 1992.

Pivdenmash ("The Southern Machine Works," known also by its Russian acronym Yuzhmash) was headed by Leonid Kuchma (future prime minister and president of Ukraine). He is to my right, with the plant's chief engineer, Dr. Koniukhov, to my left. Kuchma showed me the general conveyor, where already at that point Ukrainian strategic rockets were no longer being constructed. Ukraine was the first in the world to voluntarily turn away from its nuclear weapons-making capabilities. This factory complex was one of the most successful industrial undertakings in Ukraine, which made the decision to halt construction of the ballistic missiles all the more weighty and difficult.

17. At the Yavoriv Training Range in the Carpathian Military District in 1992.

This was taken during an inspection of one of the military units of the Carpathian Military District that had been put on alert during the night for military firing exercises at the Yavoriv Training Range. This was one of the tank crews that I talked with to get a sense of what they were doing, and how their training and daily life were in general. It was at this time that I found out that the soldiers who spoke Ukrainian were still forced to speak to their officers in Russian. And so, out of this review came my decree that officers had to speak with soldiers in the language of their homeland—Ukrainian.

18. Near Chernivtsi in the Carpathian Military District, 1992.

This was during an inspection of a training division in Chernivtsi, in the Carpathian Military District. I was learning the social situation of the officers and soldiers there—and their families. In this photograph I am meeting with the commander of the Carpathian Military District, Gen. Vasyl Sobkov, who was my appointee to that position. At that time there was a debate among the officers there whether to reconstitute the system for officer selection as it had existed in the Soviet Union or to accommodate the new system that I had instituted. By giving consideration to all sides in the matter, I was able to avoid a potentially destabilizing situation.

19. With Raisa at Konch Zaspa in the environs of Kyiv, September 1992.

This is a location where many government officials had their dachas as official perquisites of their positions. On weekends Raisa and I had a chance to get away from my duties. It is a lovely location. When I resigned my position I was matter-of-factly asked to give up the dacha. Eventually it was "privatized" and, as much as we loved it, we have not been able to go back to it.

20. With Gen. John M. Shalikashvili and the military commandant of Kyiv City, November 1992 (*photo by Ya. Zubkova*).

This photograph was taken during Gen. Shalikashvili's first visit to Kyiv. At that time he was the NATO supreme Allied commander, Europe. It was at my invitation that he visited Ukraine. This was an informative meeting for both Shalikashvili and for me. I wanted to establish contacts with European and NATO defense structures, with an eye toward possible cooperation. And so I initiated a series of visits by various European ministers of defense and other important figures in the Euro-Atlantic defense system.

21. Victory Day (May 9) in 1993, with President Leonid Kravchuk, Prime Minister Leonid Kuchma, Speaker of the Parliament Ivan Pliusch, and Gen. Ivan Gerasimov (head of the Committee of Ukrainian Veterans of World War II).

Ukrainian authorities are preparing to lay flowers on the monument to Ukrainian soldiers in Park Slavy (Park of Glory) in Kyiv. From left to right: head of the Committee of Ukrainian Veterans of World War II, Gen. Gerasimov; Prime Minister Leonid Kuchma; President Leonid Kravchuk; Speaker of Parliament Ivan Pliusch; and myself. It was extremely important to maintain good relations with veterans' organizations and to honor the many sacrifices that Ukrainian soldiers have made under different flags.

22. With the Command of the Ukrainian navy in Sevastopol, July 1993 (*photo by K. Bezkorovainyi*).

The situation with the Black Sea Fleet remained difficult throughout my tenure, but there were a number of patriots in the command structure there who realized the importance of the Fleet for Ukraine's long-term security. Despite very strong Russian counter-measures and pressure of every imaginable kind, we did manage to establish the basis of a Ukrainian navy and did not allow the Russian government the total control over Sevastopol and the naval facilities there that it desired.

23. Checking plans for new uniforms with President Kravchuk, September 1993 (*photo by Pavlo Poschenko*).

President Leonid Kravchuk, as the head of the Defense Council of Ukraine, acquaints himself with the new Ukrainian-based designs for insignia for the uniforms of our troops. This was one month before my resignation.

(con't from p. 100)

force exercises. Furthermore, I had no definite role to play either in planning or in directing those exercises. Needless to say, I found this a rather peculiar invitation.

"Why was I expected to attend?" I asked, again rather naively. "Who decided that I should be there?"

General Chechevatov replied that General Varennikov had simply informed him, "Take Morozov with you, and we'll meet in Pryluky." When I asked whether the commander in chief of the air force knew about my invitation to this event, the answer came back: "No, you inform him. That's your business."

I decided to confirm these plans with the command post of the air force in Moscow and to inquire whether I had truly been assigned to leave Kyiv and fly to another garrison. The central command post knew nothing about such plans, and no one could give me any further information. Although I knew that Marshal Shaposhnikov would be at home at such an early hour, I asked the command post officer to phone me, either at work or at home, as soon as Shaposhnikov came in. This change in the schedule had to be the result of a mistake of some kind, for I couldn't imagine why Chechevatov and I would have been invited to an event of this kind. No need to make special preparations, I told myself. Somehow my superiors would resolve this matter.

General Chechevatov later phoned to tell me that he would leave for Kyiv the next morning when the plane arrived. He also said that a mistake had been made: the General Morozov who was to accompany him to Pryluky was the General Morozov who was the commander of the Odesa Military District, not me. This news gave me a deep sense of relief and satisfaction since it confirmed that I had correctly assessed the situation.

As soon as the flight plans were prepared, I checked to see whether General Varennikov's flight from Moscow to Pryluky had been scheduled. I found his name included only in a supplementary flight plan indicating that he was flying not to Pryluky, but to Kyiv. In addition, there was no indication that the minister of defense would be in Pryluky or that military exercises would be held there. The only conclusion I could draw was that no ceremonies were to take place in

Pryluky after all and that General Varennikov's Sunday flight had been arranged as part of a surprise inspection of the Kyiv Military District.

The only other possibility, it seemed to me, was that this flurry of activity was connected to the personal plans of the military's top brass—a practice that I found particularly irritating, if not offensive, because we were often forced to change our plans, summon flight crews for additional assignments, and prepare flight plans just in order to satisfy the personal whims of a senior officer. I had always opposed such abuses, and although my outspokenness had not caused me any immediate problems, no doubt the top brass frowned on commanding officers who questioned the necessity of their travel arrangements or took an interest in the treatment of flight crews and the inappropriate use of military equipment. Nevertheless, I remained clear and consistent in opposing such excesses.

On Sunday, a crew left for Crimea as planned and picked up Chechevatov at the Bilbek airport for the return flight to Kyiv, where he met with Varennikov, recently arrived by plane from Moscow. Then the military district's headquarters ordered that I arrange for a return flight to Bilbek on the same day. This request convinced me that all this commotion was designed to satisfy the personal plans of the top brass, who, I concluded, were simply flying to Crimea for a vacation. Varennikov, no doubt, was probably planning to have some rest and relaxation at Chechevatov's dacha. But why had Chechevatov been summoned to Kyiv, and why had his vacation been interrupted? Whatever the case, I was satisfied that the flight crew was back on duty, that these flights had been approved by the air force central command, and that we were able to carry out this request without straining our resources.

The plane again left for Bilbek, this time with both Chechevatov and Varennikov on board. After ordering that preparations be made for the plane's return to Kyiv, I went home about noon on Sunday, August 18. After supper I heard from the command post that the plane had returned, its mission accomplished, and all was in order.

I instructed the district headquarters that I be informed whether there were any further plans to transport the top brass and that, if not, the flight crew be given a chance to rest. In most respects this had been a typical weekend for me, an air army commander involved in a number of special transportation assignments. Although we didn't know it at the time, the curious incident involving unscheduled flights for the top brass was part of the preliminary planning for the coup. It turned out to be a prelude to much more dramatic events.

During the next few days the veil of mystery around this flurry of activity on August 17 and 18 was quickly lifted. As I soon learned, Varennikov had been one of the key representatives of the military involved in planning the August coup. On August 17, he had requested that Shaposhnikov, who had been left out of the inner circle plotting the coup, keep a special plane ready to fly him to Kyiv, supposedly on a military inspection mission. Shaposhnikov had accepted this explanation. After arriving in Kyiv on August 18, Varennikov met up with Chechevatov, and the two of them flew to Crimea, where they joined the Moscow delegation, which apparently confronted Gorbachev and attempted to persuade him to support the coup. When Gorbachev refused, most members of the delegation flew to Moscow to confer with their colleagues on the next steps they would take. Varennikov, however, had been designated to ensure the support of all three military district commanders in Ukraine for the plot and to gain the support or acquiescence of Ukraine's senior political elite. Thus, he returned to Kyiv, where on the morning of Monday, August 19, he was to supervise the implementation of the plans of the State Committee for the State of Emergency (SCSE).

That morning I was awakened at 6:00 a.m. by a call from the chief of the 17th Air Army's political department. His voice full of excitement, he told me to turn on my television and listen to the news that Gorbachev was ill and that an emergency committee had been formed to oversee the affairs of state. Although I had planned to arrive at headquarters by 7:30 in order to review the reports submitted by all military commanders and chiefs of departments, I stayed glued to my TV set. Like everyone else in Ukraine and throughout Russia, I was "entertained" by scenes from Tchaikovsky's "Swan Lake."* Every so often, the programming was interrupted by a single news story read monotonously by an announcer specially selected for the occasion: The president of the USSR had fallen ill, and the Soviet leadership had issued an appeal to the Soviet people. After listening to several repetitions of this news bulletin, I called for my driver to take me to headquarters.

The formation of the eight-man SCSE was an extraordinary event, a sign that the situation in the country had changed radically overnight.* I realized that I had to get to my post quickly and receive the latest information so that I could help keep the military situation under control. As a rule, in emergency situations, the garrisons wait to receive information and instructions so that they know whether they have to change their regular schedule. But there was nothing like this in our planning books, of course. When I reached my office, I learned that the district headquarters had issued orders to assemble all military personnel and place all units on alert. Under such conditions troops have to wait for special instructions, while all officers who are away on leave have to return to their units. While this status is in force, commanders are expected to stay at their posts where they confirm action plans, account for personnel, supervise communications systems, and so forth. No other forms of activity are foreseen. Typically well prepared for situations of this kind, military personnel go through all these procedures during special training sessions or when they are preparing for an inspection. Technically it makes no difference to them whether this is an exercise or whether the alarm is for real: they prepare for it as if they are truly in a combat situation.

The reports I received that morning confirmed that all military personnel were in place and were following the usual schedule. Asked for further instructions, I ordered that everyone should be prepared to follow our previously established plans. I insisted on issuing this command, since the 17th Air Army was involved in very intense training activities, and I wanted to ensure that it took advantage of all the available daylight hours. Eight military schools were under the jurisdiction of our army, which was heavily involved in training future pilots.* We were already behind schedule in our training, and our planes had to fly in two or three shifts.

When I tried to report to the district headquarters (I had direct access neither to the district's commander nor to the chief of staff), I discovered that their senior officers were constantly in meetings. I then decided to consult with the commander in chief, General Shaposhnikov, but according to the duty officer, he was attending meetings with the minister of defense. Since no additional instructions from the central air force headquarters were forthcoming, I decided to follow, as much as possible, our normal routine. I knew what had to be done in such situations.

Still I was concerned, for example, that we continue fulfilling our daily in-flight training plans, for the weather was good and the conditions for working with trainees from the military colleges were excellent. Thus, I decided to proceed in accordance with the plan that we had used during the previous week. That is, I instructed the command post to inform all the aviation regiments and schools to prepare their flight plans. On my own initiative, I added that no one should be told to cut short a vacation. This was a particularly painful issue for many of our personnel, because the flight timetable was so intense that it was difficult to find opportunities for certain specialists to get away from their work. Once they had gone, all commanders waited for their return so that a new party could be sent off to rest. It was therefore undesirable to modify this timetable.

I finally managed to contact Marshal Shaposhnikov in between his meetings. I asked him what he thought of the situation and whether he had any additional instructions for me. He replied that he had received a directive from the minister of defense and had begun working on the appropriate instructions for the air force. Soon, he said, I would receive a coded message with further information. He then asked me about the activities of the army I commanded, and I informed him that we were not wasting time and were continuing to work with students from military schools, implementing our existing training plans. He did not directly comment on this activity, but he did not dissuade me either. I even sensed that although Shaposhnikov's spoken comments were noncommittal, he agreed with what I was doing. After this conversation I felt even freer to proceed as I best saw fit, and I ordered that all those scheduled for a second or third shift be allowed to go home so that we could proceed with our original plans.

There is a strict rule in the air force—if everything before a flight is not done according to regulations, then the flight must not take place. It was essential that flight crews be calm, have an opportunity to rest and prepare themselves for the next shift. In addition, to maintain order and avoid any possible panic, I halted the distribution of weapons and ammunition, even though this was standard procedure in a situation of heightened combat readiness. I instructed my subordinates that the army would continue with its regular functions. We would continue to fly, and our command post passed that same message on to the central command post in Moscow.

It was of great help to me that Marshal Shaposhnikov never tried to pressure me or force me to act hastily, without carefully considering what I had to do. These were essential qualities for me to maintain my air force command, for it was important that my orders or inquiries not promote confusion at lower administrative levels. The more complex the situation, the calmer the process of exchanging information should be. To maintain my authority it was essential for me to act in a measured, deliberate fashion. I had to be careful, even in the most complex situations, to do nothing to promote confusion among my subordinates.

Still, I found myself in a difficult situation. In the past I had never had any difficulty interpreting Shaposhnikov's commands. This time, however, something was wrong. A long time passed before I received the coded message he had mentioned, and when it did arrive, it contained nothing to explain the state of emergency and prepare us to deal with this new situation. It simply stated that a State Committee for the State of Emergency had been set up, that our activities should be in accordance with plans to maintain an increased combat readiness status, and that all measures should be taken to defend our weapons and ammunition. (A number of weapons recently had been stolen from military bases, and in a confused or chaotic situation criminals could take advantage of these circumstances. Measures to secure the weapons sounded reasonable, but Shaposhnikov's message portrayed them as being tied specifically to the implementation of the state of emergency regime.)

After reading this telegram, I was more convinced than ever that the army under my command should continue its normal everyday activities. I decided that we would not carry out any additional measures to increase our combat preparedness. I cannot say that this was because I realized that the state of emergency had been declared by reactionaries or that a surprise of some kind was being prepared for us. More likely, it was simply because I wanted to continue preparing student trainees without disrupting our regular schedule. I did not want to get involved in intrigues that would lead to regrets about wasting valuable time for no good reason.

In our initial conversations during the state of emergency, Marshal Shaposhnikov and I had to maintain a certain degree of reticence, which was only natural, given the circumstances, for he could not openly tell me that I should ignore the coded message he was sending me. He could not be sure how I would react. At the same time I could not tell him that I found the situation rather confusing and would simply ignore the instructions because I did not want to waste valuable training time. In any crisis I had to accept full responsibility for my actions and then later—with the benefit of perfect hindsight—assess whether those actions were right or wrong. Thus, I told Shaposhnikov that I would not fully implement the state of emergency and would continue training military students. He replied that if this were my decision, I should go ahead with it. He did not give me clear instructions, and he did not tell me that I shouldn't pay attention to the coded message, but at least he knew my stance.

At the same time the mass media were reporting Marshal Shaposhnikov's statements, which could be interpreted as indicating his support for Boris Yeltsin. In particular, I recall a television program that repeatedly aired film clips showing various buildings in Leningrad with signs that read "Pilots are for Yeltsin." Shaposhnikov himself telephoned me later in confidence, and I sensed that those film clips were accurate in their assessing the true state of affairs in the air force.

During this turbulent period, Shaposhnikov began to formulate his position concerning the role of the political organs and the CPSU organizations within the armed forces, a position he confirmed after

119

he became the defense minister of the USSR. "They must be immediately expelled from the armed forces," he told me in a confidential telephone conversation. Unfortunately, there was no one at the time—other than my wife Raisa—with whom I could discuss this potentially explosive situation. My deputies and the majority of senior officers either took a position opposite from mine, or they were afraid to speak out. I sensed that Marshal Shaposhnikov was in a similar situation.

In hindsight, it is thanks to what Shaposhnikov was doing in Moscow that Boris Yeltsin was able to take control over the armed forces during the period of the putsch. Generals Samsonov, Grachev, and Kobets also played roles, but it was Shaposhnikov's role from the very first moments of the putsch that was the most important. I understood even then that his responsibility for his actions would be even greater than my own and so felt an even greater respect for him given the actions that he took.

Shaposhnikov was supporting Yeltsin in Moscow much the same way that I was supporting Kravchuk and the decisions of the Ukrainian Parliament in Kyiv. Realizing the bankrupt nature of the Communist Party, which had spent its last ounce of strength defending its own pernicious ideology rather than the people—and which had ominously and dangerously tried to drag the armed forces into that absurd process of self-preservation—Shaposhnikov, with his innate sense of justice and honor, distinguished himself as one of the first to act against that tide. And his subordinates sensed how he distinguished himself.

Shaposhnikov later noted, "I didn't see any Party apparatchiks on the barricades in Moscow who might have tried to avert the bloodshed. Yeltsin was there and already outside the Party, and Rutskoi, who had been tossed out of it."

After the putsch, in September 1991, I traveled to Moscow as the designated minister of defense of Ukraine. Our party of Ukrainian political leaders was there to discuss the possibility of an economic union. I saw there Gorbachev, completed defeated and able to speak only in generalities. Having lost the chance of reconstructing the Union on a political basis, he had placed his hope on a last ditch effort, to recreate the Union on an economic basis. Shaposhnikov understood and saw all of the details of the political situation then in a way that some of the politicians of the time did not. But later, when he became chief of the armed forces of the Commonwealth of Independent States (CIS), he came to defend the interests of reintegration of the republics on the basis of those armed forces. He no longer understood the dynamic and interests of the other republics where the process of building on independence could not be turned back.

But back to the putsch. Sketchy as it was, the information available to us on television at that time made it obvious that we were being lied to. There were too many contradictions in the reports about how the country was being run. I remember my very first impressions on hearing about the declaration of the state of emergency. I could foresee that, no matter what was actually taking place, we would receive instructions to hold a Party meeting, gather together all officers, formally discuss and approve what we were told to approve, and then prepare an official letter that would be coded and then approved by our army's political organs. Thoroughly disgusted at the thought that I would have to be involved in all this rubbish, I sensed that what was happening reflected an offensive of the forces of reaction. From the radio and television reports available to us (newspapers commenting on these events came out only on Tuesday, August 20), it was clear that those implementing the state of emergency were categorically opposed to the growing authority of the democrats.

I was not the only one who thought this way. Although most of the officers under my command were afraid to voice their opinions, I knew how they felt. I was quite confident that I would find many who shared my views among the field grade officers—that is, the majors, lieutenant-colonels, and colonels. To be on the safe side, however, I called some of them into my office and, while discussing our activities and the information that we were receiving, I tried to determine how they felt about the reports of Gorbachev's "illness" and the establishment of the SCSE.

Personally, I had no illusions about the intentions of those behind the SCSE, which represented an offensive by reactionary forces against democracy in the Soviet Union. Its primary beneficiary was the Communist Party, which was being widely and openly criticized at the time, and I had no doubts that I had to do what I could to oppose this offensive. It soon became clear that the pro-coup forces had taken direct aim at the democratic movement in Ukraine and planned to exert pressure on Gorbachev, to force him to agree to harsh measures to restore "order" in society. If he refused, he was to be pushed aside, at least temporarily, on grounds of ill health. This was, in fact, what was done—at least for a few days in August.

The State Committee for the State of Emergency—a small group of irresponsible individuals—had decided to implement a number of brutal measures to crush the democratic movement and remove its leaders. Afterwards they planned either to reinstate Gorbachev and give him greater powers as the senior representative of the Communist Party, or to put forward another candidate to lead the country, like, for example, Lukianov. In essence, however, the aim of the coup was to renew the Party's traditional dominance of the state.

This scenario is much clearer now in hindsight, although even at the height of the August crisis, there were plenty of reports circulating from which we could infer these leaders' motives. We certainly felt the anxiety of living in complete uncertainty. Nonetheless, at the time my subordinates were greatly disoriented by the uncertainty of the situation in which we found ourselves. Thus, when I met with the officers on duty at the command post and tried to get a sense of their attitudes toward the current events, it quickly became clear that, hungry for leadership, they respected my judgment and would support the position I took. They recognized in me, I think, the ability to bring those leadership qualities to bear on this immediate crisis: namely, they knew what to expect of me; they knew that they could rely on me and that I would not deceive them.

Already many field grade officers were aware of how I felt about the Communist Party's platform, which had been widely discussed in the military. Some others, however, had been in favor of radical measures to impose their version of "order" on society and were ready to implement them. In particular, I was surprised how few senior officers—generals, colonels, and above all, deputy commanders—shared genuine pro-democracy sentiments. Most had always been afraid to speak their minds, and before the declaration of the state of emergency, I was not aware of their political views.

Discovery and Resignation

The next sequence of events showed just how serious conditions had become. On Monday, August 19, it finally became clear that we found ourselves in a very serious situation. Other armies began taking a variety of measures to implement the state of emergency, summoning officers back from their vacations, preparing planes to take on extra equipment and weapons, and activating offensive systems. In effect, most of the armed forces went on full military alert. I knew about these preparations because information from the military district headquarters reached me through my representatives in the command post.

That morning, when I held a meeting to discuss our activities for the day and our flight plans, the officer on duty at the command post informed me that Varennikov had ordered that his plane be recalled from Moscow. I was surprised to hear that Varennikov was in Kyiv, since I at the time knew nothing about the specific role assigned to him by the SCSE. I had concluded that he was still in Crimea and would return to Moscow directly, without retracing his steps through Kyiv. Varennikov, however, had never left Kyiv after returning from his visit with Gorbachev. Instead, he had spent the night in the Military District's headquarters, and in the morning he had issued orders to implement the increased combat readiness plan.

Varennikov's role in the coup finally began to fall into place for me when I discovered that on Monday morning, accompanied by Chechavatov and the chief of the political department of the Kyiv Military District, he had held a meeting with Kravchuk and some of the latter's associates.*

Later I called the chief of the military district's political department, General Sharikov.

"Why did you go to see Kravchuk?" I asked point-blank.

"I went with the Military District's commander to discuss some important issues," he replied.

"Such as?"

"Well, uh, I'm not really free to share the contents of that conversation."

"At least tell me in what capacity you attended the meeting," I said.

"You know that very well already. I'm sure you know. I attended as head of the political department and a member of the district's military council."

This was exactly what I was waiting to hear. Although I was a member of the military council, I had not been invited to this meeting. What's more, I had not even been informed about it.

"It is entirely inappropriate for the council to be divided into secretive clans," I objected.

"Well, uh…, Comrade-General Morozov, perhaps you…uh…should address your questions to General Chechevatov himself, as head of the council."

"I won't be turning to anyone for explanations. Moreover, I will suspend my activities in any military council that acts in this fashion." With that I promptly hung up the telephone.

It was infuriating to find out that the military council, a senior administrative body, could behave in this way in the absence of its full membership. Even with the sparse information available to me, I was ready to take a stand, and I definitely would have done so if I had been allowed to participate in the military council's meeting with Kravchuk. But the military district's commander and the head of the political department had acted independently, following their own specific agenda, which was shaped by nostalgia for the days when the Communist Party always had the final word. My colleague in the political department, of course, was the commander's right-hand man where political issues were concerned, and these political officers all called themselves "representatives of the Party's Central Committee" in the armed forces.

Now it finally became possible to start fitting together the pieces of this puzzle. I realized that it was unlikely that Varennikov had flown to Crimea for a vacation; rather, he was probably a member of the SCSE delegation, which, as the media were beginning to report, had met with Gorbachev the previous day. Immediately after this meeting the members of this group left for Moscow, leaving Varennikov behind to take charge of the situation in Ukraine. After all, Ukraine was a critical region for the coup leaders, probably even more important than the Baltic republics. Thus, Varennikov's conversation with Kravchuk and Kostiantyn Masyk, the acting head of government at the time, was clearly designed to put pressure on the Ukrainian authorities. I learned more about the details of this meeting a few days later when the text of Masyk's article, entitled "Behind the Scenes of the Coup," was published in the newspaper *Vechirnii Kyïv*. According to that article, Varennikov's behavior was truly outrageous. Who was this general from Moscow, and what gave him the right to deliver ultimatums to Ukraine's most senior political official?

Later that morning—that is, August 20—Varennikov flew to Moscow. Late the night before, or early on the 20th, he had confirmed that Gorbachev was continuing to refuse to cooperate with the SCSE, and he thus had to meet with the other figures involved in the coup to decide on their next steps. We learned about these developments only on August 22 or even the August 23, after Gorbachev returned to Moscow. However, before the fate of the coup became clear, a number of dramatic developments took place on August 20 that required decisive action.

As commander of the Kyiv air army, I was responsible for managing all air traffic over Ukraine's territory. Our army was in charge of the zonal air traffic management center, which also had branches in Lviv and Odesa, and we were responsible for coordinating the plans of all three air armies stationed in Ukraine. Any plans we approved had to be coordinated with the air defense forces whose commander and staff were also responsible for maintaining order in Ukraine's air space.

All of a sudden, without any preliminary warning from the appropriate authorities, I discovered that a large number of transport planes from the Baltic region was being transferred to Kyiv and

125

would be landing at the Boryspil Airport just to the east of the city. Furthermore, because of the nature of the bases from which they had departed, I concluded that these planes must be carrying troops. I had not received any flight plans for these planes, had not approved their entry into Ukraine's air space, and had not given any instructions for these planes to be monitored. As if that were not enough, we were informed that these planes had been instructed to fly directly over Kyiv.

Imagine an armada of some thirty heavy transport aircraft flying low over this city in clear weather. Military and political strategists knew exactly what an impact such a show would have on the citizens of Kyiv and all of Ukraine. It was an effort to exert psychological pressure on Rukh activists and, more significantly, on the leaders of Ukraine, who, as the coup leaders saw us, were insufficiently eager to support them. Certainly I did not know of any official measures by senior officials in Ukraine to support the coup plotters.

Since I was not involved in planning the flight of these aircraft, I did not have the right to order their crews to return to their bases. I categorically forbade them, however, to fly over the city. In all likelihood this operation was being managed directly from the headquarters of the Kyiv Military District, and I assumed that a senior air force official from Moscow was in Varennikov's group. Since he would have direct contact with the central command post in Moscow, he probably gave the orders for this particular route to be chosen. He must have provided the flight crews with detailed instructions and cleared them with the command post in Kyiv, only a few minutes before this aviation group reached my zone's borders. I could, however, control their flight path in the vicinity of Kyiv. At this point they were only thirty kilometers (less than twenty miles) from Kyiv and were heading for the center of the capital. Here, reducing their altitude, they were to prepare to land at Boryspil Airport.

When I tried to intervene, the officer in charge of the command post, a colonel, protested that he had very specific instructions from Moscow and that the military district headquarters, with Varennikov present, was controlling the situation. I reminded the officer, however, that by giving him alternative instructions, I was relieving him of responsibility and assuming it myself. This is a routine way of handling such changes in plans, but I had to remind the colonel of this practice since he was stubbornly insisting on carrying out his original instructions. I was not sure why he was so insistent. Maybe someone had spoken with him before I came by, maybe he had volunteered to carry out these instructions, or maybe he had been warned about the significance of this mission. He was literally trembling at the thought that I, appearing out of the blue, was trying to countermand his original instructions. However, I emphasized the importance of my decision and directly ordered him to follow my instructions. I also informed him that if he wished to do so, he had every right to send a report to Moscow about my decision to change his original instructions.

My office received a number of calls from the district headquarters complaining about my decision, and the chief of staff reminded us that the original orders had been confirmed, that this was a very important matter, and that Varennikov was supervising this operation. However, I told my subordinates to reply that they were simply following *their* commander's orders, and everything proceeded according to my instructions. The planes thus crossed the northern part of Kyiv Oblast and kept at least thirty kilometers away from Kyiv. Although the troops landed at Boryspil and stayed there for two days, I believe, they were not deployed in any way, nor were they even allowed to set up camp, and their living conditions must have been terrible. There was no attempt to satisfy even their most basic human needs, and they must have been terribly confused by the situation in which they found themselves.

The Ukrainian leadership did not come out with any statement regarding the coup attempt on August 19. I saw, however, that the senior Ukrainian leadership showed no signs of supporting the putsch. They did not require me to take any initiatives or assume additional duties against the dictates of my conscience, and I greatly appreciated their support. Thus, I supported our leaders by simply ignoring the declaration of the state of emergency and proceeding with our usual schedule.

In addition, I instructed my subordinates that if they received any orders to issue arms or ammunition to military personnel, they were to inform me immediately before taking any action. This decision surprised certain officers, for we found ourselves in a critical situation, and the safe thing to do was to stand aside and not interfere in what was happening. I made a firm decision, however, not to issue weapons to the students in military schools or allow soldiers to use live ammunition on street patrols and at public meetings or demonstrations. I knew all too well what a disaster "loose cannons" could produce.

Some readers might ask why I am dramatizing the situation if the air army I commanded was unlikely to be assigned a combat role, given that its primary job was to train cadets from military schools. In crises, however, any military force, including our army, could have suddenly been shifted to combat status. Thus, I began to monitor the behavior of the commanders of the garrisons within my jurisdiction, in order to know exactly what instructions they were issuing to our aviation units. Within this zone there were many garrisons, more than 20 airports, 8 large military schools, and more than 10,000 cadets and as many soldiers. The total force number was around 37,000 men.

I was concerned that arms and ammunition might be issued to these cadets and soldiers, who might then use them to suppress the democratic forces, supposedly in the interest of supporting "public order." This interference could be accomplished by restricting people's movement, preventing public meetings, and prohibiting the use of pickets and other forms of protest. Orders to engage in such activities could have been expected in many garrisons, for the situation that was unfolding on August 20–21 was complex, delicate, and not subject to easy solutions. Aviation commanders in isolated garrisons could hardly be expected to know exactly what to do.

For example, in many cities and villages, Communist Party members held meetings to support the coup leaders' decisions. In addition, the garrison commanders, who were directly subordinated to the Kyiv Military District command, were heavily influenced by the positions and decisions taken by this command. It, in turn, was controlled and directed by Varennikov, who had remained in the headquarters of the Kyiv Military District for much of August 20 to supervise developments in Ukraine. Thus, my main preoccupation was to maintain control over the forces under my command and to monitor the instructions issued by the garrison commanders and the district headquarters. In particular, I wanted to ensure that the personnel of the 17th Air Army would never be used against the democratic forces in Ukraine.

The information I received was often incomplete or contradictory. For example, the unofficial memos I received were "corrected" by explanations emanating from official sources, and vice versa. And how much energy was expended to demoralize the democratic movement in Ukraine! Pro-coup forces issued various appeals and statements, painting the situation in Ukraine in very black colors. According to these statements, the democrats were inciting the population to disobedience, threatening social harmony, and challenging the very existence of the Soviet Union by opposing efforts to maintain its integrity.

The coup leaders considered that the turbulent political developments in Ukraine posed a serious threat to the survival of the system that they represented, and this is why such a large force of airborne troops was sent to Ukraine. However, the pro-coup forces distrusted me and did not assign me the task of organizing and transferring successfully the airborne division to the Boryspil garrison. My stance on political issues may not have been immediately obvious to this element, but no doubt they inferred it through conversations with some of my fellow officers.

Whatever we might have felt prior to the coup attempt, the dramatic events of August, 1991 greatly encouraged me and other like-minded officers to participate directly in the process of democratization rather than remain mere observers. I remember, for example, how impressed I was when, in the August 20 issue of *Vechirnii Kyïv*, I read a press release from Rukh openly stating, for the first time in Ukraine, that the declaration of the state of emergency represented an attempt by the forces of reaction to overthrow the state. The main targets of the coup leaders, according to that article, were the democratic forces and the ideal of a democratic society.

I was so impressed by this courageous statement, and so thoroughly agreed with its authors, that on August 21, I decided to call Kravchuk to tell him how I felt about the recent developments in Ukraine. In our conversation I told him that the 17th Air Army was fully under my control, that the coup attempt would not find support in Ukraine, that I fully supported the democratic forces in our country, and that I was prepared to help ensure the stability of the situation in Ukraine.

On August 22, I contacted Kravchuk for a second time through one of his assistants. I reiterated that the 17th Air Army did not pose a threat to the democratic process and that the armed forces in Ukraine were under firm control. I was eager to demonstrate my support for a distinctive Ukrainian stance on the coup, one that was not dictated by events in Moscow. Moreover, I wanted to confirm that my position was in perfect harmony with that of the current Ukrainian leadership. In particular, I believed that we should work together with the new democratic forces in Ukraine, which, united in Rukh, espoused ideals that I myself held.

The Party's role in the August crisis increasingly preoccupied my attention. What's more, I was still a member of the Party, and I decided that I should move quickly to resolve this contradiction. My decision was based on both my assessment of the political turbulence in Ukraine and the broader interests of my fellow officers and the army that I commanded. I had concluded that the Party should cease its activities in the armed forces. The military's purpose was to serve the people and defend the state's territory against external aggression. It was not to try to tip the political scales in favor of one cause or another. Still, I felt that each officer should have the right to make a personal decision concerning his Party membership, which should not be forced on anyone or terminated by executive decree.

I was convinced that the Party's involvement in the coup was anti-constitutional, anti-democratic, and thoroughly reactionary. On August 22, I shared my thoughts on this matter with my fellow officers, including the head of the air army's political department, his deputy, and the secretary of the Party committee. Further, I proposed that the officers under our command be given the opportunity to make their own independent decision concerning their Party membership. Needless to say, my recommendation did not draw rounds of applause from my colleagues, for it was truly unprecedented. Since my fellow officers did not support my general proposal, I told them that I would confirm my personal decision concerning my Party membership at a meeting the next day—that is, Friday, August 23.

I'm quite sure that the authorities in Moscow were informed about my decision immediately after the meeting on August 22, but I had acted very deliberately in taking this step, and was not concerned about any possible consequences. At 8:15 a.m. the next morning, I addressed the daily meeting of admin officers.

"Do you think it necessary to make any changes in the structure of CPSU activity in the armed forces?" I asked the secretary of the Party committee.

"It is probably premature to raise that issue," he responded.

Turning to the other officers, I called upon them to voice their opinions, although I knew that they found themselves in a difficult situation and I did not really expect them to speak out. After all, I had prepared myself for this meeting. They, on the other hand, were still waiting to determine how the situation would evolve during the next few days.

I made it clear that I was not accusing anyone, nor forcing anyone to make an immediate decision. As of August 21, however, I had ceased to consider myself a member of the Communist Party of the Soviet Union. Each officer was free to make up his own mind, and whatever his decision, I would accept it. But for me, the only decision I could personally live with was contained in a written statement of resignation, which I had prepared at home the previous evening. To ensure that I was following proper procedures, as soon as the meeting was over, I submitted the statement to the secretary of the appropriate Party Committee. With that, I resigned from the Communist Party.

I did not consider myself to be a hero. I made this decision not in my capacity as a commander but as a human being, and I wanted no less for each army officer, who should have the same right to act according to conscience. Resignations from the Party became a widespread phenomenon within just a few days, as people took their cue from Gorbachev himself.* Privately I was glad that I made my decision before it became the popular thing to do.

My newfound freedom coincided, it turned out, with Ukraine's. At the time I had no idea that Ukraine was moving so rapidly toward full independence and that the historical decision to make that declaration, as the next chapter discusses, would occur in just two days—August 24, 1991.

7 Ukraine's First Minister of Defense

As news of the attempted coup d'état and its aftermath spread throughout Ukraine, concern about the stability of the military deepened. The democrats in particular wanted to learn how the armed forces were responding to the coup and whether, if given a command to fire on civilians, the soldiers would obey. Images of recent violence in Sumgait, Tbilisi, and Vilnius fueled the fears of many Ukrainians who asked whether the army might turn against the residents of Kyiv, Lviv, and Kharkiv.

Because of the important role the three military districts and the Black Sea Fleet in Ukraine played in Soviet military strategy, a disproportionately large number of military personnel was stationed on their territory. The majority of those servicemen had no familial or other ties to Ukraine other than that they had been assigned to various posts inside this republic.* Moreover, the military had access to and control over an enormous storehouse of weapons, both nuclear and conventional, creating a potentially volatile situation that caused the democrats much concern.* Thus, they did their best to gather information about internal developments within the armed forces and search for a senior military officer they could trust.

Cautiously the democrats began to inquire about individuals in the armed forces who might have positive attitudes toward democratic reform and Ukraine's independence. A number of Rukh members met first with company and field grade officers (but not general officers) whose opinions about democratization were well known. These officers could be trusted to pass along confidential information about senior commanders who might be sympathetic to Rukh's objectives and who recognized that democratic ideas were gaining a foothold in Ukraine. Because of their positions and the interdiction against military personnel engaging in political activities, these senior officers were not able to speak out. No doubt my name was among those that Rukh members added to their list of officers who might support Ukrainian independence and statehood.

I had always been interested in politics and sociology, but the military world I had known for most of my life had greatly limited my imagination and my activities in these areas. In turn, many of the democrats whom I met felt intimidated by the military, which for them represented something of an arcane and rather threatening world. During the immediate post-coup period, I met several representatives from the Narodna Rada parliamentary faction,* democrats in the Supreme Soviet including Ivan Drach, who suggested that I allow officers working in the headquarters of the army I commanded to meet with leaders of the democratic movement. I readily agreed to his proposal.

Such a meeting was, of course, unprecedented. Under normal circumstances it most assuredly would have been banned, and I cannot conceive that such a meeting could even have been contemplated in the days before the coup attempt. But here we were—a number of well-known democrats and military officers, all assembled in a large conference hall, openly participating in a question-and-answer exchange. Far from challenging the authority of the powers that be, this meeting was intended to help clarify issues related to the coup attempt and prevent future misunderstandings between the leaders of the democratic movement and those officers who were under my command.

But who at the time could have been absolutely sure what would happen next? How would the armed forces react to the ongoing struggle for power in Moscow? Would the tensions between the Yeltsin-led forces and the hard-line Communists, apparently supported by some factions within the military, spread to Ukraine? Looking for answers to such questions, the democrats in the Ukrainian Supreme Soviet suggested that several meetings be held to promote a better understanding of the conditions—both psychological and military—within the armed forces stationed here. Parliamentary deputy Larysa Skoryk, for example, expressed a desire to meet with the students and officers of the Kyiv Higher Military Engineering School, a contingent of over a thousand people. I authorized this meeting and asked my staff to help organize it.

Those who knew almost nothing about the theory and practice of democracy listened intently to the proceedings, while those who with a greater interest in politics put questions to Skoryk as speaker. Even if one disregards the political impact of this meeting, it was very important to ensure that military officers, who led a highly regimented life, had access to independent sources of information about current events, and also that those active in politics learned something about the military. To this end, I recommended that our army's military council include several parliamentary deputies who could then learn more about the circumstances in which the army found itself and convey this information to their colleagues. I felt that this interaction would help build trust by eliminating the mutual fears and suspicions widespread among both civilians and military personnel. Unfortunately at the time this proposal was rejected. This proposition, together with others concerning the "democratization" of the situation in the military, was sent to Marshal Shaposhnikov (by then he was already the new minister of defense of the USSR). However, I did not receive any response from him, and I could not detect any support for my ideas in his speeches. I assume that these proposals were seen as encouraging a rather extreme level of openness, a level which even today is considered unacceptable.

Gradually, many democratic politicians and what I might call the more enlightened military leaders came to recognize that we had a great deal in common. My contacts, both indirect (largely through intermediaries) and direct, with the democratic forces intensified dramatically during the summer of 1991. In one exchange (through intermediaries) with Ivan Drach, whom I had not yet met face-to-face, and Volodymyr Muliava,* a Rukh activist with a great interest in military affairs, I was asked outright whether soldiers would obey commands to fire at peaceful demonstrators or picketers. How could I respond? Speaking only for myself, I could assure them that where I had influence and where I was in a position to take the appropriate decisions, the military would not be used against civilians. Drach and Muliava were as much surprised that I used their first names and patronymics in addressing them as they were pleased that they could find some common ground with a Soviet general. Perhaps it was my categorical statement that the military forces under my command would not resort to violence against peaceful demonstrators that encouraged them to trust me.

As our communication continued, I was able to convince them that I merited their trust, and we eventually began to discuss issues of a more theoretical nature, such as the role to be played by the military if the democratic forces in Ukraine's Supreme Soviet were successful in winning support for their political platform. Muliava informed me that there were military officers in Ukraine who not only shared Rukh's ideals but had even cooperated with the organization. These officers, I was told, saw Ukraine as an independent country with its own armed forces, a country soon to be integrated into the European community of nations. Various opinions as to how to achieve this goal ranged from a step-by-step, evolutionary transition to armed struggle against the USSR. Moderate forces with the Union of Officers of Ukraine (UOU) were sufficiently strong and in general opposed to the more violent means so long as progress could be made in other ways. Further correspondence with Drach and Muliava made it clear that these plans for an independent Ukraine with its own armed forces was no by means a merely theoretical issue.

I must make a note here of my first face-to-face meeting with Drach, which took place during the putsch, either on the 19th or 20th, and was an important milestone for me. Drach appeared unannounced at my office and started talking to me as if we were long-time acquaintances. My first response was surprise. Here was a man whose voice I knew well—I had listened to him on the radio, I had read his published articles, we had corresponded and carried on contacts through third parties. Now he was actually standing before me, talking to me.

In a very real sense, however, I realized that I knew this man, knew him almost as a friend—despite the fact that he had been continually misrepresented by the Communist Party press and other propagandists. Having listened to his public speeches and studied his ideas about the country's tasks at hand, I had come to my own conclusions about him. Meeting him that day confirmed for me that Drach was no extremist in any sense of the word and that he was far from being a traitor. I took great satisfaction in knowing that I had developed an independent point of view based on what I myself saw, heard, and read. Even though it did not coincide with the official point of view, that judgment, I knew, was right. That realization, for me, proved to be an enormously liberating experience

The Act of the Supreme Soviet Declaring Ukraine's Independence

On Saturday, August 24, the day after I had announced my resignation from the Communist Party, I came to work at 8:00 a.m. Although it was not officially a working day, because of the turbulence of the preceding week many of us senior officers found it necessary to handle a large backlog of old business as well as deal with a variety of new matters that had arisen. However, I also wanted to keep track of the rapidly changing developments in Ukraine's Supreme Soviet, whose extraordinary session was to be broadcast that morning. Eager for any new information, but not without a small twinge of anxiety, I switched on the television set in my office and soon found it difficult to tear myself away from the parliamentary debates.

Clearly something unprecedented was happening. Deputies representing several parties were engaged in a vigorous debate over some document, which at first I could not identify. Many, including those whom I considered to be democrats, disagreed sharply over its content. A majority of the democrats, however, demanded that a vote be taken immediately and the document be adopted before anyone was permitted to leave the chamber. As tensions rose, I turned up the volume and, fascinated by the proceedings, closely studied the deputies' gestures, facial expressions, and interactions.

Taking a wait-and-see attitude, several deputies urged caution and expressed concern that any precipitous action could lead to civil unrest and bloodshed, or at least could cause Moscow to intervene in Ukraine's internal affairs. Others pointed out that we were wasting valuable time, that the political situation in the Soviet Union could continue to deteriorate, and that the tanks which had earlier rumbled down the streets of Moscow could still appear in the streets of Kyiv. Now was the time to seize the opportunity, these deputies urged. Now was the time to take control of Ukraine's future.

The deputies argued at length, seeking further to improve the wording in the document that held everyone's attention. Then, after a short break, Dmytro Pavlychko, the head of Tovarystvo Ukraïns'koï Movy (the Ukrainian Language Society), stood up to read a draft of what turned out to be Ukraine's Proclamation of Independence.

The parliamentary debate continued to take unpredictable twists and turns as tensions rose over exactly when and how Ukraine would declare its independence. As the time approached to put the proclamation to a vote, Volodymyr Hryniov, the deputy speaker, asked that he be allowed to present his point of view. Although Kravchuk knew his position and was reluctant to let him speak, he nevertheless granted Hryniov the floor. "Let us ban the Communist Party first," Hryniov argued, "then declare Ukraine an independent state. Such a ban would make it clear, throughout the entire country, that the Communist Party would no longer determine the nature of our political life."

The Hryniov proposal was sidetracked for the moment in favor of more pressing issues (the next day, in fact, the Presidium corrected this oversight by banning the Communist Party in Ukraine). Soon afterwards, when more evidence emerged of the Communist Party's complicity in the coup attempt, its activities were suspended.* Other deputies such as Ivan Zaiets and Larysa Skoryk then presented arguments supporting Ukraine's immediate break with the Soviet Union. Prominent members of the national-democratic opposition and rather emotional individuals, both deputies were quite passionate in making their arguments.

Debates continued throughout the day, but by 5:00 p.m. on August 24, it came time to take a vote on the declaration, the final version of which read as follows:

138

Act of Declaration of the Independence of Ukraine

In view of the mortal danger surrounding Ukraine in connection with the state coup in the USSR on August 19, 1991,

- continuing the thousand-year tradition of state building in Ukraine.
- based on the right of a nation to self-determination in accordance with the Charter of the United Nations and other international legal documents, and
- realizing the Declaration on State Sovereignty of Ukraine, the Supreme Soviet solemnly

DECLARES THE INDEPENDENCE OF UKRAINE AND THE CREATION OF AN INDEPENDENT UKRAINIAN STATE—UKRAINE.

The territory of Ukraine is indivisible and inviolable.

From this day forward, on the territory of Ukraine only the Constitution and laws of Ukraine are valid.

This act becomes effective at the moment of its approval.

SUPREME SOVIET OF UKRAINE
August 24, 1991[*]

The full proclamation was adopted to the cheers of the deputies who stood in ovation, and at this heady moment all the major political conflicts dividing these deputies were the farthest things from their minds. The deputies congratulated each other on a job well done. Although their work had only just begun, now that Ukraine was independent of the USSR—in name, if not yet in fact—we could openly state that *we were living in our own country.* No one, however, even the most prescient among us, could have imagined the kinds of problems that would soon face us. It is one thing to declare the country's territory inviolable, quite another to enforce that declaration against those who might take advantage of the new nation's uncertain first steps.

Thus, at the same time that the deputies began to debate independence, they also took up the issue of the military installations and personnel within Ukraine's boundaries. They were deeply concerned about how the large, powerful, and well-equipped army stationed in Ukraine would accept these dramatic changes in the country's status and political allegiance. The army's support, or its acquiescence, would largely seal the acceptance of Ukraine's independence and send a strong message that a peaceful transition of power in the country was possible.

The resolution of Parliament (in English we use this term, not "Supreme Soviet" after the act of Independence) on the military was intended for distribution among all military units in Ukraine. One section of the resolution asserted Ukraine's right to self-determination and explained why the events associated with the recent coup in Moscow should be considered a deadly threat to human rights in Ukraine and to the republic's very existence. The other section provided a preliminary indication of Ukraine's military policy. For example, it stated that Parliament and the country's leaders were fully aware of deep-seated problems such as inadequate salaries and the lack of proper housing for military personnel and their families. By preparing this document, the deputies sought to decrease tensions and to keep military personnel from falling under the influence of other sources of information which might foster discontent and set them against the country's independence.

A Meeting with Drach

Soon after the Ukrainian independence was proclaimed, I was sitting in my office when it was announced that Drach himself had arrived and wished to confer with me. Hardly had this announcement been made when Drach appeared.

Drach inquired how the military generals in Ukraine were reacting to Act of Declaration of Independence that had been approved by Ukraine's Parliament. In connection with this he asked me whether I, personally, was planning to leave Ukraine. I replied that generals were human beings like everyone else and that each one had his own point of view on independence. As far as I was concerned, I had immediately and absolutely accepted Ukraine's independence. Since I had been born here and had grown up in Ukraine, and since all my family, including my parents and my wife's parents, lived or

140

were buried here, I certainly had no plans to leave.

This made a very positive impression on him. I could sense that he quickly understood that we generals were not a monolithic group and that among them he could find not only someone with whom he could have a normal conversation but who also might share his views. I don't know the exact content of the negotiations that were then being conducted by the People's Council with Leonid Kravchuk, the parliamentary speaker. Drach, however, in view of his great authority and influence on the future president, no doubt played a crucial role in my future role in an independent Ukrainian government.

A Roundtable Meeting of the Generals

After the adoption of the act proclaming independence, the parliamentary executive decided that a special meeting of the senior commanders of all military formations on Ukraine's territory would be called for August 27. Its purpose was to provide information and to allow a dozen or so high-level specialists a chance to express their opinions on the role of the military in the new Ukraine. The recently established Union of Officers of Ukraine (UOU) had already prepared some proposals, but they were at best sketchy. As the commander of the 17th Air Army, I was invited to attend, along with the senior commanders of three military districts (Kyiv, Odesa, and Carpathian), the Black Sea Fleet, all armies in Ukraine, the civil defense forces, railroad troops, and the commanders of certain divisions. The meeting was chaired by the speaker of the Parliament, Leonid Kravchuk.

I fully expected to find myself in a very difficult situation, and in that regard I was not disappointed. I knew, for example, that many of the senior commanders, on the one hand, would have viewpoints diametrically opposed to the position Kravchuk would likely present. On the other hand, Kravchuk clearly intended to use this meeting to assess the positions taken by these commanders and gauge the nature of the support he could expect from them. As a result of my meetings with deputies from the democratic camp, I knew that plans were afoot to create an independent defense system for Ukraine, thereby implementing one of the provisions of the 1990 Declaration of Sovereignty. How would the senior military commanders react to this proposal?

To support these commanders' probable objections and in all likelihood to continue controlling the situation in Ukraine from the old "center," General Vladimir Lobov, chief of the General Staff of the USSR in Moscow, was also invited to attend this meeting. Kravchuk, with Lobov on his right and Kostiantyn Masyk, acting head of the government, on his left, presided over the meeting. I was assigned a place two seats from Lobov, but within a few feet of all the senior commanding officers. Members of the Presidium sat around the other tables—the chairmen, I believe, of various parliamentary committees.

The session itself took place in the meeting room of the Presidium of Ukraine's Parliament. Confident and independent, Kravchuk was masterful in conducting it. Even his dress signaled an air of distinction and self-confidence. Whereas all of us generals were dressed in our military uniforms and the Communist Party functionaries wore their traditional and rather dull brown or gray suits, Kravchuk sported gray wool pants and a navy blue jacket with bright gold buttons. Having fully assumed his role as Ukraine's leader, he had no desire to be subservient to the power brokers in Moscow, and both his demeanor and his dress indicated that he was now his own man, ready to do business and take charge of the situation.

Kravchuk began by summarizing recent developments in Ukraine, particularly those revolving around the Parliament and its act declaring independence a few days earlier. He briefly addressed the Presidium's plans to continue promoting democratic practices. Various appointments, for instance, had to be made as soon as possible. Then he turned to the main business of this meeting, indicating that he hoped to hear from each commanding officer about the role he saw the military taking in the new republic.

Beginning with those on Kravchuk's right, the generals spoke in order of rank. The commanders of the three military districts and the Black Sea Fleet in Ukraine detailed their reasons for taking uncompromisingly negative positions—not with respect to Ukraine's independence, which they had accepted as a legitimate act of the Ukrainian Parliament—but with respect to the proposals for implementing

142

independence. Ukraine could not properly manage this new challenge, they argued, for it was beyond the country's capabilities. The structure of the armed forces was such that one could not even contemplate tearing an enormous chunk out of this organic whole. Moreover, these leaders vehemently opposed the idea of creating an independent defense system, and to be fair, it must be stated that at the time no one—including the heads of parliamentary commissions and the leaders of the democratic factions in the Parliament—had any idea what this army would look like and how it would be structured.

As the discussion moved inexorably around the table, some generals briefly stated their arguments, underlining the costs of operating independent military force and the difficulty of providing it with the supplies and equipment it needed. Others spoke at length, taking much longer than the few minutes each of us had been allotted. Some speakers seemed to be delivering a public lecture, one that they had prepared days in advance of this meeting, in an attempt to educate a group of people who supposedly had absolutely no idea what they needed to do. General Chechevatov, for example, had probably been instructed to conduct a propagandistic "political briefing" session, and he performed accordingly.

I could see that my turn to speak was fast approaching. I knew that I did not have time for a lengthy presentation, nor did I have all the facts I needed at hand. I was simply required to make a brief comment on how I felt about establishing a separate Ukrainian military, but I felt as if I were about to step out onto a high wire with no net below. So far, the tone of this meeting had been set by the commanders of the military districts, whose armies were much larger than the air army I commanded. Still, no matter how high that wire or how delicate my first step, I knew that I could not change my convictions or compromise my principles just to please the people sitting around that table. It was also clear to me that brevity, at least at this meeting, was the appropriate tactic to take.

By virtue of the fact that I was seated on Kravchuk's right near General Lobov, I would be one of the last to speak. Only two more people would make presentations after my comments, and I was very much aware that I would be the first—and probably the last—

speaker to support Kravchuk. His views on the question of the Ukrainian military were hardly a secret to anyone at the table. After all, he had maintained an independent and relatively progressive stand, not only in the recent parliamentary debates, but also in his high-profile performance at the Novo-Ogarevo meetings when he and other leaders of the Soviet republics had met with Gorbachev to discuss a restructuring of the union treaty. It was up to me to take a stand with him in the presence of all of Ukraine's top brass.

I had a small notebook with me, and as I listened to the other speakers, I jotted down a few sentences on one page. Finally it was my turn, and I still remember my brief statement as if I had spoken those words only a few minutes ago. I stood up, greeted my distinguished colleagues, and spoke for seven or eight minutes in Russian like everyone else at the meeting. I stressed that I fully supported the legitimate strivings of the Ukrainian people toward self-determination and their right to defend their democracy. I then offered a few comments about how we might go about creating the foundations for Ukraine's armed forces, noting that it was difficult for me to present a detailed blueprint of how to achieve this objective since I had not yet had time to think systematically about this matter. Under the circumstances the best I could do was to express an opinion, but nevertheless one that was grounded in my personal values and convictions.

Four basic principles guided my thinking about the role of the military in the new Ukraine and were reflected in my comments. First, only Ukraine's political leaders—not a bureaucracy of military personnel taking orders from professional military commanders—should control the armed forces on this territory. Second, in regards to provisioning, training, and evaluating the armed forces, I believed that some kind of unified structure could be developed to coordinate those activities throughout all the new republics. Third, I envisioned a Ukrainian military that would consist of the forces currently in Ukraine, but reduced in numbers. These forces would be subordinated to the military leadership of a coalition armed forces structure, which would comprise the separate militaries in each of the former Soviet republics. Fourth, this subordination would have to be mediated by our Ukrainian leaders, in consultation with the appropriate members of Ukraine's Parliament.

I finished my statement and glanced around the table. My colleagues sat in stony silence, their expressions betraying the deep skepticism they must have felt for the arguments I had presented. They were not given an opportunity to put forward a rebuttal, but I could sense that my comments had not won me great support from the most powerful military leaders serving in Ukraine. Yet when I sat down, I felt satisfied that I had stated my position as openly and clearly as I could. My presentation may not have provided specific details, but no one at the meeting could doubt that I strongly supported democratic ideals.

General Lobov was the last to speak before Kravchuk concluded the meeting. Although very diplomatic, Lobov lent his weight to the negative opinions already expressed on creating an independent military in Ukraine. Instead of independence, he stressed the need for cooperation. The Ministry of Defense in Moscow, he said, had prepared several versions of a plan to create national military formations that would be part of a larger armed forces structure. These national formations would have specific functions such as dealing with natural disasters. However, he insisted on maintaining what would be, in essence, a pan-Soviet structure for the military, ultimately under Moscow's control.

After all the speeches were completed, Kravchuk's face revealed volumes of disappointment. I could tell he was distressed that a dozen generals, representing the most senior command posts, had spoken in such a negative fashion about the prospects for an independent armed forces for Ukraine. Still, he was unsure of how to close the meeting, for while he did not wish to appear vanquished, at the same time he could not simply say to the generals, "Well, my good fellows, I guess you yourselves know that we won't be needing you now." He was too much of a politician to end the meeting in such a fashion.

Being the only one of twelve generals to express a positive opinion on this issue, I think that my presentation provided Kravchuk with some support. My public resignation from the Communist Party paled in comparison to the professional stance that I was taking before my peers, all of whom ostensibly disagreed with me. For the first time in my life I had taken a stand that clashed with the majority opinion, and I knew that this act would have serious consequences.

Kravchuk ended the meeting in characteristic fashion. He had a marvelous way of bringing participants together at the end of a meeting so that they would not part as enemies. No doubt he was aware how dangerous it would be, in the current circumstances, to alienate any of these generals. Thus, he neither contradicted General Lobov nor openly supported the position I had taken, for he knew that by doing either, he would only add to the existing tensions. After delivering a brief summary, he simply allowed the meeting to end. He thanked the assembled generals for their comments and stated that it was important to continue these consultations since this was a new, complicated, and extraordinarily important issue for Ukraine. Always the statesman, Kravchuk let everyone know that he had expected something different from this meeting. The generals, he thought, had adhered to an old-fashioned style of thinking. How much he would have appreciated a more constructive attitude from them! After all, he pointed out, the Parliament of the new Ukraine had already made clear its position in this matter and would certainly maintain its current course toward democracy.

An Offer I Could Not Refuse

The weather in late August was perfect for the rigorous training program our military school students were undertaking, and I continued with my busy schedule as if the August 27 meeting had not taken place. Quite unexpectedly, on August 29, I received an invitation from Kravchuk, in his capacity as parliamentary speaker, to meet him the following day.

I speculated on what he might want to discuss with me. Certainly it was necessary to plan the next steps that Ukraine's leaders would take to establish firm control over the military forces within Ukraine's borders. Perhaps he also wanted to initiate a discussion on how best to create a superstructure under which all of Ukraine's military forces would be united and managed. Such a plan would require a great deal of study and work.

Because of the stand I took during the coup attempt and particularly at the August 27 meeting of generals, I thought that I might be considered for a senior appointment in Ukraine's future ministry of defense. As I had argued before the generals, however, I was convinced that the person heading the ministry should be a civilian. If Ukraine was to be a democratic state, I believed that we should learn from the example of other democratic countries, which stressed the principle of civilian control of the armed forces. In the structure I imagined, I saw myself occupying the position of a deputy minister or special assistant or advisor to the minister of defense.

I met Kravchuk in his office on August 29. He was very relaxed and gracious.

"So, Kostiantyn Petrovych, what did you think of our meeting with the generals?" Kravchuk asked.

"Much as I had expected," I replied. "I wish only that I had had more time to prepare a plan for reducing the size of the military forces and ensuring that control of the army lies with the people and their representatives."

"Not the most popular position to put forward at this time in our history, do you think?"

"Perhaps it's not," I said, "but sooner or later it will happen. The armed forces must ultimately be in civilian hands."

"What would you say to making it later?" Kravchuk asked, his eyes focused on me like searchlights.

"I'm not sure what you mean, Leonid Makarovych."

"In a word, Kostiantyn Petrovych, I propose that the Presidium at its next meeting nominate you for Ukraine's first minister of defense."

It is impossible to describe what thoughts and emotions rushed in upon me when I heard this: shock, surprise, pride, trepidation, to name a few. I quickly composed myself and asked Kravchuk to clarify some issues for me.

"Does the Presidium know that I have never worked at the level of the General Staff? Do the deputies know that I have no political experience, that I have never served as a military attaché, and that I have never participated in international negotiations? What's more, are they aware that I have no concrete proposals yet for dealing with the enormous challenges facing Ukraine's future military?"

"All that and more," Kravchuk replied with an enigmatic smile. "The Presidium is fully aware of your background and qualifications. The deputies want to give your candidacy serious consideration."

Whatever the outcome of our discussion, I now had a clean conscience. I myself had informed Kravchuk about my lack of experience for certain aspects of the job.

"If this goes through, I will need a great deal of assistance from you and others to fulfill my responsibilities."

"And you will get it, Kostiantyn Petrovych. But thank you for being so frank. Often what we perceive as deficiencies are so only in our own eyes, and the Presidium may be looking for other qualifications for the post which you have discounted. Let me assure you that the deputies have thoroughly discussed all these concerns. But they realize that they have to act quickly to resolve the problems facing Ukraine in the military sphere. It's time to begin creating a system of comprehensive control over the military forces on Ukraine's territory."

Kravchuk led me to understand that this nomination was not intended as a reward to me for the stance I had taken at the meeting, but was the result of very serious deliberations sparked by the difficult circumstances in which Ukraine found itself. Not one of the senior generals in the Ukrainian military had shown a willingness to support democratic ideals. Thus, someone else had to assume responsibility, someone who knew the military environment as well as the prevailing mood among the officers. Furthermore, it had to be someone who could properly control the situation.

"This is such an important decision that I have no right to give you an immediate reply," I said to Kravchuk.

"Of course," he replied. "Take a few days to think and discuss the proposal with your family. Then phone me, either at work or at my dacha."

Before parting, we talked briefly about General Lobov's proposition to retain a common chain of command and control with the remainder of the Soviet armed forces, while special units under Ukraine's command would deal with natural disasters and issues of a local character. Kravchuk gave me the documents describing Lobov's proposal and asked me to examine them carefully.

In a mere twenty minutes the meeting was over, and I left his office, both a lighter and a heavier man than when I had entered.

A Lesson in Democratic Politics

During the next few days I thought about nothing else than the offer of this ministerial post. Why me? I asked myself. Probably it was because I had so closely identified myself with the democratic forces in Ukraine, and their leaders clearly understood how important it was for Ukraine to create its own system of national defense and its own ministry of defense. Still, before I agreed to assume the post of minister of defense, I needed more clarification on issues that troubled both me and Ukraine's leaders. Before I had a chance to call Kravchuk to discuss these issues, however, I was invited to attend a meeting of the Presidium of Ukraine's Parliament on September 3.

This meeting was arranged to give the members of the Presidium a chance to become acquainted with me and assess my background. After I was officially introduced, the Presidium was informed that Kravchuk had already spoken with me and that he was asking the Presidium to consider me as a candidate for minister of defense. A number of questions then followed.

Dmytro Pavlychko, the poet and activist in the Ukrainian cultural renaissance, led off the questions:

"Kostiantyn Petrovych, do you think you can master the Ukrainian language?"

Having listened to his speeches in Parliament and read some of his writings, I felt that I knew him well enough to address him similarly:

"Dmytro Vasylovych, after all, you are the head of the Ukrainian Language Society. May I count on you to help me improve my Ukrainian?"

My answer must have amused him greatly, and this was enough to relieve some of the tension of this interrogation.

The next question came from Ihor Yukhnovskyi, the physicist and professor at Lviv University. It was not a technical question; rather, it raised a sensitive issue that was in everyone's mind.

"According to Ukraine's Declaration of Sovereignty, in the future Ukraine is to become a non-nuclear state. Is it your opinion that Ukraine should transfer its nuclear weapons to Russia, or should we destroy them here on our own territory?"

"It would be a great inconvenience," I replied without hesitation, "to transfer these weapons physically to Russia. After all, that would mean dismantling them and shipping them over long distances, thus running the risk of contamination, theft, or increased danger to civilians. In my opinion they should be destroyed. I have to say, however, that I have not yet fully considered the technical aspects of how this elimination could best be carried out, and would welcome suggestions from you and your colleagues."

This answer met with the approval of many members of the Presidium, for it probably coincided with their own views on this issue.

Other questions followed, all of which probed into the nature of my support for Ukrainian statehood. As this meeting came to an end, I thought that I would be given additional time to consider my final decision. Immediately after the questioning, however, the Presidium announced that it was officially supporting my candidacy for this ministerial post, even though others—most prominently the deputies Vasyl Durdynets, Oleksandr Yemets, and Yevhen Marchuk*— were also mentioned as possible candidates. I do not know whether individual deputies put forward their names or whether parliamentary committees had formally evaluated their candidacies, but all those considered for the post of defense minister were fervent patriots of Ukraine and very able individuals who, like me, had pursued careers in the armed forces or in the security apparatus.

When the members of the Presidium reconvened after a short break, they informed me that my nomination was ready to come to a vote. Shocked at the speed of the proceedings, I took a long, deep breath and pondered the heavy responsibility about to be placed on my shoulders. I was escorted to the loge occupied by members of the Presidium, and as I sat down, I felt very conspicuous. All the deputies knew who I was and why I was there.

The parliamentary speaker announced that the Presidium had already considered the nomination of Major General Morozov, commander of the 17th Air Army for the position of minister of defense for Ukraine. He then asked me to approach the podium. Reading a short statement, he mentioned a few details about my education, my life, and the positions I had occupied. Then he stated that I had explicitly and publicly expressed my support for Ukraine's course to create the foundations of its statehood.

Then it was my turn to speak. For this I was totally unprepared, because I did not have a single firm idea how Ukraine's military should be constructed. Although I had crossed the country from one end to the other many times over, I felt that I had hardly enough opportunity to get to know its history, its traditions, and its people. After all, I had lived in Ukraine less than four years as an adult and had only just begun educating myself in things Ukrainian. I was unsure even how to address this distinguished group of patriots, much less what to say to them.

I formulated a few thoughts on the spot. My brief speech has remained imprinted in my memory to this day. Quite unexpectedly—for me and for my audience as well—I began my speech in Ukrainian:

"Esteemed deputies, I am very grateful to you for your trust, and I am honored that I am standing before you today. I do not yet have a concrete plan of action, but I am prepared to support the establishment of Ukraine's armed forces and would like to work together with you to achieve this goal. I understand Ukrainian, but I have spent the last twenty-five years of my life in the armed forces, where only Russian is used. Thus, I will respond to your questions in Russian."

The audience erupted into applause. I had the impression that the deputies supported my nomination and would confirm me as minister of defense. I was surprised, however, that the next round of questions addressed to me were much more concrete than those posed in the earlier session. For example, several deputies asked about the optimal mechanism for establishing Ukraine's military. Others wanted to know where I stood on the fate of certain military testing grounds. I confess that I had difficulty replying to many of these questions, but I did my best to answer diplomatically without committing to something that I could not follow through later. In general, the deputies and I seemed to agree on most issues.

At the conclusion of this interview, Kravchuk put the issue of my appointment to a vote. The results: 323 votes in my favor, 11 against me, and a few abstentions. By a constitutional majority, I had been approved as Ukraine's first minister of defense.

8 A Test of Will and Resolve

That fall, the rumor mill worked at peak capacity. Speculation that my close ties to Kravchuk had won me the appointment as minister of defense dogged me everywhere: I was said to be one of "Kravchuk's people," a man whom he could control and manipulate, a reasonable alternative to the Communist sympathizers or hard-line generals who vied for the position to which I had just been appointed. Some must have seen my appointment as a means for the new president to extend his grasp over both civilian and military institutions so that what had happened to Gorbachev in Russia would not happen to him in Ukraine.

My association with Kravchuk was cordial and cooperative, but never so conspiratorial as those rumors suggested. Before the coup attempt, I acted in my formal capacity as a senior military officer and participated in a variety of festivities and meetings, which Kravchuk himself attended, but I had conversed personally with the president only once—that fateful day he invited me to his office and quizzed me on my attitudes toward Ukraine's independence and the need to establish an armed forces structure separate from that of the USSR. Although I knew that our brief association in no way could type me as a member of Kravchuk's inner circle, the very presence of those rumors, coupled with my own sense of the job's enormous responsibilities, caused me to question the deputies' motivations for nominating and electing me as the first minister of defense for Ukraine.

Initial Doubts

Why *did* Kravchuk choose me for this position? I had no formal experience in international negotiations, had never served on a high-level political delegation, and was still a beginner in and had just begun educating myself in Ukrainian history and culture. From every possible angle I could see, I clearly lacked the political and diplomatic experience this position required. After all, Ukraine had just taken the first steps to becoming a new east-central European state, a player on a new world stage. The impression we made in presenting ourselves, arguing our case, and describing our plans for the future would determine—perhaps for many generations—the image our neighbors and other countries of the world formed. The work of a negotiator at this level seemed far beyond my experience and capacities.

Second, at the time I was still convinced that the minister of defense should be a civilian. This principle stemmed from my conviction that in a fully constituted democracy, the person who holds the top military job must ultimately be responsible to the people, just like the army that protects them. Many patriotically minded deputies, however, were of another mind, and I gradually came around to accept their point of view. They were concerned primarily about the question of loyalty: In the fall of 1991, approximately 750,000 to 900,000 troops were stationed on Ukraine's soil,* many of them from republics of the Soviet Union far removed from Ukraine in both geography and culture. Could these military personnel be expected to show an iota of allegiance to the newly independent Ukrainian state and its government or its citizens? The deputies argued that in order to maintain peace and ensure the people that the current armed forces would not take up arms against them, the Parliament would have to appoint a *military* officer as the minister of defense. This person would have to be acceptable to military servicemen, someone who could command their respect and loyalty, while participating in international negotiations that were bound to arise now that Ukraine, laden with a nuclear arsenal it did not need, had declared independence.

154

Moreover, the deputies wanted a candidate who had made his career as a commander in the armed forces rather than in the KGB or any of the other security agencies. This was both expedient and practical, for the quickest way of enlisting the support of the armed forces would be to select a person who knew the intricate workings of the military and who at the same time did not have close ties with or owed favors to the secretive security agencies.

As I saw it, there were several potential candidates for minister of defense who had distinguished careers in the armed forces. Normally such a high-ranking appointment would have been made at the level of the commanders of the military districts. It would never have been offered to a mere major general who was associated with a particular service branch of the military such as the air force. Among those under consideration were General Viktor V. Skokov, the commander of the Carpathian Military District, General Viktor S. Chechevatov of the Kyiv Military District, and General Ivan S. Morozov of the Odesa Military District (to whom I bore no relation). In addition, Admiral Mikhail M. Khronopulo, the commander of the Black Sea Fleet, was a potential candidate. All four commanders, however, had refused even to consider the possibility of establishing a separate military for Ukraine. Thus, in the eyes of the parliamentary deputies, there were no viable alternatives to my candidacy for the post of Ukraine's defense minister.

As I mentioned earlier, although I strongly supported the idea of civilian control of the armed forces, I came to agree that it was still too early in the development of an independent Ukraine to talk about a civilian occupying this post. Because neither the deputies nor the government had a clear understanding of the military and the attitudes that prevailed in the officer corps, the minister of defense had to be an individual who could closely monitor the military, someone who could influence or control developments and help guide the positions taken by the officers within his jurisdiction. He also had to propose a strategy for improving the poor living conditions of servicemen and ensuring their future well-being—two issues that could easily lead to serious unrest within the military. Above all, he had to ensure that the Soviet armed forces stationed on Ukraine's soil would be gradually and peacefully transformed into the new country's future military.

Finally, I was deeply concerned that I had no clear plan of action on how to deal with any of these problems. Yet I was expected to appear before Parliament and inform the deputies about my next steps as defense minister. When I look back at this time of uncertainty, it's clear that this was the most fundamental of my concerns. Although I was worried about my ability to transform the military, I recognized why my candidacy proved as popular as it did with the parliamentary deputies. Over the four years since my reassignment to Ukraine, I had gained considerable experience as the chief of staff of the 46th Air Army (1986–1988), then as commander of the 17th Air Army (1988–1991). Moreover, I had engaged in both short-term planning concerning operational issues and long-range planning concerning the possible use of the army's strategic aviation—that is, the long-range bombers that could carry nuclear warheads if a global conflict between the superpowers and their allies were to break out.*

I myself, however, had never worked at the level of the General Staff and had no experience dealing with high-level strategic documents.* Thus, I was especially concerned about the challenge of preparing a conceptual framework for the establishment of Ukraine's armed forces. I knew that the General Staff under the Soviet Ministry of Defense included highly qualified specialists who knew a great deal about restructuring the military and promoting military reform. My lack of familiarity with their practices was a serious barrier to my effectiveness as a leader. To remove this obstacle, I began enlisting the assistance of several specialists who had worked with the General Staff and had experience with military restructuring efforts.

Democracy in Action: The Union of Officers of Ukraine (UOU)

The creation of the Union of Officers of Ukraine (UOU) represented a logical extension of the historical traditions of the Ukrainian national liberation movement.* Rukh and most other political organizations established to promote the state's national interests had to concern themselves at some point with military issues and the defense of Ukraine's independence. Ukrainians had learned a hard lesson from history in that deficient military planning had led to the loss of Ukrainian statehood on several occasions, most notably after the Bolshevik Revolution of 1917. One of the biggest mistakes of Ukraine's first independent government was its lack of serious military preparations in response to the civil war in Russia. That turmoil eventually spread to Kyiv in the early part of 1918, as Ukraine was caught between the German and Bolshevik armies and forced to sign the Treaty of Brest-Litovsk with Germany, Austria-Hungary, Bulgaria, and Turkey. The painful lessons of the past made it all too evident, even to those who were lukewarm to the idea of national independence, that it was essential for Ukraine to have its own system of national defense.

Although the UOU had held its first formal congress (*z'ïzd*) in July, 1991, to discuss the establishment of Ukraine's armed forces, my military duties had not permitted me to attend. Now, however, I determined that as a first step I would study and evaluate the proposals this group had formulated. As a sign of respect for their work, I visited the UOU leaders on September 4, the day after I was appointed minister of defense. I wanted not only to meet these individuals, but also to hear about the plans they had prepared and to obtain copies of their proposals, which, I hoped, would provide me with some insight.

Originally established within the framework of the Rukh movement headed by Ivan Drach, the UOU sought to propose a defense policy for a future independent Ukraine. The first head of the UOU, Colonel Vilen Martyrosian, for instance, began his career as a democrat and representative of the military in the Congress of People's Deputies of the USSR, and he always took a bold stand on the need to eliminate the widespread abuses and corruption in the armed forces.* As a member of the organizing committee of the UOU and later as head of the organization, he continued his vigorous activities along the same lines.

The founders of the UOU were true patriots committed to the idea of Ukraine's independence; however, none of them was a senior officer with operational-strategic experience. Thus, the officers who examined and studied this issue had undertaken an extremely complex task. After decades of Soviet domination, even UOU members found it difficult to imagine that Ukraine might actually create its own armed forces. All of us faced a real psychological barrier: How could this enormous entity—the Soviet armed forces—be divided? How could this military structure, centralized in and controlled by Moscow, be safely dismantled, at least insofar as Ukraine was concerned? Many officers argued that, given existing circumstances, the most we could do would be to establish Ukrainian military units or battalions that would function under the authority and control of the Soviet armed forces. Ukraine could not simply declare, as was done in the Baltic states, that the Soviet forces on its territory constituted an occupation force. For one thing, in the fall of 1991, a large percentage of the military personnel in Ukraine, especially those in junior positions, were either residents of Ukraine or of Ukrainian origin, and were thus future citizens who could form the "core" of the Ukrainian military.* Second, the Soviet forces in Ukraine were disproportionately large, well-armed, well-organized, and commanded by very capable officers. Those who supported an evolutionary path argued that declaring all these military personnel *personae non gratae* would have posed a danger to the very existence of an independent Ukrainian state.

The proposition advanced by some activists—namely, that at some distant point in the future Ukraine would have its own armed forces—did not meet with widespread approval, even within the ranks of the UOU. That such forces might be created was a possibility not to be dismissed entirely, but it was considered so farfetched and controversial that it was not even mentioned in the first of the UOU draft proposals.

The democrats and certain members of the UOU proposed several alternatives. Although not everyone recognized it at the time, the most revolutionary of these proposals would have certainly led to heightened tensions and, in all probability, armed conflict. It suggested setting up new military structures, parallel to the existing ones, manned by nationally conscious personnel (first and foremost, members of the UOU). These new structures would have consti-tuted, from day one, Ukraine's armed forces.

A second proposal called for a transformation of the Soviet mili-tary formations on Ukraine's territory into Ukraine's armed forces. Military personnel would be given the option of declaring their loy-alty to the new state of Ukraine or receiving a transfer to another location in the USSR. The structures in which these military person-nel functioned would themselves undergo major changes appropri-ate to Ukraine's new status as an independent democracy, and the Ministry of Defense would attend to the selection of command per-sonnel who could be trusted to act in the national interest. This approach was approved by the UOU even before an independent Ukrainian state was proclaimed.

Although a lengthy process, this "transformation" was better suited to the circumstances in which Ukraine found itself. In the Baltic states, for example, the local population was extremely hostile to the Soviet armed forces and everything it represented, whereas similar sentiments were found primarily only in western Ukraine. In other words, the Soviet armed forces had a fair amount of legitimacy in Ukraine, with the exception of its western regions. Although sig-nificant, the military presence in the Baltic states—including per-sonnel, infrastructure, and the military-industrial complex itself—was not as great as that in Ukraine. In addition, the number of Baltic-origin personnel in the Soviet armed forces in the Baltic states was lower than that of Ukrainians in the Soviet armed forces in Ukraine. Creating a brand new military was viable in the Baltic states, whereas in Ukraine transforming most of the existing Soviet armed forces on the country's territory into a military force serving Ukraine was the more viable alternative.

In essence, the transformation was only partial, since much of the old Soviet military structure was simply renamed and re-subor-dinated to Ukraine. Ambitious restructuring plans—for example, the relocation of troops and infrastructure away from Ukraine's western borders—could not be implemented because of financial and other reasons. Some dramatic changes, however, were introduced in, among others, the sphere of political education, with the replacement of the Soviet main political administration, which was responsible for propagating Soviet ideals and propaganda messages, with a social-psychological service intended to promote Ukrainian patriotism.

Needless to say, even the proposition of such modification and transformation did not meet with unanimous approval from military personnel. In the late summer and early fall of 1991, a significant propaganda campaign against the UOU was conducted within those segments of the military loyal to the USSR. The authors who prepared the documents advocating separation—despite the fact that at the time it was forbidden even to consider the possibility of the creation of a Ukrainian military—were treated almost as traitors, and their activities were constantly monitored. In fact, certain documents prepared by the UOU and given directly to me after the proclamation of independence show that some individuals, who portrayed themselves as among the founders of the UOU, were actually among its harshest critics when it began its activities. These critics argued that the organization was engaged in destructive activities that would lead to social unrest and military conflict. The heads of several political departments in the military sent reports to Moscow, describing the UOU in extremely negative terms as an organization that posed a threat to society and could provoke a breakup of the military. In this context, however, the term "breakup" was interpreted as meaning that part of the Soviet armed forces would break away and become the foundation of the national armed forces of Ukraine.

I won't deny that at times I had mixed feelings about some UOU actions. Sometimes its leaders engaged in very emotional rhetoric, and some of their expressions and resolutions offended some officers in Ukraine and provoked tensions in the armed forces. Even more important, their activities often provided powerful ammunition for anti-Ukrainian groups in the armed forces, which did their best to discredit the UOU as soon as it emerged. The impulsiveness characterizing some of the UOU's activities reflected the nature of its leadership, and sometimes more experienced officers found it quite easy to neutralize those activities by discrediting UOU proposals or the individuals behind them.

Several UOU priorities generated considerable debate and controversy. They included, for example, the rapid introduction of Ukrainian military traditions (including those connected to Ukrainian Cossackdom and UPA activities during World War II) within Ukraine's military to replace Soviet military traditions, and the rapid introduction of the Ukrainian language in all spheres of military activity to replace Russian. In fact, knowledge of Ukrainian was perceived by some UOU activists to be a criterion of loyalty. UOU activists insisted on the strict application of the loyalty oath as well as the use of other measures to test the loyalty of anyone indicating a desire to serve in Ukraine's military. They also wanted to import large numbers of ethnic Ukrainian officers serving outside Ukraine and to discourage ethnic Russians from serving in Ukraine's military. UOU activists attempted to play a major role in decisions regarding the appointment of military cadres, and in some regions of Ukraine such as the Carpathian Military District, they apparently did have, at least briefly, some influence over the cadre policy, which many military personnel greatly resented.

Moreover, after it began its public activities, the UOU attracted many people who had grievances against the military—some legitimate, some not. Unmoved by the UOU's loftier goals, these people simply wanted to voice their complaints or defend their rights. Some of them eventually came to dominate the organization itself, unintentionally playing into the hands of those who wished to discredit the UOU. Its detractors argued that the organization attracted malcontents who wanted to push their negative agenda and destroy the armed forces.

I was never a member of the UOU or even an interested observer who would always support its activities. Prior to my appointment as minister of defense, however, I was aware of the UOU because of Soviet armed forces intelligence reports about it. (An example is included in the documentary appendices.) Even before the unsuccessful coup attempt, I tried to understand their program. By no means did I share those evaluations—sent to us by the KGB or the political organs in the military—that UOU members were turncoats or destructive individuals with criminal intentions. I regarded their activities as a healthy consequence of the democratization of society, which could not help but affect the armed forces.

A Transfer to the Ukrainian Military

My own transfer from the ranks of the Soviet armed forces to the post of minister of defense of Ukraine stirred up something of a controversy because it set an important precedent for the transfers of other officers. Officially it was handled without major political or military conflicts—I did not lose, for example, my posts as a military commander and as a member of the military council of the Kyiv Military District. I kept in reserve the option of resigning from the Soviet armed forces, but fortunately I never had to use it. Marshal Shaposhnikov informed me that as of October 1, 1991, President Gorbachev had simply issued a decree relieving me of my responsibilities as commander of the 17th Air Army and member of the Kyiv Military Council, and transferring me to the disposition of Ukraine's government. Although this procedure "legalized" my assumption of the position of Ukraine's minister of defense, interestingly enough, it did not formally relieve me of my duties in the USSR armed forces. At the time of its issue, Gorbachev and others were assuming that Ukraine's forces would remain part of the USSR's unified forces. Thus, issuing that decree revealed how Moscow was underestimating the significance of political and military developments in Ukraine.

As a matter of principle, I believe that continuing one's service in the armed forces of Ukraine should be considered a matter of honor, as long as a person acted out of his own free will, openly and honestly declared his intentions of serving Ukraine, and suffered no humiliation or loss of standing among his fellow officers. An officer's transfer from the Soviet armed forces to Ukraine's military had to take place naturally, provoking neither indignity nor humiliation from the authorities responsible for it or from the leaders of the military unit in which the officer served. I was eager to establish a precedent that other officers could use by which they might regard such transfers as normal, nonconfrontational events. They were to understand that a transfer was their right, that the Ukrainian state would guarantee their security once they took this momentous decision.

Because my transfer was the first, the central military authorities in Moscow spent a great deal of time devising a procedure that would allow them to deal with my specific case. They had no ready formulas or timetables for handling such requests in the first place. The entire process took over two months. Not only did the authorities have to invent a formula and establish a precedent, they also debated whether it was possible even to consider such a transfer.

On September 9–10, 1991, the USSR Ministry of Defense sponsored a meeting in Moscow of military leaders from all the former republics except the Baltic states. The delegates from Ukraine were Vasyl Durdynets, the head of Ukraine's parliamentary commission on defense and state security; Yevhen Marchuk, the minister of state in charge of defense issues, national security, and emergency situations; and various experts on military affairs. I served on the delegation in my capacity as minister of defense. For two days we participated in extensive meetings in the Soviet Defense Ministry's two monstrous buildings on the Arbat, but we acted in an entirely professional manner, and our behavior must have dashed any hopes that military leaders of the USSR may have had that we could be swayed in our resolve to defend Ukraine's independence.

At the conference some in Moscow raised the question of whether a single military force, with members drawn from each of the republics and Russia, might not be a viable alternative to a hodgepodge of separate units, each identified with a separate nation. Perhaps out of desperation, some Moscow officials suggested that I retain the post of commander of the 17th Air Army, which would remain part of a joint force serving the Soviet Union no matter what form it ultimately assumed—that is, a federation or a confederation. Simultaneously I would serve in the Ukrainian government as head of a committee that would deal with defense issues and take responsibility for coordinating Ukraine's military programs with those of the Ministry of Defense in Moscow. In all of these discussions, however, they could not even utter the term "minister of defense."

"The idea of Ukraine as a non-bloc state has already been entrenched in the Declaration of State Sovereignty of 1990," I argued. "With a public referendum set for December, Ukraine will soon be a fully independent state. It is therefore nonsense to talk about a united army made up of battalions from various republics."

Our counterparts at this meeting could see that we would make no compromises on the matter of Ukraine's integrity and its right to form and maintain a separate army. Thus, we decided to move quickly to resolve future personnel problems by establishing an orderly procedure for transfers.

Given this level of resistance from Moscow, it is no wonder that official transfer took two months to be approved. The delay, however, worked to our benefit, for we gained valuable experience and support for the course Ukraine had taken. Once the appropriate orders and decrees had been issued, my colleagues and I smoothed the way for transferring a number of senior officers to Ukraine's armed forces. Our primary criterion for appointing candidates to leadership positions in the military was dedication to Ukraine's independence, and this conviction guided me in choosing those to serve at the highest levels of the Ministry of Defense.

Team-Building

Immediately after assuming my new post I sought to attract officers who could help me deal with the many difficult challenges facing my fledgling ministry. From day one, I searched out highly qualified officers who had worked at Soviet General Staff headquarters and had experience in planning and carrying out organizational reforms within the military. I considered individuals whom I had met during my career in the military and whom I could trust. Luckily I found a number of capable officers, both in Ukraine and sometimes beyond its borders, who were eager to join my team. Although they were primarily of Ukrainian background, that was not universally the case. I knew, however, that each one supported the idea of a free and independent Ukraine.

From the moment I took over as defense minister, I began receiving scores of letters and appeals from military personnel throughout the Soviet Union who wished to serve in Ukraine. In addition, I had to respond to a large number of similar appeals that the parliamentary commission on defense issues had begun receiving as soon as the declaration of sovereignty had been issued in 1990.

Although there were many worthy candidates for various lower-level military posts, it soon became clear that there were no suitable candidates in Ukraine for the posts of deputy ministers with responsibility for the country's four operational-strategic formations. Specialists with the appropriate background and skills could be found only beyond Ukraine's borders, either in the General Staff headquarters or in other military districts. Simply put, we needed individuals who had worked at this level or had experience commanding similar operational-strategic formations; moreover, they had to be individuals who could work together with me as a single team.

At the same time I was constantly pressured by the democratic deputies in Ukraine's Parliament to appoint junior officers to important command posts. I understood the motivation behind these requests, and whenever possible, I tried to satisfy them. If these junior officers were both capable soldiers and dedicated patriots of Ukraine, in a few years they might become excellent specialists and, even more important, they represented the future of Ukraine's military. The senior-level positions, however, created another set of problems: Without delay, we had to appoint a number of high-level specialists who could assume responsibility for the restructuring of Ukraine's armed forces and implementing those reforms.

I held talks with colleagues in the General Staff headquarters and received several statements of interest from generals who were not only of Ukrainian background, but were also loyal to the idea of Ukrainian statehood. Two of the most promising candidates for senior appointments were General Heorhii Zhyvytsia and General Ivan Bizhan, both of whom had worked in the General Staff headquarters. General Bizhan, in particular, had experience in commanding an army.* I sent an official request to Soviet Defense Minister Shaposhnikov inviting both Zhyvytsia and Bizhan to Ukraine to prepare proposals for the future structure of the Ukrainian armed forces. Shaposhnikov gave the appropriate instructions to the chief of the General Staff, General Lobov, and he summoned these generals, gave them their instructions, and sent them off to Ukraine.

After the first month I asked for an extension to their invitation. Whether as a result of rumors or our tough negotiating position on the military's future, I could sense that Zhyvytsia and Bizhan were already distrusted in the General Staff headquarters. Their participation in several difficult meetings in Moscow must have added fuel to the assumption that they had contributed to the uncompromising stance Ukraine was taking. I suggested that they leave their posts in the General Staff headquarters and that they be transferred to work for Ukraine's Ministry of Defense. We ensured that their transfers were handled quietly and legally, and on January 3, 1992, these generals were part of the first group of Ministry of Defense officials who took the oath of allegiance to Ukraine and worked closely with me in planning and setting up the framework of Ukraine's armed forces.

Because General Zhyvytsia had significant practical experience of high-level organizational work, he proved to be of great help to me in the early phase of our work. He certainly knew how to handle structural and organizational issues. For example, he was the first to elaborate and introduce the proposals that were included in the concept of the armed forces of Ukraine, which was ratified by Ukraine's Parliament in November, 1991. This document later provided the basis for the laws on the Defense of Ukraine, which were approved in December, 1991. In addition, Zhyvytsia deserves much credit for organizing the ceremony on January 3, 1992, in which officers swore the Oath of Loyalty to the new country. He had a sharp tongue, however, and could never be mistaken for a diplomat. Many officers criticized his behavior, and he soon developed the reputation of an individual who had difficulty working with others. Finally, in 1993, he was retired from active duty service and released into the reserves.

General Bizhan was a more tactful, diplomatic individual who ended up participating in various Ukrainian delegations at international meetings and negotiations. As deputy defense minister, he has defended Ukraine's interests in negotiations such as those over the Black Sea fleet and the treaty governing conventional forces in Europe.

With the assistance of Generals Zhyvytsia and Bizhan, I worked out a plan by which the general structure of the Soviet armed forces would be maintained, although a gradual downsizing would take place. Meanwhile, more radical (and expensive) restructuring efforts including the transfer of troops and accompanying infrastructure from western Ukraine, where it was most heavily concentrated, would be undertaken at a later date. Their transfer to other regions of the country, especially along the border with Russia, required a high level of improvisation, since in the fall of 1991 it was difficult to predict how many Soviet armed forces officers would agree to serve in Ukraine's military.

Each day we signed letter after letter asking the commanders of various military districts, as well as the main personnel administration of the Soviet armed forces in Moscow and even the defense minister and the chief of the General Staff of the Soviet armed forces, to grant permission for other officers to be transferred to Ukraine. The Ukrainian authorities, however, did not properly organize this transfer process, and it did not have an adequate financial base.* From the very beginning the transfers occurred quite spontaneously, often as a result of the efforts of the Union of Officers of Ukraine, or of parliamentary commissions, or following an analysis, by the Ministry of Defense, of the approximately 20,000 letters and petitions it received from those wishing to return to Ukraine.* We did our best to prepare all the necessary documents and asked local authorities in the regions where the transferring officers served to do everything possible to ensure that careers and families did not suffer as a result of the decisions these military personnel took.

In various republics, however, largely because of the intervention of the main administration of cadres and the leadership of the Ministry of Defense of the USSR, those wishing to transfer often did not receive the appropriate support and assistance. Many of them had to cover the costs of their transfers out of their own pockets and in the process lost several months of pay. Officers ended up living in dormitories while their families stayed with friends or relatives. Motivated by patriotism, however, they persisted in spite of these difficulties, and they deserve our respect.

I'm convinced that the majority of the officers who transferred to Ukraine after the events of August, 1991, did so out of patriotism. Some of them may have transferred for selfish reasons, but they were a small minority. I know a number of officers who, motivated by high ideals and love of Ukraine, moved here with their families, despite the great barriers placed in their path and the losses they endured.

General Volodymyr Antonets, for example, had been one of my friends in the Gritsevets Kharkiv Higher Military Aviation School and later in the Air Force Academy. I remember from our student days that he seemed much more Ukrainian than I. He usually spoke Ukrainian, for instance, which came naturally to him, given that he hailed from Poltava, one of the less russified regions of central Ukraine. In the course of serving many years in the Soviet armed forces, however, he had no opportunity to use Ukrainian and switched to Russian. In 1991, when I was appointed minister of defense, Antonets was serving as the first deputy commander of the air army in the Baltic Military District, where he was stationed in Riga.* A pilot and a fine general, he desperately wanted to transfer to Ukraine. He went on to become a lieutenant general, a deputy defense minister, and air force commander in Ukraine's military.

About this same time, General Strogov, the commander of the air army based in Lviv, was preparing to retire. I knew perfectly well that the Soviet armed forces administration in Moscow would try to take advantage of this forthcoming vacancy by quickly appointing someone who would oppose the democratic changes taking place in Ukraine. Accordingly, I moved rapidly to arrange for Antonets' transfer through the regular personnel administration officials, only to find that all sorts of obstacles had been put in the way. At one point I was told that a decision about Antonets would be made shortly, whereas another source informed me that a replacement for the retiring general had already been found. The new man, who was the deputy commander of an air army in the Moscow Military District, was to be flown the next day to Lviv and introduced to the administrative officers of the Lviv air army. General Petr Deneikin, who had been appointed commander in chief of the Soviet air force after Marshal Shaposhnikov was appointed minister of defense, was to accompany him.

I was acquainted with this general whom the authorities in Moscow supported. Although he was very experienced, he was not originally from Ukraine, and in comparison to Antonets it was clear the Moscow candidate was not suited for the Lviv post. In essence, this situation had all the marks of a test of wills between the authorities in Moscow and me. Believing it was time to show who was actually in charge in Ukraine and knowing that this decision would have a significant impact on the interests of the Ukrainian state, I phoned Moscow and stated that we would not appoint General Kozachkin, the candidate supported by Deneikin. I stressed that I did not wish to create new tensions by making a unilateral decision and that I wanted to continue the current process for resolving problems in our mutual interests, so long as officers and their families did not suffer. I held my ground, however, by objecting to the planned flight from Moscow to Lviv and even denying permission for the plane to land in Lviv. In the end the authorities in Moscow blinked first.

General Antonets was thus appointed to the post in an order signed by President Kravchuk. After his appointment was confirmed, Antonets quickly found in the local administration of Lviv a group of people with whom he could work. The head of the Lviv Oblast council was Mykola Horyn, and the president's representative (after December 1, 1991) was Stepan Davymuka; both of them were fervent Ukrainian patriots.* In addition, they had a deep understanding of the military issues and were sensitive to what needed to be done to maintain stability in Ukraine. The four of us met frequently, and General Antonets did everything possible to keep the lid on tensions in the air army under his command. He was one of the first, for instance, to propose that conscripts who were not from Ukraine be allowed to return quickly to their native republics. He also arranged for the immediate transfer of all the officers—and there were many of them—who refused to declare an oath of allegiance to

Ukraine and who needed assistance to get home (usually their destination was Russia).* Because he coped so brilliantly with these challenges, I later recommended him for appointment as commander in chief of the Ukrainian air force.

I also later heard complaints that certain of the officers who began working with me in the fall of 1991 simply took advantage of Ukraine's atmosphere of uncertainty to advance their own careers in ways that they could not have if the old Soviet armed forces had continued. I categorically reject these insinuations, for I know these officers very well, the majority of whom are true Ukrainian patriots—not necessarily in terms of their ethnic backgrounds, but in spirit at least, because they either had put down roots in Ukraine or were convinced that Ukrainian independence was a just cause.

In the fall of 1991, thirty officers worked with me in at most six rooms set aside for the ministry in the same building that housed Ukraine's parliamentary committees. Working conditions were truly primitive. What made matters even worse was the fact that we had no means at our disposal for administering effectively the military formations on our territory. At the time, all military personnel on Ukraine's territory were subordinated to Moscow, and the Soviet Ministry of Defense and the General Staff continually reminded us of this condition.

To take one example, we had to manage the transfer of all kinds of goods in large quantities from storehouses in Ukraine, in accordance with instructions from Moscow. These included antique and trophy weapons, provisions, and all kinds of military equipment. I received information about this transfer from two main sources—members of the UOU and those parliamentary deputies who were democrats. We had no effective mechanism for reacting to these events, however. We could use the regular municipal phone system, which gave no guarantee of security. We had a few fax machines that we had received as gifts from diaspora Ukrainians. And we had about twenty officers who, taking a great risk, became part of our organizational group. I saw what they experienced, and I also felt the frenzied resistance to the implementation of our decisions to develop Ukraine's own armed forces. Even those who, quite obviously, were not opposed to what we were doing, were still administered from Moscow.

Moreover, senior commanders, undoubtedly following instructions from Moscow, were skeptical about, if not dead set against, the formation of an independent Ukraine military. Those who agreed to help me were actively discouraged from doing so, either by colleagues or by their own family members. As soon as I became minister of defense and it became clear that Ukraine was serious about setting up its own armed forces, a flood of phone calls and encrypted telegrams—no doubt originating in Moscow—went out to the commanders of the military districts in Ukraine. Officers were forbidden to get in touch with me and to cooperate with me. They were told that the Soviet Ministry of Defense was "studying the situation" and would make "appropriate" decisions in this matter.

We began to actively create groups of officers who supported our work in various units. Without revealing their names, we would contact them in various places: Odesa, Lviv, Vinnytsia, Kyiv. I did not know these people personally, but in each large command structure we had thirty to fifty of them. It was precisely these men who made our control of the situation possible.

Our ministry had two old Volga cars and one UAZ similar to a van to which I had access as the now former commander of the 17th Air Army. Between September and December, 1991, I made frequent requests to the Kyiv Military District command and, in particular, to General Viktor S. Chechevatov, for help with transportation, but I received no response. Later some officers informed me that in November, 1991, General Chechevatov expressed a readiness, if instructed to do so from Moscow, to arrest me rather than help me out. I have good reason to believe that the commanders of the other military districts in Ukraine, in Lviv and Odesa, were of the same mind and inclined their subordinates to think the same way.

Despite these obstacles, we were able to put together a cohesive team of officers and generals who worked day and night. Moreover, we put certain mechanisms in place which allowed us to study and control the existing situation as it unfolded. For example, a network of UOU members was formed throughout all of Ukraine, responsible for keeping an eye on local command personnel and monitoring military developments. They informed me and my associates of any developments they considered worthy of attention.

The large foreign military presence on its territory posed a direct threat to Ukraine, and it was imperative to administer an oath of loyalty to the officers who wished to serve in Ukraine. Only then could we take full control of the entire system for administering the military. Beginning in January, 1992, therefore, we took over the headquarters and administrative offices of the Kyiv Military District, administered the oath to officers, shut down the communications system linking the district to Moscow, and fired the commanders of the three military districts.

It was clear I had to act fast and decisively.

9 Radical Restructuring and the Oath of Loyalty

After nearly eighty years of rule, occupation, and suppression by a more powerful neighbor, how does a newly independent country go about building its own armed forces and giving it some semblance of credibility? How can it accomplish this goal if it does not yet officially have the approval of its citizens in a democratic referendum, if it is not yet recognized as a sovereign country, and if it lacks a secure, recognized, and legitimate structure for diplomatic and international relations? And how does it accomplish all these objectives in only three months? Among scores of other economic, social, and political issues, these questions presented formidable challenges to the people leaders of Ukraine between mid-August and December 1, 1991, the date set aside for the referendum on our independence.

Many Ukrainians—including my wife Raisa and daughter Eva—asked why it was necessary to wait so long. As they saw it, the political situation was so tense and the military one so unstable that it was essential to take immediate action. This moment in our nation's history, they argued, should not be allowed to slip through our fingers. The people of Ukraine were ready for independence, and they should have the right to express their views now that the immediate outcome of the August coup was known. In retrospect, however, the decision to hold a referendum was justified.

Taking Control of the Forces at Home

Although the coup attempt had failed, Gorbachev did not weather the storm well. He appeared weakened and incapable of retaining his grip on power. Boris Yeltsin, then president of the Russian republic and challenger to Gorbachev (although he had supported Gorbachev during the coup attempt), became increasingly popular, and his high-profile stance against the leaders of the putsch gave new life to democratic reformers.

The actions of these two leaders stirred up passions among both supporters and detractors, and the political scene in Moscow remained thoroughly confused during the fall of 1991. By no means immune to this volatility, we Ukrainians were nonetheless assured that the troublesome events in Moscow would not result in an armed conflict with Russia. This was not in the cards, so to speak. As the Soviet Union continued to unravel, no one was quite sure at the time how far it would go, yet many seemed eager to tug on any available string, testing the strength of Ukrainian identity and freedom. With a popular Yeltsin more or less in control, an invasion and a protracted war to suppress popular movements in other republics seemed highly unlikely.

Despite all the arguments in favor of taking immediate action to mark Ukraine's independence, there was a clear logic behind the decision to wait three months. For one thing, the officials of the new government faced enormous economic, social, and political problems, which took precedence, I might say, over military ones, at least for the time being. These problems included (in no particular order) dealing with separatist sentiments among some local politicians and part of the population in Crimea, deciding what to do with the Communist Party and its officials in Ukraine, creating a foreign policy apparatus almost from scratch, pacifying a population increasingly impoverished by the rapid decline of Ukraine's economy, and satisfying some of the demands of vocal social groups such as miners in the Donbas region.

Moreover, from a legal point of view the status of a newly declared independent Ukraine was not so clear. As a part of the USSR, the republic did not have the constitutional authority to appoint a minister of defense or establish its own military. The August proclamation had asserted that right—and the representatives in Parliament had approved it—but simply declaring it did not make it so. For the three months from late August through the end of November, Ukraine legally did not exist as an independent state, since technically it did not have the sanction of the people until the December referendum. Various proposals for military reform went before the Commission on Defense and National Security, and later that fall the Parliament approved a number of constitutional amendments allowing the president to appoint senior members of the military. But from August to December, it could be argued, Ukraine had no duly elected president, hence no fully legitimate legal authority we could fall back on.

As well, military leaders both in Kyiv and in Moscow were deeply concerned about the reaction of the armed forces to democratization. Would the army sit idly by while the politicians vied for control? Would it accept the wishes of the majority as determined in a nationwide referendum? Indeed, where did its loyalties lie?

Because of the large number of servicemen and military equipment in Ukraine—between 750,000 and 900,000 military personnel, not to mention the kinds and large amount of matériel we had on our territory—this was a major unknown factor in our moving toward national autonomy and separating our armed forces from those of the USSR. The Soviet army in Ukraine was so large because it formed a part of the second echelon of troops, comprising units not only in Ukraine, but also in Belarus and the Baltic republics. These forces, especially those in the Carpathian and Kyiv Military Districts, supported the first echelon of troops based throughout Eastern Europe.* In addition to guarding the sizable nuclear arsenal on Ukrainian territory, these military personnel facilitated the transfer of troops, artillery, and supplies from Russia to military units on the USSR's western borders. In short, they saw to it that the primary Soviet defense system was always combat ready and that they were prepared to defend against an aggressor if a war broke out.

Moreover, the Black Sea Fleet and the three Ukrainian military districts—that is, the Carpathian, Kyiv, and Odesa districts—represented an extremely strong military force technically still under the control of the USSR Ministry of Defense. This made it all the more essential to discover quickly what attitudes its soldiers, warrant officers, officers, and generals had toward Ukraine's declaration of independence—a question that the democrats had studied long before independence was formally declared. A majority of the senior commanding positions had been assigned to Russian personnel in order to help control the situation in Ukraine and to prevent officers from falling under the influence of radical political movements in the republics and then spreading their views to other officers. Although not so strong as it once was, the Soviet army's grip in these three Ukrainian military districts was so firm that it could easily choke the infant democracy even as it was being born.

A commander in one of these districts had to have parents of Russian nationality as well as roots in Russia. Practically speaking, one had to have been born in a Russian city or region. By creatively juggling appointments and transfers, military officials had managed to exclude native Ukrainians from senior positions of authority in the military districts. Ukrainian officers were most likely to be sent to remote locations, ranging from the western border of East Germany to the Kuril Islands north of Japan, or to any point between Russia's northern or southern boundaries. The underlying purpose of this policy was to loosen the connections these soldiers might have with their native land and to diminish any influence that the people of a region might exert on enlisted men.

The major exception to this element of Soviet cadre policy was that warrant officers themselves could choose a service location where it might be possible for them to live with parents or other relatives. In the last years of its existence the Soviet army experienced serious housing problems for its enlisted men; thus, the requirement of nonresidential service was waved for warrant officers who, in accordance with the law, might live in their native cities or wherever their parents resided. It was not unusual, therefore, to find Ukrainian warrant officers stationed in the three military districts in Ukraine. A number of junior and mid-level officers might be Ukrainian and thus sympathetic, consciously or unconsciously, to the democratic forces behind the move toward independence. Their support, however, did not bother those responsible for cadre policy: After all, the highest army commanders in the three districts were nonresidents who were Russians.

176

All three districts' commanders openly opposed the idea of Ukrainian statehood and a military force separate from that of the Soviet Union; moreover, their staffs in each military district argued that the independence of Ukraine was an absurd idea and that the creation of a separate Ukrainian army amounted to an act of high treason.* From the beginning of my appointment as defense minister, I worked at the highest levels of the government to find a way of removing and reassigning these three commanders. That extraordinarily difficult process presented a major problem for us. As long as these three commanders continued to define the situation within their districts, they posed a potential threat to Ukraine. Moreover, their presence prevented the officers under their command from freely expressing their opinions. Under immense pressure to remain loyal to Moscow, those junior officers found their activities rigorously controlled and their careers—not to mention their families' futures—threatened by the three military district commanders.

Any attempt to get rid of these commanders would be sure to set an important precedent. As a Soviet republic, Ukraine did not have the authority even to appoint a minister of defense. Now, however, the sovereign country of Ukraine was claiming that right. The Ukrainian Commission on Defense and National Security approved various proposals recommended by the legislature that would allow the president to fill senior military positions. This approval gave us the confidence we needed to act decisively. Of course it helped that we were not trying to reconfigure a Soviet-style Ministry of Defense; rather, we were creating one from scratch, albeit a bureaucracy that inevitably retained many Soviet characteristics.

It is also important to note that at the time the democratic forces in Ukraine had a great impact on shaping the consciousness of military officers. These officers were well aware who was setting the tone in politics and who deserved their attention. The democrats positively influenced the government, the president's administration, and the leadership in Parliament, thus creating a favorable set of circumstances for implementing our plans to set up a defense ministry and build Ukraine's military.

The Early Ministry of Defense

In the fall of 1991, the Ministry of Defense consisted of myself and a group of thirty like-minded individuals. Most of these people were colleagues who knew me well from having worked with me at previous posts, and several of them had supported me even before I was appointed minister of defense.

The primary criterion I used in putting my team together was trust: The team members had to trust me and each other, and I had to trust them. As difficult as it was, building the ministry from the ground up had several advantages. First, we argued that we had the moral and legal authority to attract to our ministry only those officers who, during the turbulent period preceding my appointment, had shown that they could be fully trusted. For the most part, these officers were well known to the democrats in Parliament or to activists in the UOU. Even if I did not know these people personally, I believed that I could trust them.

I had to be persuaded, however, that they fulfilled my second criterion—namely, that they had the experience and expertise, especially in those areas of military strategy and organization where my personal experience was insufficient. That is, as trustworthy as they might be, these appointees had to have the professional experience and training to make up for potential gaps in my own background. Occasionally my political advisors and I argued over who should be appointed to a particular position, but I consistently maintained that candidates had to have more than just dedication. For example, I myself had had very little experience organizing and managing large groups of ground forces; thus, I needed someone on the team who could take responsibility for that activity. Beside Zhyvytsia and Bizhan, I asked that Generals Oleksii Lavreniuk, Vitalii Radetskyi, and Vasyl Sobkov be transfered to command positions.

In addition to this, I was concerned about maintaining at the ministry staff level a proper balance of specialists from the military service branches. As the former commander of the 17th Air Army, I knew that there could likely be an element of resentment and rivalry among the officers, especially those who came from other branches of the armed forces. In this respect, the tensions in Ukraine's military were no different from those in other nations' armies. Because of their perceived condescension toward ground forces, air force officers—whether deserved or not—are typically regarded as haughty and elitist.

Judging a candidate's patriotism and support for Ukraine's independence proved more difficult, given the fact that some of the most experienced military personnel did not have Ukrainian parents or relatives and had served in other regions of the Soviet Union for many years. Still others had established roots in Ukraine by virtue of the fact that they served there for some time and had a good sense of the country's culture, language, and history; moreover, they often had no particular desire to return to Russia or the other republics where they were born. I used myself as an example of how we should approach the issue of ethnicity. I was born and reared in the russified Donbas, spoke Ukrainian quite poorly when I was appointed minister, and had for some time believed that my mother was Ukrainian and my father was an ethnic Russian. My background could be taken as evidence to other officers that Ukraine was not favoring individuals on the basis of their ethnic origins—after all, when my appointment was confirmed by the Parliament, no one had an inkling that my father was actually of Ukrainian background. It was assumed that he was a "passport" Russian.

We informed the officers that if they were born in Ukraine or had family roots in Ukrainian soil and considered Ukraine rather than some other republic as their homeland, then they would be treated as patriots of Ukraine and would have our full trust. Once this criterion was satisfied, they would be assigned to positions on the basis of their professional qualifications, their personal qualities, and their leadership capability. Of course, there were many cases of dubious individuals with no clear connections of any kind to Ukraine, who insisted that they were keen to serve on behalf of Ukraine and would agree to all conditions imposed on their service in its armed forces. While we did not automatically distrust such individuals, we adhered to the principle that patriotism was not simply a slogan, but that it should be supplemented either with service for a considerable time in Ukraine or with direct Ukrainian family ties.

Aware of the fact that I supported the democratic forces in Ukraine, General Grigorii Avdeev came to see me long before I was appointed defense minister. He was Russian by birth but had served in this country for many years, primarily as a logistics and quartermaster specialist—that is, one who assumed responsibility for the efficient flow of provisions and other supplies from the "rear" during a conflict. He did not speak Ukrainian well, although he was diligently trying to learn the language, as was I. We trusted each other and had worked closely together for some time. In the fall of 1991, when we were just beginning to find our way in the ministry, we needed to establish an effective communications system and some way of reducing the theft of military property. General Avdeev helped us take control of the supply units and quickly resolve many problems in the supply lines. He made a considerable contribution to the development of Ukraine's armed forces, and his ethnic background was irrelevant to his performance. Avdeev made mistakes—for example, he continued to hire contractors with dubious reputations, a practice common with the USSR armed forces, but not to be tolerated under the new regime. When I discovered that he had made illegal purchases of automobiles for a minister, I quickly put a stop to his activities.

The main criteria guiding our cadre policy, in short, were trustworthiness, a high level of professionalism and extensive experience, loyalty to and support for the cause of Ukrainian independence, and those intangible human qualities that distinguish true leaders—in particular, a sense of responsibility, high ethical standards, and respect for others. Only by adhering to these criteria could we create a Ministry of Defense that from a practical point of view was capable of building a military force dedicated to preserving Ukrainian statehood and inoculating it against the virulent negativity that infected the Soviet armed forces.

Not Just the Military

I must mention, even if briefly, that we in the military were not the only ones faced with an epic task. An independent country must have not only a military, but also an apparatus with which to conduct its relations with other sovereign countries. Although Ukraine technically had its own foreign affairs establishment (by virtue of the fact that Stalin had tried to grab more seats in the United Nations by insisting that Ukraine and Belarus have separate representation there), in reality the new, independent Ministry of Foreign Affairs (MZS) had virtually to start from scratch. In numerous engagements with MZS personnel I found a commonality of purpose and dedication to the cause of an independent Ukraine. Among those who were most helpful to me in that early period was the deputy minister for foreign affairs, Borys Tarasiuk, whom I have come to value greatly for his dedication to Ukraine, high level of professionalism, and personal humanity. I was greatly pleased later to work with him in Brussels, when he was the Ambassador to the Benelux and I was a Minister-Counselor for NATO relations and Deputy Head of the Ukrainian Mission to NATO.

Loneliness at the Top

In the first few days after President Kravchuk told me that he would nominate me for minister of defense, I experienced what many people call loneliness at the top. I felt isolated, unable to share my thoughts and concerns with colleagues, while the matter of an appointment was being debated by members of Parliament. As a result, I invited Captain Oleksandr Fedorenko, a communications officer in the headquarters of the air army, to join me as an assistant. I had great trust in him, and after I was appointed minister, he and several other junior officers helped me organize the ministry's first activities. Although only a captain at the time, Fedorenko was quite open and sincere, willing to correct a general when he knew he had a good argument and could gather the evidence to support his case.

Some other individuals, however, initially declared their full support for Ukraine's independence, but upon reflection changed their minds. General Anatolii Basov, an ethnic Russian, was a decent, honest officer and a very fine specialist. He was my deputy when I commanded the 17th Air Army, and in the fall of 1991, I recommended him to take over my post, for he knew the situation in this army very well and had the respect and support of its officers. He eagerly accepted my proposal, and I trusted him. However, a few months later, influenced by personal considerations (he had very strong family ties in the Russian Federation) and possibly because of pressure from Moscow, he announced that he could no longer fulfill the duties of a commanding officer and swear an oath of allegiance to Ukraine. As he himself requested, I agreed to relieve him of his duties. The propaganda machine in Moscow asserted without warrant that I had rejected and fired generals such as Basov, who were decent people and good specialists, simply because they were Russians. Nothing could be farther from the truth.

When I spoke to those well-educated officers who had expressed a desire to serve in Ukraine's armed forces, I emphasized the importance of their being able and willing to support the cause of Ukrainian independence and all the processes of building a new state. After all, it was only normal that the officers of Ukraine's armed forces be expected to support the state they were supposed to serve. No other country, at least as far as I could determine, had admitted officers whose loyalty might be compromised or questioned. Most of my audience had no difficulty grasping my argument, and as a sign of their concurrence, I'm proud to say that our policies did not provoke any organized protests or open demonstrations of opposition.

True, not everyone was happy with the position to which he was assigned, and no doubt some officers looked upon their service in Ukraine as only temporary, hoping that they could fulfill their duties here for a period of one, two, or three years, then receive a transfer to Russia. Always prepared, we were more than willing to assist officers who desired to make such a move. However, we did not want Ukraine's armed forces to become a way station for officers. We wanted to establish, from the beginning, a solid foundation not only for the everyday life of Ukraine's new military, but also for the system of education and training within the forces.

A Blueprint for Action

In October, 1991, the Ministry of Defense received new quarters, authorized by the Commission on Defense and National Security, which allotted several rooms to us on the fourth floor of a building in the center of Kyiv. The former offices of an arm of the central committee of the Communist Party, this facility was an immense improvement and boosted our morale. I even received my own room, and to our great delight we finally had a place where we could hold large meetings, a necessity when it came time to welcome the representatives of other states and discuss Ukraine's position on military issues. Beginning in the fall of 1991, we met with various ambassadors and senior officials—dignitaries such as Manfred Wörner, the Secretary General of NATO; Supreme NATO Commander General John M. Shalikashvili, later chairman of the U.S. Joint Chiefs of Staff (1993–1997); ambassadors and military attachés from numerous countries that had been accredited to Moscow; as well as advisers to the presidents of the United States and France—all of whom were curious as to what exactly constituted this new nation, Ukraine.

Staffed primarily by volunteers from the military, the Ministry of Defense enthusiastically began the process of building Ukraine's armed forces. We attracted a great deal of attention—more than we anticipated—since our activities were closely followed by parliamentary deputies from all parties, particularly the democrats who had supported the creation of the ministry.

Through December 8, 1991, the day on which the Soviet Union formally ceased to exist, the Soviet authorities also monitored our work closely. Thereafter, officials of the Russian Federation watched our every move. Long a vigorous opponent of the separation and autonomy of armed forces in the various republics, the USSR Ministry of Defense as of December 8 could no longer legally stand in our way as we worked to create Ukraine's defense system, but we found plenty of resistance—some of it covert—in other places. For starters, the personnel, intelligence, and resources of the USSR Ministry of Defense were now divided between two new organizations, both of which strongly opposed our efforts in Ukraine. After the December collapse of the Soviet Union, a new Ministry of Defense was formed in Moscow for the Russian Federation. Also in December, the former republics of the Soviet Union established the Commonwealth of Independent States (CIS) and formed a joint military command headed by Marshal Shaposhnikov. Both organizations shared control over the information, plans, and documents relating to the USSR's armed forces and their deployment. The General Staff of the old USSR Ministry of Defense continued to operate as a unit even after it was absorbed into the Russian Ministry of Defense. Although the transition from the old to the new system appeared smooth, there was plenty of confusion in Russia and in the other republics, which gave us the perfect opportunity to act.

We took advantage of this situation by quickly making several strategic decisions regarding our armed forces. First, we ensured that Ukraine maintained peaceful relations with neighboring states. The proclamation of independence advanced no territorial claims against any other state and regarded no state or people as a potential enemy. Throughout history, of course, Ukraine had been a prize of warring nations, often subjugated by its more powerful neighbors or subjected to political pressures from them. The hard lessons of Ukraine's history—including its often tragic and repetitive loss of independence and, at times, its complete disappearance from the map—were not lost on any of us as we sought to promote a tradition of neutrality and mutual respect with our neighbors.

Second, largely because of the instability of the USSR and the legal uncertainties surrounding our independence, government leaders in Ukraine—the democratic deputies and parliamentary leaders, as well as other officials working with the Ministry of Defense—took pains to build a comprehensive legal foundation for the national defense system. In conjunction with the declaration of sovereignty, we prepared an entire dossier of official documents on military issues. When completed, it helped neutralize arguments that Ukraine

184

had no experience in this area, no legal right to set up its own armed forces, and no means of dealing with this challenge.

Some of these documents broke new ground. For example, Ukraine was the first post-Soviet state to adopt a resolution on the social welfare of officers and their families. We knew that our separation from the Soviet armed forces would cause a great deal of consternation among the officers, many of whom had devoted their entire careers to service in the military. Would their shift of allegiance cause them to lose their pensions or threaten their seniority? What would happen to their families if they took an oath of loyalty to Ukraine? Would they forfeit their housing or other material benefits for which they had worked so long?

Taking stock of these concerns, the Ukrainian Parliament passed several laws on defense issues, which must have impressed many CIS leaders. We were keen to preserve the system whereby officers' families would be guaranteed housing. By adopting a law on the social protection of military personnel and their families, Ukraine was the first former Soviet republic to create a legislative basis which, despite its many deficiencies, began to address some of the most painful problems facing military personnel. This helped preserve a sense of normalcy in the armed forces, so that even those who had little appreciation for Ukraine's new statehood found it difficult to oppose our initiatives. Although other CIS leaders might have been planning to act along similar lines, none had yet taken concrete steps to do so. Both they and the Russian Ministry of Defense merely criticized us for rushing headlong into these matters.

Given what was at stake, however, we had no choice but to act quickly and decisively. We had to think constantly about what might exacerbate tensions and provoke resistance. Once the appropriate legislation was passed, we had to press on with implementing the new laws, although we had no clearly established mechanism to guide us.

The dossier we prepared played a critical role when the Russian Ministry of Defense attempted to assume control of the strategic forces in the former Soviet republics. A great controversy arose over how to define "strategic forces." In Ukraine we interpreted this term to mean strategic nuclear forces, and we agreed to negotiate how best to resolve problems over the future deposition of this matériel. When Moscow attempted to broaden the definition of strategic forces to include a wide variety of other aspects of the military, we presented something of a fait accompli regarding the Ukrainian armed forces. While officials in Moscow argued over the interpretation of strategic forces, we pressed ahead with our plans to create our own armed forces. Officers who supported our position voluntarily took an oath of loyalty to Ukraine, and because these actions had firm legislative support, their legitimacy was not questioned by the leaders of the CIS states. On December 30, 1991 a CIS document was signed in Minsk that acknowledged the legitimacy of the individual armed forces for the CIS countries. It also recognized the legal basis and preparatory work of Ukraine for a legitimate armed forces.

Third, we were able to withstand repeated attempts to pressure us into creating a joint armed forces with other former republics that had declared independence. The first of these came in late November at a meeting of parliamentary representatives and administrators from former Soviet republics in Moscow. Unprecedented in the long history of the Soviet Union, this meeting was characterized by the democratic-like deliberations of equal partners, sovereign states that had come together to discuss military and other important matters. Joining my colleagues on November 29, just two days before the national referendum on Ukrainian independence, I had the honor of defending Ukraine's interests and addressing the assembly about the legislative actions our Parliament had taken to establish a separate armed forces.

Yet another attempt to exert pressure came from Marshal Shaposhnikov, the former USSR minister of defense who in December, 1991, became commander in chief of the joint CIS armed forces. He proposed a joint armed forces structure within the CIS framework, one of the positions he took that caused us much concern. Although we sometimes disagreed—for example, over the definition of "strategic forces"—Shaposhnikov generally adhered to democratic views, and as a highly professional military officer, he always studied carefully all aspects of a situation where he was obliged to fulfill his responsibilities. Thus, he respected Ukraine's Parliament and the legislation defining Ukraine's defense policy, and I could usually reason with him.

Our delegation to the meeting of newly independent states in November included a number of deputies with a particular interest in how we military types would defend Ukraine's military interests. As representatives from Ukraine's Parliament, the members of this delegation gave our position a legislative validity. In addition, we got a firsthand look at the kind of resistance we would have to deal with. Marshal Shaposhnikov conducted the meeting, but sitting next to him and openly disagreeing with his stance was Pavel Grachev, who at the time was head of the Russian parliament's committee on defense issues. The differences in their positions were obvious, and we took this as a sign that our initiatives would meet with growing opposition from Moscow. In fact, the Russian press was already accusing Shaposhnikov of allowing the republics—first and foremost Ukraine—to gradually build up their own armed forces and thus to undermine the authority of the Soviet Union.

During this meeting a number of issues required the resolute but patient defense of our position. We wanted to make sure that those attending this meeting, including deputies from Russia, Ukraine, and other republics, understood that we were willing to listen to them, and that we were not just being obstreperous. Reminding the delegates that in just two days—on December 1, 1991—the referendum would demonstrate our citizens' support for Ukraine's independence, I argued that it was nonsensical for senior politicians and military professionals to speak of maintaining a common army. My observations provoked a number of sarcastic comments from those attending the meeting. Russian delegates to this meeting had no idea that Ukrainians would demonstrate such an overwhelming vote of confidence in independence.

The public referendum on December 1 gave us an enormous boost. Ninety-two percent of those voting, including many ethnic Russians and a majority of the population in the heavily russified eastern and southern regions of the country, said "yes" to Ukrainian independence. Buoyed by this support, we decided to present

Ukraine's officially sanctioned plans for its own armed forces to the Alma-Ata meeting of CIS heads of state on December 22, 1991. Ukraine's leaders wanted to demonstrate that we were doing everything possible to maintain peace and harmony both in our country and with our neighbors. Moreover, we wanted the residents of Ukraine, including those with no particularly strong patriotic attachment to the country, to understand that we had consulted frequently and openly with the leaders of other CIS countries over this important step toward full autonomy. Our CIS colleagues showed great interest in the documents we prepared for this meeting, many of which discussed the mechanics of setting up a military force independent of Moscow's control.

Because the Alma-Ata meeting was not prepared to make a final decision on the matter of separate armed forces, the question was not brought to a vote and discussion was postponed. The Ukrainian delegation, therefore, requested another meeting to be held the following week in Minsk. On December 31, this time with President Kravchuk taking the lead, we again met with the heads of the CIS states and made a concerted effort to gain formal approval for our military plans. With their approval secured, we took the first giant step toward implementing our plans on January 3, 1992. On this date the first group of Ukrainian officers and generals swore the oath of allegiance to Ukraine.

The Oath of Allegiance

The preparations for administering an oath of allegiance had occupied us for several months. It was not some hastily prepared document created for a single occasion, but one that had been thoroughly discussed and edited, judiciously pruned of some lengthy excerpts taken from various historical documents. In fact, on December 6, 1991, Vasyl Durdynets, who headed Ukraine's Commission on Defense and National Security, had stood before the parliamentary deputies to read out several changes in the oath of loyalty. Short but effective, a final draft was approved and I was the first to take it—in front of the Ukrainian Parliament.

Having recently returned from meetings in Moscow, I had attended this parliamentary session and had listened intently as the measure was adopted. When Durdynets read out the oath, I wrote down its text and proposed that I be the first to swear allegiance, without any delay, in the parliamentary chambers. The speaker of the Parliament, Ivan Pliusch, agreed that this would be an appropriate symbolic gesture confirming the steps that the deputies had taken.

I recall having left the government loge and approached the podium with the text of the oath as I had written it down. There were no official ceremonies, no letterhead, no television cameras in the parliamentary chambers to record this event for history, but I had studiously transcribed the oath, signed my name, and written the number "1" on the document—the first out of thousands of others that we would begin administering in January. I saw this as a once-in-a-lifetime act, an event that had profound historical significance. While the deputies sat in rapt attention, I read out the text:

> *I, Kostiantyn Petrovych Morozov, upon entering military service, solemnly swear to the people of Ukraine always to be faithful and devoted to them, to conscientiously and honestly execute my military duties and the orders of my superiors, to steadfastly uphold the Constitution and laws of Ukraine, and to safeguard state and military secrets.*
>
> *I swear to defend the Ukrainian state and to firmly stand for its freedom and independence.*
>
> *I swear never to betray the people of Ukraine.*

Immediately the chamber erupted with applause and cheers. In that heady moment I recall embraces and handshakes on all sides as the deputies congratulated me and each other on having taken such a giant step toward affirming our new independence.

Upon returning to the government loge, I received more congratulations from deputies who greeted and warmly embraced me. One of the national democrats, Mykhailo Kosiv, must have known that the oath would be approved that day because he was ready with a bouquet of flowers to mark the occasion. Again, the deputies stood to renew their applause and cheers.

December 6, the day I swore allegiance to my newly independent country, has been designated Ukrainian Armed Forces Day. It is a day I will never forget. Years before, when I was a new recruit in the armed forces, I had taken another oath of loyalty, this one to the Soviet Union. At the time, I was very young and impressionable, and although I took that first oath seriously, I felt that the oath to defend Ukraine had a great deal more significance. Perhaps it was because I was older, or because I realized the importance of the precedent I was establishing, or because even though it was a very young country (technically only five days old), Ukraine had a tangible reality that the abstraction represented by the large and diverse Soviet Union did not have. Perhaps my reaction had a lot to do with the responsibility I felt my position carried, or maybe it was so strong because I was the first to swear allegiance (what if other senior officers refused?). At the time, I was still deeply involved in thinking through the strategy to be adopted in further developing Ukraine's armed forces.

I am proud that I was the first to take this oath and grateful that I had the opportunity to do so. All military personnel should be proud of their courageous decision to swear allegiance to the people they serve. Taking an oath of loyalty is important not only from a legal point of view and as a sign of a military officer's allegiance to a particular state, but also from a moral point of view. The act imposes a moral and civic responsibility on those taking the oath, linking them to the soil and the people they have sworn to defend. One's formal duty to defend the state is underlined in the legislation of those states that require all young men, even in time of peace, to serve in the military. Furthermore, the oath of loyalty adds an important moral component to one's formal duty, emphasizing the responsibility to serve one's people and obey the orders of those to whom the country's defense has been entrusted.

Arguments that one has only one chance in a lifetime to make such a commitment—that is, once allegiance is sworn, it can never

be retracted—did not persuade me that my action was morally inde-
fensible. As I saw it, I had earlier taken an oath to serve the people of
the Soviet Union, but now the context involving that group of people
had changed radically. My new allegiance was to the people of
Ukraine. However fine these distinctions, the moral dilemma posed
by the sudden creation of a newly independent political entity—
Ukraine—did not deter the critics from lashing out.

On December 7 and for some time thereafter, it was widely reported that General Morozov, the new minister of defense, had rejected his former fatherland by swearing an oath of loyalty different
from the one used in the Soviet armed forces. I was so involved with
my new responsibilities as minister of defense that I hardly had time
to pay much attention to these critics. I felt that my decision was
thoroughly principled and politically justified. In addition, while it
would not solve all our problems, administering the oath would provide us with essential information about how military personnel felt
toward an independent Ukraine; thus, we would be in a much better
position to gain control over those forces stationed in our territory
and lay the foundations for establishing Ukraine's own military.

Planning the logistics of administering this oath to the officer
corps in Ukraine represented the main thrust of our work that December. Soon after the Parliament approved the official text, we met
with the country's military commanders and told them to begin preparing the officers to take this oath as early as January 3, 1992. During this period we relied heavily on a core of enthusiastic volunteers
who felt a strong moral duty to be involved in this historic process
and who were willing to assume full personal responsibility for their
work. We were not surprised to find a wide range of opinions within
the officer corps concerning the oath. Some officers, who greeted
Ukraine's independence and unambiguously regarded this new state
as their homeland, clearly had been waiting for this opportunity.
They would prove instrumental in helping us determine how we
should proceed.

Another category of officers, however, was in principle ready to
swear loyalty to the state and people of Ukraine, but they wanted to
be assured that Ukraine's position had a firm, legitimate foundation.

They did not clearly understand which structure or institution was capable of resolving this issue but, in general terms, considered that it was within the competence of the CIS to decide whether Ukraine had the legal right to establish its own armed forces. They argued that they would be fully protected only if Ukraine's actions were approved within this broader political framework. In view of their concerns, the Ministry of Defense worked hard to create an appropriate juridical basis for implementing Ukraine's defense policy, and we were constantly involved in negotiations with military authorities in Moscow.

There was yet a third group. Approximately fifteen percent of the military officers and conscripts stationed in Ukrainian territory refused to take the oath of allegiance and expressed a desire to return to their own republics. From January to March, those officers and conscripts were gradually transferred to their home regions, largely at our expense. This transfer was an accomplishment in itself, involving over 10,000 military personnel and their families. By peacefully and methodically arranging for their transfers—we provided as much assistance as possible, including financial aid*—we not only set a precedent for other CIS states to follow but also neutralized any negative propaganda that officers opposed to our program might generate. As it turned out, our strategy worked brilliantly.

Opposition from Russian officials was less blatant than we might have expected. The central military authorities nevertheless went to great lengths to emphasize that the Soviet Union's armed forces and their property could not possibly be split up. They placed numerous obstacles in our path. The central administrative organs in Moscow, for example, maintained close contacts with military units in which many officers were reluctant to swear loyalty to Ukraine or in which a commanding officer adopted an anti-Ukrainian position. This strategy allowed Moscow to closely monitor military developments in Ukraine and provide assistance to the commanding officers opposed to our plans.

Well-known figures in Russia often had to take a less conspicuous role. At the time of the coup attempt in Moscow, for example, both Marshal Shaposhnikov and General Pavel Grachev had identified themselves with the democratic forces in Russia by supporting Yeltsin on the barricades outside the Russian White House. Now, however, they had to defend Russia's national interests and answer to politicians whose agendas were far from being democratic. Either trying to preserve the idea of a Soviet Union or to create a new entity dominated by Russia, both to some extent represented a long-standing tradition of imperial ambitions.

Overcoming Resistance

Despite the heavy majority of support for Ukrainian independence, elements of organized resistance to the oath of loyalty did spring up. How much of this resistance was home grown, how much was inspired by outside forces is unclear, but we were successful in avoiding the use of force and in settling conflicts peacefully. Thus, we prevented the Russian forces or those of the CIS from intervening in our domestic affairs.

Our success in identifying pockets of resistance came from two main sources: new commanders that the Ministry of Defense had appointed and assigned to various military units, and grassroots members of the Union of Officers of Ukraine (UOU). The newly appointed young officers were our eyes and ears in the garrisons and military posts throughout the country, and from them we gathered reliable information on emerging centers of resistance. With this kind of advanced warning, we were able to take immediate control of the situation and work with a dissatisfied group of officers to resolve their problems.

The UOU comprised various military personnel, many of whom were close to retirement. As a purely advisory group, the UOU did not officially influence decisions of the Defense Ministry, but its members provided us with information, offered advice, and at times even criticized our activities. They continued to put forward their own demands, but always in the form of consultation. Thanks to them, we had a lever of influence within military units in every oblast of Ukraine.

The UOU was especially valuable as a source of information about units where it was hard to know exactly what was going on. A number of commanding officers, for instance, had difficulty accepting Ukraine's need to create a separate armed forces. Remaining in constant touch with their superiors in Moscow, these senior officers and their deputies had ways of suppressing the younger officers in a given unit who favored joining Ukraine's armed forces. In such a delicate situation, these young officers did not express their views openly for fear of jeopardizing their careers and their families' livelihood. At the same time, military authorities in Moscow attempted to discredit us by claiming that the UOU harbored traitors, incompetents, or careerists who should have been released from service in the Soviet armed forces. I remain convinced, however, that most UOU members were patriots who had no designs on senior posts in their units. In many cases they were simply good specialists who were close to retirement, and as Ukrainian patriots they closely followed what was happening around them.

We at the Ministry of Defense had to defend the right of young officers to express their loyalty to Ukraine and to protect them from reprisals. But we needed reliable information about their commanders' views on Ukrainian sovereignty and the oath of loyalty. Even after the oath was administered, an officer might well behave in a manner that was not in line with the commitments he had assumed.

Early in 1992, a group in the Vinnytsia garrison formed the Alternative Union of Officers of Ukraine apparently in response to a number of tactless statements that some representatives of the UOU and commanding officers made regarding the military and the new order. This alternative group hoped to appeal to two sorts of officers: those who refused to swear the oath of loyalty in the first place and those who had taken the oath only later to discover, under some pressure, that they had changed their minds.

Had the Alternative UOU gained the influence that its organizers had hoped for, the group might have posed a serious threat to Ukraine. A number of patriotic officers, however, provided us with information that enabled us to monitor this challenge closely. Refusing to interfere with this alternative group's meetings and its leaders' decisions, I instructed the commanding officers of Vinnytsia garrison to meet with representatives from the Alternative UOU. When the group summarized its demands in a document ready to be circulated among all officers in Ukraine, I stepped in to invite the leaders to meet with me in my office and air their grievances. Sensing that I genuinely wanted to learn about their situation and reach a mutual understanding, they agreed.

They probably didn't expect me to take the position I did. Rather than launching a counterattack, I informed them that I wanted to study their demands and complaints. By entering into a dialogue with these officers, my deputies and I were able to defuse the potential crisis. Leaders of the Alternative UOU had to understand that they were pushing the limits of what was acceptable. As a result of our meeting, they agreed to cease their activities, and their grievances never gained any significant support among the officers in Ukraine.

The Congress of Officers' Assembly

The oath of loyalty placed an enormous obstacle in the path of those beyond our borders who hoped to foment opposition within our military. At the Congress of Officers' Assemblies held in Moscow in January, 1992, we heard virulent speeches condemning the radical restructuring that we had undertaken in Ukraine. Critics raised the same objections we had heard so often before—namely, that a united military should be preserved at all costs, that our position had created so wide a breach that no one at the congress could depend on the support of the military in Ukraine. Several speakers at this congress directed their most hostile criticism at Ukraine's leaders, arguing that President Kravchuk should be summoned to Moscow immediately and made to reverse this act of rebellion. It was, of course, inconceivable that he should attend this meeting, where he was sure to be called on the carpet for allowing the democratic forces to undermine the solidarity of the Soviet Union. Despite the officers' vehement demands, Kravchuk showed remarkable restraint by not reacting to them at all. He closely followed the broadcasts, which described the proceedings of the congress, and I communicated with him regularly, providing a personal assessment of the events.

We were now witnessing a radical restructuring not only of Ukraine, as it wrestled with its own military problems, but also of the Soviet world as we had known it. Russia was, after all, now a foreign state.

At the congress, the dialogue—to use the term loosely—increasingly took on a tone of frenzy, prompted by the delegates' extreme frustration with the dissolution of centralized power that once was the Soviet Union. This tone helped confirm for us, however, that we were on the right track. If the delegates' deep feelings were representative of all officers' sentiments, then many more officers in Ukraine would have mobilized against the country's legislative action to create its own armed forces. A great many more of them would have attended this congress in Moscow seeking its support, but in fact, few of them did.

The radical restructuring of old institutions, which accompanied the parallel creation of Ukraine's armed forces and security agencies, also finally put an end to the old Soviet system whereby representatives of the KGB were found in all military units. The responsibility for monitoring the Ukrainian military fell to the Sluzhba Bezpeky Ukraïny, or SBU, the national security agency headed by Yevhen Marchuk. His challenge was to restructure the old KGB rather than create a new security agency, a task no less daunting than the one I faced, given the cohesiveness and secrecy exhibited by the KGB. When Marchuk determined that some official had to be dismissed or a new person appointed, he was caught between a hammer and an anvil. He had to take great care in reforming the state security system because it had such powerful means at its disposal that it readily could have been exploited to undermine the Ukrainian state. At the same time, Marchuk was under constant pressure—as I myself was—to acknowledge the demands of democrats who demanded a thorough purging of the institution under his control.

The SBU played a vital role in helping us control the rapidly changing situation within the military. Thousands of officers and conscripts were relieved of their duties when they refused to take the oath of allegiance or when they resigned because they could not accept the new system that the Ministry of Defense introduced. The enormous number of personnel changes brought on a set of complicated problems, many of which the SBU and the ministry worked together to resolve. Marchuk's support and the cooperative relationship between the Defense Ministry and the SBU were essential to the success of our program. I had almost daily contacts with a number of security officials. Colonel Oleksandr Skipalskyi, head of the SBU's military counterintelligence administration, and Colonel Hryhorii Omelchenko, one of the founders of the UOU, helped me understand the reforms taking place within the SBU and provided the ministry with valuable information about the reception of political and military changes in the armed forces.* Our dealings with each other were open and sincere, and I felt their trust in me grow as they witnessed the concrete, practical steps I took to reform the armed forces.

Of all the initiatives I took to establish a credible military force in Ukraine, the oath of loyalty stands foremost in my mind. It represents for me and for millions of Ukrainians the moral, political, and military commitment to defend our country at whatever price, and it stands as one of the major symbolic gestures to a free and independent Ukraine. Viewed in the broader context of Ukraine's military presence vis-à-vis the former republics of the Soviet Union as well as our neighbors in Europe and beyond, restructuring the Ukrainian military and administering the oath of loyalty were two of the most important steps that we took in 1991 and 1992. There remained, however, the question of what to do with the armaments that remained in Ukrainian territory. What should be returned to Russia and how should the transfer take place? What dangers lay ahead for our citizens and the military personnel who had sworn to protect them? How should we now negotiate with those who had so vehemently opposed the creation of a separate military force in Ukraine?

With the oath of loyalty we had taken a gigantic step only to discover there lay in our path tremendous obstacles that would require our sharpest strategy.

Conclusion

It is not often that people are placed in a situation where they have to make a decision that affects them to the very core of their identity. In my life there have been just such incidents, when I have had to make choices that I knew would not only influence the circumstances of my future life, but also would affect something that must be qualified more substantially and called "destiny." In the 1960s after I completed high school, I chose for myself the profession of a military pilot. I therein tied not only my own fate, but also that of my family, with a life of service and responsibility. I served in fifteen different assignments over thirty years that lead up to the decisions that I had to make during those August days of the putsch. I had to balance three fundamental issues in my decision-making of that critical time. First, I had to look at the social consequences of my actions for my country. Second, I had to evaluate the actions and prospects of others—especially the democratic forces active at the time. And, third, I had to answer the fundamental question, "Who am I?"

Soon it will be ten years since the central events described in this book. But even now I am asked by many people, "How is that you, with an excellent career as a Soviet general, decided to support Ukrainian independence and the formation of an independent Ukrainian armed forces?" The history set forth in this book is my answer to those questioners. Perhaps the particular way in which I reacted to untruth and injustice as I perceived them was determined already in my childhood, by the moral and spiritual compass set in place by my mother and our family's circumstances. Whatever its source, this innate reaction helped me to see the truly dangerous and corrupt nature of the ideology of the Communist Party of the Soviet Union at a critical juncture. Simply stated, I perceived the Communist Party's actions during the time of the putsch as illegal. I also saw the essential illegality and peril for masses of people—my people!—that came from the readiness of many Party leaders to make use of the Soviet armed forces against the public. The danger was two-fold. The obvious danger was the possibility of bloodshed among the civil population. But even then I perceived the more subtle danger—that our officers might be so misused that their potential for achieving a just and moral position within civilian society would be permanently destroyed.

The Party leadership, as throughout history, put its own interests before the interests of the people, of the law, and of justice. For me, the result was that it stimulated my own sense of the rectitude of the Ukrainian people's reaction to these unjust developments. And with that sense of the justice of their cause, grew my conviction that the people of Ukraine had a right to undertake actions that would form the basis for self-government on a moral and just basis. That sense increased under the influence of my meetings with representatives of the democratic movement—men and women who over many years had continued the struggle for Ukrainian independence. My respect grew even firmer for those political leaders who selflessly worked to form the infrastructure necessary to attain the goal of independence.

My own heritage and the heritage of my family also was important for me. At a very fundamental level, my family and I had always viewed the Ukrainian Republic (whether in its Soviet or independent incarnations) as our homeland. No other land or country ever replaced that essential relationship. My family also was graced by the fact that we held similar ideas on political and social issues. Raisa, Eva, and I did not hold significantly different views toward the political developments of the time and we supported each other in our reactions to those events. With that crucial support from those that I cared for most, I left the Communist Party, condemned the SCSE, guaranteed the non-intervention of forces under me against democratic groups, supported Ukrainian independence as a just cause, and drew closer to the political leaders and representatives of the

(con't on p. 217)

Photo Collection III

24. With Secretary General of NATO Manfred Wörner in Kyiv, February 22–23, 1992 (*photo by NATO Photo Services*).

This picture was taken at the Ministry of Defense, during our first day operating on the base of the Kyiv Military District Staff Headquarters. Ukraine entered a new stage in its relations with other world leaders when NATO Secretary General Manfred Wörner visited Kyiv and invited Ukraine to join the North Atlantic Cooperation Council (NACC). The Council was established to bring together the NATO countries and the Newly Independent States of the former Soviet Union. On March 31, 1992 I took part in the first meeting of the NACC (at the ministerial level) in Brussels. In 1997, NACC became the Euro-Atlantic Partnership Council (EAPC), an important sphere in which all of these former adversaries work together to ensure peace and stability. In that year both Ukraine and Russia signed charters establishing a special partnership with NATO. After our meeting in 1992, Sec. Gen. Wörner and I—as colleagues and as fellow pilots—exchanged watches. I still have his German Artos Bund watch (no. 511567). It reminds me of a meeting with an extraordinary man and outstanding politician.

**25. Washington, DC, April 13, 1992, with U.S. Secretary of Defense
Dick Cheney at a Full Honors Ceremony for Morozov.**

*During my first visit to the United States I had the opportunity to meet with
Secretary of Defense Dick Cheney at his office in the Pentagon. This was a
remarkable event, considering that our Ukrainian armed forces was less
than a year old. As I recall, we were discussing the military tradition in
Ukraine and in the United States when this photograph was taken. During
that same visit, I traveled to several military installations in the United
States: the Pentagon, a navy training center outside of Chicago, an army
armored cavalry regiment at Fort Carson near Colorado Springs, the Air
Force Academy, Nellis Air Force Base in Las Vegas, and the U.S. Military
Academy at West Point. Secretary Cheney and I developed a very good rela-
tionship—not only professionally, but also personally. My wife and I both
think highly of him and his family. The third person in the photograph is
George Sajewych, a very talented State Department interpreter.*

26. With Raisa and Major General Nicholas Krawciw, US Army (ret.), at a meeting with the Ukrainian-American community, April 1992 (*photo by Yaroslav Kulynych*).

I had meetings with wonderful, huge groups of Ukrainian-Americans in various cities: New York, Chicago, and Washington, DC. This particular meeting was in New York. At the podium is Maj. Gen. (ret.) Nick Krawciw, an American of Ukrainian heritage and a man that I tremendously admire. This also reminds me of the dedication and great contributions that men and women of Ukrainian heritage have made in the United States military, from Sgt. Michael Strank (of Carpatho-Ukrainian heritage and the leader of the Marines who raised the American flag on Mt. Suribachi at Iwo Jima in February 1945) to Gen. Krawciw (who is one of the highest ranking Ukrainian-Americans ever in the U.S. military). It is important, too, for me to note that Raisa traveled with me during this trip to represent our young country and also was very active in our meetings with the Ukrainian-American community.

27. With Raisa and the Hon. Roman Popadiuk, the United States' first Ambassador to Ukraine, April 1992.

This picture was taken in Blair House, across the street from the White House. Mr. Popadiuk was appointed the first Ambassador of the United States to Ukraine and presented his credentials to President Kravchuk three months after this picture was taken. He remained the Ambassador to Ukraine until October 1993.

204

28. During a visit to Nellis Air Force Base (Las Vegas, Nevada), when Morozov flew a U.S. F-16, April 1992.

At Nellis AFB in Las Vegas, Nevada, I had the opportunity for the first time in my life to fly a non-Soviet aircraft. The plane was an F-16. I was very excited by the flight and my American colleagues could see that. So, they proposed that I take the picture and the commander of the base made up a special plaque for me with the picture and a certificate commemorating the flight, which he signed. It now hangs in my study in Kyiv. Many people then asked me how the F-16 differed from, say, the MiG-23. That is a delicate question to answer, because it gets into a fundamental difference between Western and Soviet and post-Soviet fighter design. The operational goals of the craft are similar, but our fighter designs have always relied on the pilot's abilities to accomplish many of those goals, whereas the Western aircraft had mechanical means of achieving the same thing. This in turn explains the extreme focus on the health and psychological state of our pilots that I talk about in the text. This is not to say that Western pilots are any less fit than our pilots are, just that—from our point of view—they get to fly much more "comfortable" aircraft. The year after this photo was taken I had the opportunity to fly an FA-18 from the U.S.S. George Washington—my first time flying from an aircraft carrier and likewise an extraordinary experience.

29. The full Ukrainian delegation at Nellis AFB, April, 1992.

*This was our full delegation during the trip to Nellis. To my right are O.
Orlov (our translator), Gen. Yurii Prokofiev, Dmytro Pavlychko (Member of
Parliament), Yurii Kulyk (representating our embassy in Washington), Gen.
Yaroslav Skalko (also in a flight suit), and Yu. Bubnovsky (assistant minis-
ter). To my left are Volodymyr Muliava (head of the administration of the
Ministry of Defense), Kostiantyn Gryschenko (head of the administration of
the Ministry of Foreign Affairs; now Ambassador of Ukraine to the United
States), and Valentyn Lemish (Member of Parliament).*

30. At a state-level meeting to discuss forces disposition (especially with regard to the Black Sea Fleet) at Dagomys, Krasnodar Oblast, Russian Federation, June 23, 1992.

As the minister of defense, I took part in many meetings of heads of the CIS countries. This was the meeting in Dagomys (June 23, 1992), when the decision to divide the Black Sea Fleet was made. Pavel Grachev is on the far left. Yuri Dubinin, head of the Russian negotiating team for the Black Sea Fleet issue, is to my left and Volodymyr Lanovyi, Ukraine's minister of the economy and vice-prime minister, is to my right. President Kravchuk and President Yeltsin are in the foreground.

31. Signing a bilateral military accord with Poland, February 1993

This photograph was taken after the signing of a memorandum of under-standing on military cooperation with Poland. I am shaking the hand of my counterpart, Janusz Onyszkiewicz, the Polish minister of national defense. Third from his right is Ukrainian Foreign Minister Anatolii Zlenko. To his left is Ukraine's Ambassador to Poland Hennadii Udovenko (he later became the minister of foreign affairs of Ukraine and also president of the 52nd Assembly of the UN). In front of them is Academician Ihor Yukhnovskyi, head of the Parliamentary commission. In light of our historical conflict, it was a very positive step to establish friendly, cooperative relations with Poland. In fact, Poland was the first country to recognize Ukrainian independence and has consistently supported Ukraine on the international stage.

32. At the Pershotravneve [Pervomaisk] Missile Complex in Mykolaïv Oblast, May 1993 (*photo by Oleksandr Klymenko*).

President Kravchuk, an officer of a Strategic Rocket division, and I stand in front of a missile silo at Pershotravneve (in Russian, Pervomaisk) in May of 1993. I am briefing the president about the decommissioning of active warheads from these sites. Behind the president is Anton Buteiko (then the presidential foreign affairs advisor). Ukraine from its outset declared its intent to become a non-nuclear state. However, the decommissioning process was extremely complicated and, moreover, expensive for our fledgling country. Ukraine went from having the third-largest nuclear force at independence to having no nuclear weapons today. I hope the world never forgets the example that we have set.

33. Signing a bilateral military accord with Turkish Minister of Defense Nevzat Ayaz in Kyiv, July 1993.

Our relationship with Turkey is extremely important in light of our shared regional interests in the Black Sea Littoral and our desire for stability in that area. The memorandum of understanding with the Ministry of Defense of Turkey that we signed in July 1993 provided for a broad variety of cooperative measures that our respective armed forces could take—naval cooperation being an important element in them. Behind me stands the deputy minister of defense for weapons issues, Gen. Ivan Oliinyk.

210

34. The raising of the Ukrainian flag at Norfolk Naval Base in honor of Morozov's visit, July 1993.

American marines raise the Ukrainian flag during my visit to the Headquarters of the NATO Atlantic Command. I met with Admiral David Miller there, the supreme commander of Atlantic Forces of NATO. It was not the first time that I had seen the Ukrainian flag raised on American soil, but it still had a powerful effect on me.

35. With Secretary of Defense Les Aspin and Deputy Secretary of Defense Strobe Talbott, Washington, DC, July 26, 1993.

This was during negotiations at the Pentagon, when we were making prepa-rations for the signing of the first memorandum of understanding with the United States. To the right of Secretary Les Aspin (who is across the table from me), is Ambassador Strobe Talbott, who was the ambassador-at-large for the Newly Independent States (he became deputy secretary of state early the following year). On my right is Oleh Bilorus, Ukraine's Ambassador to the U.S. The signing of the Memorandum of Understanding with the United States greatly facilitated the signing of similar memoranda with other NATO countries.

212

36. With German Defense Minister Volker Rühe in Kyiv, August 1993.

This photograph shows our discussions about preparing a future memorandum of understanding on cooperation between the armed forces of Ukraine and Germany. To my right is General Anatolii Lopata, the Chief of Staff of the Ukrainian armed forces. This was one of the attempts that we instituted to establish relations with other European countries.

37. With British Defense Minister Malcolm Rifkind in Kyiv, September 1993.

British Minister of Defense Malcolm Rifkind was another of the European defense ministers to visit Ukraine during our tenure. This was our first meeting with journalists during the trip. Britain continues to be an important strategic partner for Ukraine, especially within NATO's Partnership for Peace and in our joint commitment to various peacekeeping missions under UN sponsorship. During this particular visit a memorandum of understanding was signed that foresaw cooperation between the defense ministries of our countries in a number of areas. Rifkind continued this support for Ukraine when he became Britain's minister of foreign affairs in 1995 and returned to Kyiv to mark his first official visit abroad in that capacity in September 1995.

38. With Borys Tarasiuk and Javier Solana at the inaugural meeting of the NATO-Ukraine Commission, October 8, 1997.

This was the inaugural meeting of the NATO-Ukraine Commission (NUC), which was created as a result of the Special Charter on a Distinctive Partnership between the North Atlantic Treaty Organization and Ukraine, signed in Madrid on July 7, 1997. Since that time, the NUC has met regularly at the level of plenipotentiary emissaries, and ministers of defense and foreign affairs. Among the issues examined at these meetings have been: European security and Ukraine's role in it, Ukraine's relationship with NATO (especially with regard to Ukrainian peacekeeping activity), and contingency planning for emergency situations that might arise in our part of the world. Once formal bilateral relations were established with NATO and an appropriate decree was signed by President Kuchma of Ukraine in 1998, a permanent Ukrainian Mission to NATO in Brussels was established. Borys Tarasiuk was its first Head and I was his Deputy.

215

39. With President Leonid Kuchma upon appointment as Ambassador to Iran, May 29, 2000.

After working for three and a half years in Brussels as the Deputy Head of Mission to NATO, on April 7, 2000, I was appointed Extraordinary and Plenipotentiary Ambassador to the Islamic Republic of Iran. Before my departure to Tehran, President Kuchma and I met in his office. For me this photograph symbolizes the great importance of service to our country even beyond its borders. This picture also reminds me of the important responsibility laid on my shoulders by the President, as witnessed by his words in the credentials he gave me to present to President Khatami of Iran: "Please accept him with good will and trust everything that he says on my behalf and on behalf of the Government of Ukraine." Having had my small, humble part in the building of this state and its government, I can think of no higher honor than to represent it abroad with such a charge. I never would have imagined myself a state builder when I was a young cadet. Neither would I have imagined myself as a statesman when, as a soldier, I served my country to build its armed forces and protect its government. But such has been my life and fate that I have been able to continue to serve Ukraine, wherever that service may take me.

(con't from p. 200)

intelligentsia who had, much earlier than I, created in the general public those ideals of the nation that led to independence.

Fortunately, I was not unique in the Soviet armed forces. Many of my colleagues joined me in the dangerous and weighty work of creating the Ukrainian armed forces. All of the newly assigned military district commanders, commanders of armies, corps, and their staffs were, on the whole, like minded. For a long time the situation in the Black Sea Fleet remained a serious problem for Ukraine. But even there, despite the conditions of terrible conspiracy and intrigue, officer-patriots managed to form the foundations of a serious and responsible Ukrainian navy. Moreover, in the staff of the 43rd Strategic Rocket Forces Army, which jurisdictionally was subordinated directly to Moscow, there were Ukrainian patriots who made use of their positions to support the peaceful and just transfer of control of these nuclear weapons to the jurisdiction of the Ukrainian Ministry of Defense.

An important moment in the history of the building of the Ukrainian armed forces was the Ukrainian Parliament's resolution to bring all armed forces in Ukraine under the jurisdiction of the Ukrainian government. This was expressed from the very first day of the declaration of Ukrainian independence. Equally important was the historically unprecedented decision to administer an oath of loyalty to the forces that remained in Ukraine as well as to repatriate those Ukrainian military personnel who were serving outside Ukraine at the moment of independence. That decision was very critical from the point of view of subsequent Russian military formation and the presence of Soviet forces in Ukraine. In that situation, we understood that the officers' acceptance of the oath of loyalty to Ukraine was not a sufficient criterion to ensure their loyalty, but that at the same time it was an absolutely necessary step in the creation of the core of the future Ukrainian armed forces. The wisdom of that decision has been confirmed with the passage of time.

The Ukrainian armed forces from the first days of its existence has been faced with economic crisis—the limitation of its budget that has influenced matériel, the integration of military-civil relations, and the living standards of military families in Ukraine. But the government has done everything that it can, and the Ukrainian armed forces has done everything it can as the defense structure of an independent nation. I am proud of it.

The Ukrainian armed forces today has great authority in Europe and in the world. It cooperates with many governments and armies in Europe, the U.S., and Canada. Ukraine is a special partner with NATO as a fundamental element of European security. Our armed forces takes part in peacekeeping activities in Bosnia, Kosovo, and we conduct peaceful training and military exercises on the territory of Ukraine and many other countries. Ukraine, as a contributor of European stability and security, has achieved this position due to the stability and authority of its armed forces.

Many times, I also have been asked, "Why does Ukraine need its own army? With whom is Ukraine ready to go to war?" History has shown that in order to *avoid* going to war, whether on Ukrainian territory or on the territory of any other country, it is necessary to form a Ukrainian armed forces that can make an integral contribution to the world's perception of the Ukrainian government as a reliable and predictable partner. A strong, well-ordered, democratic Ukrainian military shows that Ukraine is a country that can resolve its own domestic problems, work out its problems with its neighbors, and become an important element in the general structure of European security.

For the resolution of those problems it was necessary to undertake the difficult and dangerous task that we undertook in those heady days. And today I am proud and happy and thankful for a fate that allowed me to make the contribution that I did and to join in the marvelous state-building project that has given us an independent and free Ukraine.

Documentary Appendices

1. *The Declaration of State Sovereignty by the* Verkhovna Rada *of Ukraine (July 16, 1990)* [English translation]*

DECLARATION ON STATE SOVEREIGNTY OF UKRAINE

The Supreme Soviet of the Ukrainian SSR,
- expressing the will of the people of Ukraine;
- striving to create a democratic society;
- acting on the need to secure fully human rights and freedoms;
- respecting the national rights of all peoples;
- concerned for the fullest possible political, economic, social and spiritual development of the people of Ukraine;
- recognizing the necessity of establishing a state based on the rule of law;
- having as a goal the affirmation of sovereignty and self-rule of the people of Ukraine;

PROCLAIMS
the state sovereignty of Ukraine—the supremacy, independence, plenariness and indivisibility of the republic's authority within the boundaries of its territory and its independence and equality in external relations.

I. Self-Determination of the Ukrainian Nation

The Ukrainian SSR, as a sovereign national state, develops within existing boundaries on the basis of the realization of the Ukrainian nation's inalienable right to self-determination.

The Ukrainian SSR implements the protection and defense of the national statehood of the Ukrainian people.

Any violent actions against the national statehood of Ukraine on the part of political parties, public organizations or other groups or individuals will be prosecuted in accordance with the law.

II. Rule of and by the People

Citizens of the republic of all nationalities constitute the people of Ukraine. The people of Ukraine are the sole source of state authority in the republic. The complete authority of the people of Ukraine is actualized on the basis of the republic's

---

*English translation by Roma Hadzewycz for *The Ukrainian Weekly*. Reproduced with permission.

Constitution, directly, as well as through the people's deputies elected to the Supreme Rada and local councils of the Ukrainian SSR.

Only the Supreme Rada of the Ukrainian SSR may speak in the name of the entire people. No political party, public organization or other group or individual can speak in the name of the entire people of Ukraine.

III. State Authority

The Ukrainian SSR independently decides all issues regarding its state affairs. The Ukrainian SSR guarantees the primacy of the Constitution and the laws of the republic on its territory.

State authority in the republic is exercised in accordance with the principle of its separation into legislative, executive and judicial branches.

Ultimate oversight, as regards the precise and uniform enforcement of the law, is exercised by the Procurator General of the Ukrainian SSR, who is appointed by the Supreme Rada of the Ukrainian SSR, and is responsible to it and accountable only to it.

IV. Citizenship of the Ukrainian SSR

The Ukrainian SSR has its own citizenship and guarantees each citizen the right to retain the citizenship of the USSR.

The basis for acquiring and for forfeiting citizenship of the Ukrainian SSR is determined by the Ukrainian SSR's law on citizenship.

All citizens of the Ukrainian SSR are guaranteed the rights and freedoms provided for by the Constitution of the Ukrainian SSR and by those standards of international law recognized by the Ukrainian SSR.

The Ukrainian SSR guarantees equality before the law to all citizens of the republic regardless of their ancestry, social or property status, racial or national identity, sex, education, language, political views, religious beliefs, the type and nature of their occupation, their place of residence or other conditions.

The Ukrainian SSR regulates all immigration processes.

The Ukrainian SSR expresses its concern for and takes measures to protect and defend the interests of the citizens of the Ukrainian SSR beyond the republic's borders.

V. Territorial Supremacy

The Ukrainian SSR exercises supremacy on its entire territory.
The territory of the Ukrainian SSR within existing borders is inviolable and cannot be changed or utilized without its consent.

The Ukrainian SSR independently determines the administrative-territorial system of the republic and the procedures for establishing national administrative units.

VI. Economic Independence

The Ukrainian SSR independently determines its economic status and secures it in law.

The people of Ukraine have the exclusive right to the ownership, use and disposition of the national resources of Ukraine.

The land, its mineral wealth, airspace, water resources and other natural resources found within the borders of the territory of the Ukrainian SSR, the natural resources of its continental shelf and its exclusive maritime economic zone, and all economic and scientific-technical potential created on the territory of Ukraine are the property of its people, the material foundation of the republic's sovereignty, and are used with the aim of providing for the material and spiritual needs of its citizens.

The Ukrainian SSR has the right to its share of the all-Union wealth, especially of all-Union diamond and hard currency stocks and gold reserves which share was realized through the efforts of the people of the republic.

Issues concerning all-Union property (the common property of all the republics) shall be resolved on the basis of agreements between the republics, the principals as with regard to this property.

Enterprises, institutions, organizations and facilities of other states and their citizens and of international organizations may locate on the territory of the Ukrainian SSR and use the natural resources of Ukraine in accordance with the laws of the Ukrainian SSR.

The Ukrainian SSR independently establishes banking (including a bank for external economic activity), pricing, financial, customs and tax systems, prepares a state budget, and, if necessary, introduces its own currency.

The National Bank of Ukraine, which is accountable to the Supreme Rada of the Ukrainian SSR pay a fee for use of the land and other natural and labor resources and remit deductions from their currency receipts, as well as pay taxes to local budgets.

The Ukrainian SSR provides for the protection of all forms of ownership.

VII. Environmental Safety

The Ukrainian SSR independently determines the manner of organizing the protection of the environment on the territory of the republic and procedures for the use of natural resources.

The Ukrainian SSR has its own national committee on the protection of the population from radiation.

The Ukrainian SSR has the right to ban the construction and to halt the operation of any enterprises, institutions, organizations and other entities that constitute a threat to environmental safety.

The Ukrainian SSR cares for the environmental safety of its citizens, the genetic stock of its people and their young generation.

The Ukrainian SSR has the right to compensation for damages to the environment of Ukraine brought about by the acts of Union agencies.

VIII.   Cultural Development

The Ukrainian SSR independently decides issues of science, education and the cultural and spiritual development of the Ukrainian nation and guarantees to all nationalities living on the territory of the republic the right to free national and cultural development.

The Ukrainian SSR ensures the national and cultural rebirth of the Ukrainian nation, its historical consciousness and traditions, its national and ethnographic characteristics and the functioning of the Ukrainian language in all spheres of social activity.

The Ukrainian SSR sees to it that the national, cultural, spiritual and language needs of Ukrainians living outside of the republic's borders are satisfied.

The national, cultural and historical treasures on the territory of the Ukrainian SSR are the sole property of the people of the republic.

The Ukrainian SSR has the right to have those of its national, cultural and historical treasures that are found outside the borders of the Ukrainian SSR, returned to the ownership of the people of Ukraine.

IX.   External and Internal Security

The Ukrainian SSR has the right to its own armed forces.

The Ukrainian SSR has its own internal armies and organs of state security, which are subordinate to the Supreme Rada of the Ukrainian SSR.

The Ukrainian SSR determines how citizens of the republic are to perform their military service.

Citizens of the Ukrainian SSR perform their active military service, as a rule, on the territory of the republic and cannot be engaged for military purposes beyond its borders without the consent of the Supreme Rada of the Ukrainian SSR.

The Ukrainian SSR solemnly declares its intention of becoming, in the future, a permanently neutral state that does not participate in military blocs and adheres to three nuclear-free principles: not to accept, not to produce and not to acquire nuclear weapons.

X. International Relations

The Ukrainian SSR, as a principal of international law, conducts direct relations with other states, enters into agreements with them, exchanges diplomatic, consular and trade missions, and participates in the activities of international organizations to the full extent necessary in order to secure effectively the republic's national interests in the political, economic, ecological, informational, scientific, technical, cultural and sports spheres.

The Ukrainian SSR acts as an equal participant in international affairs, actively promotes the strengthening of world peace and international security and directly participates in the all-European process and in European structures.

The Ukrainian SSR recognizes the pre-eminence of universal human values over class values and the primacy of universally accepted standards of international law over standards of internal state law.

* * *

The relations of the Ukrainian SSR with other Soviet republics are built on the foundation of treaties entered into on the basis of the principles of equality, mutual respect and non-interference in internal affairs.

The Declaration is the foundation for a new Constitution and laws of Ukraine and defines the position of the republic in concluding international accords. The principles of the Declaration on the Sovereignty of Ukraine are to be used in the preparation of a new Union treaty.

Kyiv. July 16, 1990.

THE SUPREME RADA OF THE UKRAINIAN SSR

2. *"Telegramma Raketa" (Classified Soviet Armed Forces Dispatch) on the Activities of the Union of Officers of Ukraine (July 31, 1991)* [4 sheets]

ТЕЛЕГРАММА=РАКЕТА=

АБРИКОС, ВИТЯЗЬ, РЯБИНА, ГИТАРА, ДЕСНА, МЫС ДОЛИНА
НАЧАЛЬНИКАМ ВОЕННО-ПОЛИТИЧЕСКИХ ОРГАНОВ=

ЛЕГЕНДЫ 117 212 30 1201

В ПОРЯДКЕ ИНФОРМАЦИИ СООБЩАЮ О СОСТОЯВШЕМСЯ В КИЕВЕ СЪЕЗДЕ
ОФИЦЕРОВ УКРАИНЫ.
27-28 ИЮНЯ В КИЕВЕ СОСТОЯЛСЯ ОРГАНИЗОВАННЫЙ РУКОМ СЪЕЗД ОФИЦЕРОВ
УКРАИНЫ. ПО СООБЩЕНИЮ РУКОВОДСТВА СЪЕЗДА В ЕГО РАБОТЕ ПРИНЯЛО
УЧАСТИЕ 900 ЧЕЛОВЕК ИЗ ВСЕХ ОБЛАСТЕЙ УКРАИНЫ. ОБЪЕКТИВНО НЕ БОЛЕЕ
300 ЧЕЛОВЕК, В ТОМ ЧИСЛЕ ОКОЛО 10 ПРОЦЕНТОВ ОФИЦЕРЫ КАДРА,
ОСТАЛЬНЫЕ ОФИЦЕРЫ ЗАПАСА В ОСНОВНОМ ИЗ ЗАПАДНЫХ ОБЛАСТЕЙ УКРАИНЫ,
УЧАСТНИКИ РУХА.
        УДАЛОСЬ УСТАНОВИТЬ КОЛИЧЕСТВО ОФИЦЕРОВ КАДРА , ПРИНИМАВШИХ
УЧАСТИЕ В РАБОТЕ СЪЕЗДА: ПРИКВО-6 ЧЕЛ, ЧФ-3 ЧЕЛ, КВО-ОДВО-НЕТ.
СПИСКИ УТОЧНЯЮТСЯ.
        ДЛЯ ОСВЕЩЕНИЯ РАБОТЫ СЪЕЗДА НА НЕМ ОККРЕДИТОВАНО БОЛЕЕ 20
ЖУРНАЛИСТОВ РАЗЛИЧНЫХ СРЕДСТВ МАССОВОЙ ИНФОРМАЦИИ, РАДИО И
ТЕЛЕВИДЕНИЯ, В ТОМ ЧИСЛЕ И ЗАПАДА.
        ВОЕННЫМ СОВЕТОМ ОКРУГА И ВОЕННО-ПОЛИТИЧЕСКИМ УПРАВЛЕНИЕМ
ПРИНИМАЛИСЬ МЕРЫ С ЦЕЛЬЮ НЕДОПУЩЕНИЯ ПРОВЕДЕНИЯ СЪЕЗДА,
РАЗЪЯСНЕНИЮ ВОЕННОСЛУЖАЩИМ И ГРАЖДАНАМ УКРАИНЫ ЕГО ИСТИННОЙ СУТИ
И ПРЕДНАЗНАЧЕНИЯ.
        ВОПРОС С ПРАВОМОЧНОСТИ СЪЕЗДА И ЦЕЛЕСООБРАЗНОСТИ ЕГО
ПРОВЕДЕНИЯ БЫЛ ПОСТАВЛЕН ПЕРЕД РУКОВОДСТВОМ ВЕРХОВНОГО СОВЕТА
РЕСПУБЛИКИ. НО ТВЕРДО ВЫСКАЗАЛСЯ ПРОТИВ ЕГО ПРОВЕДЕНИЯ ТОЛЬКО
ПРЕДСЕДАТЕЛЬ ПАРЛАМЕНТСКОЙ КОМИССИИ ПО ВОПРОСАМ ОБОРОНЫ И
ГОСУДАРСТВЕННОЙ БЕЗОПАСНОСТИ ТОВ. ДУРАЙНЕЦ В.В., ОСТАЛЬНЫЕ
УКЛОНИЛИСЬ ОТ ПРИНЦИПИАЛЬНОЙ ОЦЕНКИ ПРЕДСТОЯЩЕГО МЕРОПРИЯТИЯ.
        НЕ ПРИНЕСЛА ЖЕЛАЕМЫХ РЕЗУЛЬТАТОВ И БЕСЕДА КОМАНДОВАНИЯ ОКРУГА
С РУКОВОДСТВОМ РУХА.
        В СВЯЗИ С ПРЕДСТОЯЩИМ СЪЕЗДОМ БЫЛО ПРОВЕДЕНО:
- СОВЕЩАНИЕ КОМАНДНО-ПОЛИТИЧЕСКОГО СОСТАВА,СОЕДИНЕНИЙ, ЧАСТЕЙ,
ВУЗОВ КИЕВСКОГО ГАРНИЗОНА,
- СОБРАНИЕ ПРЕДСТАВИТЕЛЕЙ ОФИЦЕРСКИХ СОБРАНИЙ КИЕВСКОГО ГАРНИЗОНА
НА КОТОРОМ БЫЛО ПРИНЯТО ОБРАЩЕНИЕ КО ВСЕМУ ОФИЦЕРСКОМУ СОСТАВУ
ОКРУГА,
- СКООРДИНИРОВАНЫ ДЕЙСТВИЯ СО СТОЯЩИМИ НА ТВЕРДЫХ ПОЗИЦИЯХ
СРЕДСТВАМИ МАССОВОЙ ИНФОРМАЦИИ И ОБЩЕСТВЕННЫМИ ОРГАНИЗАЦИЯМИ
УКРАИНЫ. ТЕКСТ ПРИНЯТОГО ОФИЦЕРАМИ ОБРАЩЕНИЯ ОПУБЛИКОВАН В ГАЗЕТАХ
,,ПРАВДА УКРАИНЫ'', ,,РАДЯНСЬКА УКРАИНА'', ,,РАБОЧАЯ ГАЗЕТА'',
,,КИЕВСКИЙ ВЕСТНИК'', ,,ПАТРИОТ БАТЬКИВЩИНЫ'', В ОКРУЖНОЙ ГАЗЕТЕ
,,ЛЕНИНСКОЕ ЗНАМЯ''. В ОБЛАСТНЫХ ГОРОДСКИХ И РАЙОННЫХ ГАЗЕТАХ
/ВСЕГО ОКОЛО 300/ ПО ЛИНИИ ТАСС-УКРИНФОРМ ОБРАЩЕНИЕ ОПУБЛИКОВАНО
В ИЗЛОЖЕНИИ

НР 19/129   В ШАРИКОВ-

224

[Translation from Russian; sheet 1, *continues*]
[Handwritten:]   <u>115</u>
           30   20 35
           (Signature)

TELEGRAM = "ROCKET"=

Apricot, Knight, Ashberry, Guitar, Desna, Cape, Valley

To the Chief Officers of the Military-Political Organs
[handwritten:]   To Comrade Yu. M. Shendrikov
            Summarize and prepare a report
                       (signature)
                       7-31-91
Legends 117 212 30 1201 =

RE: The Congress of the Union of Officers of Ukraine in Kyiv.
    The Congress of the Union of Officers of Ukraine organized by Rukh took place in Kyiv on 27–28 June. According to the Congress leadership 300 people from all regions of Ukraine participated in it, objectively—not more than 200 people, including some 10 percent officers on active duty, other reserve officers (mostly from the western regions of Ukraine), and Rukh members.
    We managed to establish the number of active duty officers participating in the Congress: Carpathian (Military District)—6 individuals, Black Sea Fleet—3, Kyiv and Odesa (Military Districts)- none. The lists are being verified.
    Over 20 journalists were accredited from various branches of the mass media, radio and television, including from the West, in order to report on the work of the Congress.
    The District Military Council and Military-Political Department had made efforts not to allow the Congress to take place, and to explain to the military personnel and citizens of Ukraine the Congress' true essence and goal.
    We raised the issue regarding the legality and propriety of the Congress to the republic's Supreme Soviet. However, only the chairperson of the Parliamentary Commission on Defense and National Security, Comrade V. V. Durdynets had firmly objected to the Congress, others evaded giving a categorical evaluation of the event at hand.
    Conversation between the District Command and the Rukh leadership did not yield the desired results.
    In anticipation of the Congress, we took the following measures:
– A meeting of the Kyiv Garrison Command-Political Corps of groups, units, military colleges,
– A meeting of the Kyiv Garrison officers meetings' representatives, at which an address to the entire [Military] District officer corps was adopted,
– Actions were coordinated with the mass media and public organizations of Ukraine that have hardened their positions. The text of the address to the Officer corps was published in the following newspapers: *Pravda Ukrainy, Radianska Ukraïna, Rabochaia Gazeta, Kievskii Vestnik, Patriot Batkivshchyny,* in the [Military] District newspaper *Leninskoe Znamia.* In oblast [regional], city, and raion [administrative district] newspapers (totaling about 300) the address was published in summarized form through the TASS-Ukrinform network.

Nr 19/129   V Sharikov— (signature)

ТЕЛЕГРАММА=РАКЕТА=

АБРИКОС ВИТЯЗЬ РЯБИНА ГИТАРА ДЕСНА МЫС ДОЛИНА
НАЧАЛЬНИКАМ ВОЕННО-ПОЛИТИЧЕСКИХ ОРГАНОВ=

ЛЕГЕНДЫ 118 291 30 1202=

БЫЛО ПРИНЯТО РЕШЕНИЕ ВОЗДЕРЖАТЬСЯ ОТ АКТИВНЫХ ДЕЙСТВИЙ СО
СТОРОНЫ ОФИЦЕРОВ В ДНИ ПРОВЕДЕНИЯ СЪЕЗДА. ЭТО СЫГРАЛО СВОЮ
ПОЛОЖИТЕЛЬНУЮ РОЛЬ, ТАК КАК ПРЕДСТАВИТЕЛИ МНОГИХ ,,ДЕМОКРАТИЧЕСКИХ
ИЗДАНИЙ ПЕРЕД НАЧАЛОМ СЪЕЗДА ОТКРОВЕННО ЖДАЛИ МАНИФЕСТАЦИЙ,
ПИКЕТИРОВАНИЯ, НАПЛЫВА БОЛЬШОГО КОЛИЧЕСТВА ОФИЦЕРОВ, ЧТО
ПОЗВОЛИЛО БЫ СПРОВОЦИРОВАТЬ КОНФЛИКТНЫЕ СИТУАЦИИ.
СЪЕЗД СОСТОЯЛСЯ В ЗДАНИИ РЕСПУБЛИКАНСКОГО ДОМА УЧИТЕЛЯ. ПРИ ЕГО
ОТКРЫТИИ И В ПОСЛЕДУЮЩИХ ВЫСТУПЛЕНИЯХ НЕОДНОКРАТНО ПОДЧЕРКИВАЛАСЬ
СИМВОЛИЧНОСТЬ ДАННОГО ФАКТА, Т.К. ИМЕННО ЗДЕСЬ В 1918 ГОДУ
ПРОХОДИЛИ ЗАСЕДАНИЯ НАРОДНОЙ РАДЫ УКРАИНЫ, ОТКАЗАВШЕЙСЯ ОТ
СОБСТВЕННОЙ АРМИИ, ЧТО ПРИВЕЛО ,,К ОККУПАЦИИ УКРАИНЫ БОЛЬШЕВИСТСКОЙ
РОССИЕЙ С ОДНОЙ СТОРОНЫ И ГЕРМАНИЕЙ И ПОЛЬШЕЙ С ДРУГОЙ''. ПОЭТОМУ
СЪЕЗД НАЧАЛСЯ ПОД ЛОЗУНГОМ ЧТО ЕМУ ПРЕДСТОИТ ИСПРАВИТЬ ОШИБКУ,
ДОПУЩЕННУЮ В 1918 Г.
СЪЕЗД РАССМОТРЕЛ ВОПРОСЫ:
-ПОЛИТИЧЕСКАЯ СИТУАЦИЯ НА УКРАИНЕ И ПРОБЛЕМЫ ВОЗРОЖДЕНИЯ
ВООРУЖЕННЫХ СИЛ,
-ГОСУДАРСТВЕННО-ПРАВОВЫЕ АСПЕКТЫ И ОСНОВЫ СОЗДАНИЯ
ВООРУЖЕННЫХ СИЛ,
-ПРАВОВАЯ И СОЦИАЛЬНАЯ ЗАЩИТА ВОЕННОСЛУЖАЩИХ.
БЫЛИ ОБСУЖДЕНЫ И ПРИНЯТЫ ПРОЕКТЫ КОНЦЕПЦИИ ВООРУЖЕННЫХ СИЛ
УКРАИНЫ, ЗАКОНА О СТАТУСЕ ВОЕННОСЛУЖАЩИХ, ПРОХОДЯЩИХ СЛУЖБУ НА
УКРАИНЕ, УКАЗА ПРЕЗИДИУМА ВЕРХОВНОГО СОВЕТА УССР ,,О МЕРАХ ПО
СОЦИАЛЬНОЙ ЗАЩИТЕ ВОЕННОСЛУЖАЩИХ, ПРОХОДЯЩИХ СЛУЖБУ НА УКРАИНЕ''.
В ОТНОШЕНИИ ПОСЛЕДНЕГО ДОКУМЕНТА БЫЛО ПОДЧЕРКНУТО, ЧТО ОН ДОЛЖЕН
БЫТЬ ПЕРВООЧЕРЕДНЫМ, ВЫНОСИМЫМ НА РАССМОТРЕНИЕ ОСЕННЕЙ СЕССИИ
ВС УССР.
НА СЪЕЗДЕ ИЗБРАН КОМИТЕТ СОЮЗА ОФИЦЕРОВ УКРАИНЫ. В СОСТАВ
КОМИТЕТА ИЗБРАНО 47 ЧЕЛОВЕК. ПРЕДСЕДАТЕЛЕМ СТАЛ В.МАРТИРОСЯН.
ПЕРВЫМ ЗАМЕСТИТЕЛЕМ-ИЗГНАННЫЙ ИЗ АРМИИ В 1989 ГОДУ,ИСКЛЮЧЕННЫЙ
ИЗ КПСС КАПИТАН ЗАПАСА ЧЕЧИЛО, ЗАМЕСТИТЕЛИ: ПОЛКОВНИК СКИПАЛЬСКИЙ
А.А.-КАДРОВЫЙ ОФИЦЕР ЗАМЕСТИТЕЛЬ НАЧАЛЬНИКА ОСОБОГО ОТДЕЛА АРМИИ
/Г.РОВНО/ ПОЛКОВНИК ЛАЗОРКИН ВИ-КАДРОВЫЙ ОФИЦЕР ПРЕПОДАВАТЕЛЬ
ЛЬВОВСКОГО ПОЛИТЕХНИЧЕСКОГО ИНСТИТУТА /ВОЕННАЯ КАФЕДРА/.
ПРИНЯТЫ УСТАВ, ОБРАЩЕНИЯ УЧАСТНИКОВ СЪЕЗДА К ВЕРХОВНОМУ СОВЕТУ
УСССР, К ОФИЦЕРАМ УКРАИНЫ, ПРОХОДЯЩИМ СЛУЖБУ НА ,,ЧУЖБИНЕ'',
ЗАЯВЛЕНИЕ УЧАСТНИКОВ СЪЕЗДА ОФИЦЕРОВ-ГРАЖДАН УКРАИНЫ.
С ПРИВЕТСТВИЕМ СЪЕЗДУ ВЫСТУПИЛИ ПРЕДСТАВИТЕЛИ ЭСТОНИИ, УКРАИН-
СКОЙ ДИАСПОРЫ В США, УКРАИНСКОЙ АВТОКЕФАЛЬНОЙ ПРАВОСЛАВНОЙ
ЦЕРКВИ /УАПЦ/
МНОГИЕ ВЫСТУПЛЕНИЯ НА СЪЕЗДЕ НОСИЛИ ЯРКО ВЫРАЖЕННЫЙ
АНТИКОММУНИСТИЧЕСКИЙ ХАРАКТЕР, СОДЕРЖАЛИ ТРЕБОВАНИЯ НЕМЕДЛЕННОЙ
ДЕПАРТИЗАЦИИ=

НР 19/129   ШАРИКОВ-

[Translation from Russian; sheet 2, *continues*]

TELEGRAM = "ROCKET"=

Apricot, Knight, Ashberry, Guitar, Desna, Cape, Valley

To the Chief Officers of the Military-Political Organs

LEGENDS 118 291 30 1202 =

During the Congress, the officers made the decision to refrain from open actions. This decision had a positive impact on the unfolding events, because before the Congress representatives of numerous "democratic" publications had openly anticipated manifestations, picketing, and large convocations of officers, which could provoke [open] conflicts.

The Congress took place in the Republican "House of the Teacher." The symbolic nature of this fact was emphasized many times at the opening and in further speeches during the Congress—it was exactly in this building that in 1918 the provisional assemblies of the People's Council [*Narodna Rada*]of Ukraine rejected creating an autonomous army, which led to "the occupation of Ukraine by Bolshevik Russia on one side and Germany and Poland on the other." Therefore the Congress began under the slogan of correcting the error made in 1918.

The Congress discussed the following issues:
– The political situation in Ukraine and the necessity of reviving a [Ukrainian] armed forces,
– State and legal issues and precedents surrounding the establishment of a [Ukrainian] armed forces,
– Legal and social protection of military personnel.

Drafts, including a concept of a Ukrainian armed forces, a law on the status of military personnel serving in Ukraine, and a decree of the Presidium of the Supreme Soviet of the UkrSSR "on measures of legal and social protection for military personnel" were discussed and adopted. With respect to the last document, it was emphasized that it should be given top priority and put before the autumn session of the Supreme Soviet of the Ukrainian SSR.

A forty-seven member [Central] Committee of the Union of Officers of Ukraine was elected at the Congress. V. Martirosian became Chairman; his First Deputy is Capt. (reserves) Chechilo, who was dishonorably discharged in 1989 and expelled from the CPSU; other deputies include Col. A. A. Skipalskii—an active duty officer and assistant commander of the Army Special Department (city of Rovno [Rivne]) Col. V. I. Lazorkin—an active duty officer and instructor at the Lviv Polytechnic University (Department of Military Studies).

Adopted were: by-laws, an appeal of the Congress participants to the Supreme Soviet of the Ukrainian SSR, an appeal to the officers of Ukraine who are serving "abroad," and a statement of the Congress participants who are citizens of Ukraine.

The Congress was greeted by representatives from Estonia, the Ukrainian diaspora in the USA, and the Ukrainian Autocephalous Orthodox Church (UAOC).

Many speeches at the Congress had a very distinct anti-communist flavor, containing demands for[…]=

Nr 19/129   Sharikov–

```
                ТЕЛЕГРАММА=РАКЕТА=


АБРИКОС ВИТЯЗЬ РЯБИНА ГИТАРА ДЕСНА МЫС ДОЛИНА
НАЧАЛЬНИКАМ ВОЕННО-ПОЛИТИЧЕСКИХ ОРГАНОВ=


ЛЕГЕНДЫ 119 288 30 1203=


АРМИИ,КАК НЕОБХОДИМОГО УСЛОВИЯ СОЗДАНИЯ СОБСТВЕННЫХ ВООРУЖЕННЫХ
СИЛ УКРАИНЫ.
    ОСОБОЙ ТЕНДЕНЦИОЗНОСТЬЮ  ОТЛИЧАЛИСЬ ВЫСТУПЛЕНИЯ ПОЛКОВНИКА
В.МАРТИРОСЯНА /ВЫСТУПАЛ ТРИЖДЫ/ ОН ВЫСТУПИЛ С РЕЗКИМИ НАПАДКАМИ
НА РУКОВОДСТВО МИНИСТЕРСТВА ОБОРОНЫ СССР, ,,КАК ОРГАН НЕ ЖЕЛАЮЩИЙ
РЕШАТЬ СОЦИАЛЬНЫЕ И ПРАВОВЫЕ ПРОБЛЕМЫ ВОЕННОСЛУЖАЩИХ'', ЗАЯВИЛ О
НЕОБХОДИМОСТИ НЕМЕДЛЕННОЙ ОТСТАВКИ ВСЕХ ЗАМЕСТИТЕЛЕЙ МИНИСТРА
ОБОРОНЫ, ЗАМЕНЫ ГЛАВКОМОВ, КОМАНДУЮЩИХ ОКРУГАМИ И НАЗНАЧЕНИЯ ИХ
ВЕРХОВНЫМ СОВЕТОМ РЕСПУБЛИКИ, РОСПУСКЕ ВОЕННО-ПОЛИТИЧЕСКИХ ОРГАНОВ,
НЕУКОСНИТЕЛЬНО ИСПОЛНЯЮЩИХ ВОЛЮ КПСС.
    В КАТЕГОРИЧНОЙ ФОРМЕ В ЕГО ВЫСТУПЛЕНИЯХ БЫЛО СКАЗАНО О ТОМ,
ЧТО ВСЕ ,,ГОРЯЧИЕ ТОЧКИ'' В СТРАНЕ СПЛАНИРОВАНЫ ЦЕНТРОМ И СЛЕДУЮЩЕЙ
БУДЕТ УКРАИНА, ЕСЛИ АРМИЯ НЕ БУДЕТ ПОДЧИНЕНА ВЕРХОВНОМУ СОВЕТУ
РЕСПУБЛИКИ.
    ОСОБОЙ АГРЕССИВНОСТЬЮ ОТЛИЧАЛОСЬ ВЫСТУПЛЕНИЕ ПОЛКОВНИКА ЗАПАСА
КУЗНЕЦОВА, ЛИЧНОСТЬ КОТОРОГО УТОЧНЯЕТСЯ.
    ОСНОВОЙ БОЛЬШИНСТВА ВЫСТУПЛЕНИЙ БЫЛА СПЕКУЛЯЦИЯ НА ПРОБЛЕМАХ
СОЦИАЛЬНОЙ И ПРАВОВОЙ ЗАЩИЩЕНОСТИ ВОЕННОСЛУЖАЩИХ И ЧЛЕНОВ СЕМЕЙ,
КАК ГЛАВНОГО ФАКТОРА, СВИДЕТЕЛЬСТВУЮЩЕГО О НЕСПОСОБНОСТИ ЦЕНТРА
РЕШАТЬ ЭТИ ПРОБЛЕМЫ И ВОЗМОЖНОСТИ ИХ ПОЛНОГО РЕШЕНИЯ ТОЛЬКО
ВЕРХОВНЫМ СОВЕТОМ УССР.
    ВСЯ РАБОТА СЪЕЗДА, ВЫСТУПЛЕНИЯ ЕГО ДЕЛЕГАТОВ, ПРИНЯТЫЕ НА НЕМ
ДОКУМЕНТЫ ПРЕТЕНДУЮТ НА ОРИГИНАЛЬНОСТЬ И ИМЕЮТ ГЛАВНУЮ ЦЕЛЬ-
ТОРПЕДИРОВАНИЕ СОЮЗНОГО ДОГОВОРА, РАСТАСКИВАНИЕ АРМИИ ПО
НАЦИОНАЛЬНЫМ КВАРТИРАМ.
    КАДРОВЫЕ ОФИЦЕРЫ БОЕВЫХ ЧАСТЕЙ,СОЕДИНЕНИЙ, ВВУЗОВ И ВОЕНКОМАТОВ
ОКРУГА,ВЕТЕРАНСКАЯ ОБЩЕСТВЕННОСТЬ РЕШИТЕЛЬНО ПРОТЕСТУЕТ ПРОТИВ
РЕШЕНИЙ СЪЕЗДА, ВЫСТУПАЮТ ЗА ЕДИНЫЕ ВООРУЖЕННЫЕ СИЛЫ.
    СЪЕЗД ПОКАЗАЛ , ЧТО РУХ СТРОГО ПРИДЕРЖИВАЕТСЯ СВОЕЙ НОВОЙ
ТАКТИКИ НА ПЕРЕХОД ОТ КОНФРОНТАЦИИ С АРМИЕЙ К ИСПОЛЬЗОВАНИЮ
ПРОБЛЕМ ВОЕННОСЛУЖАЩИХ В СВОИХ ИНТЕРЕСАХ И ПРИВЛЕЧЕНИЮАРМИИ НА
СВОЮ СТОРОНУ.
    СОЗДАНИЕ КОМИТЕТА ОФИЦЕРОВ УКРАИНЫ, КАК ОБЩЕСТВЕННОЙ
ОРГАНИЗАЦИИ ПОЗВОЛИТ РУХУ АКТИВИЗИРОВАТЬ ДЕЙСТВИЯ ПО СОЗДАНИЮ
УКРАИНСКОЙ АРМИИ, ОКАЗЫВАТЬ СЕРЬЕЗНОЕ ДАВЛЕНИЕ НА ВЕРХОВНЫЙ СОВЕТ С
ЦЕЛЬЮ ПРИНЯТИЯ ЗАКОНОВ ОБ АРМИИ И ВОИНСКОЙ СЛУЖБЕ НА УКРАИНЕ.
    СЪЕЗД ПОКАЗАЛ, ЧТО СИЛЫ, ВЫСТУПАЮЩИЕ ЗА СОЗДАНИЕ УКРАИНСКОЙ
АРМИИ, ЗА ПОСЛЕДНИЙ ГОД ПРИОБРЕЛИ НЕМАЛОЕ КОЛЛИЧЕСТВО СТОРОННИКОВ,
В ТОМ ЧИСЛЕ СРЕДИ ОФИЦЕРОВ ЗАПАСА.
    МАТЕРИАЛЫ И ДОКУМЕНТЫ СЪЕЗДА ИМЕЮТ ЯРКО ВЫРАЖЕННУЮ
ПСИХОЛОГИЧЕСКУЮ


НР 19/129          Б.ШАРИКОВ-
```

[Translation from Russian; sheet 3, *continues*]

TELEGRAM = "ROCKET"=

Apricot, Knight, Ashberry, Guitar, Desna, Cape, Valley

To the Chief Officers of the Military-Political Organs

Legends 119 288 30 1203 =

[...] abolition of the Party within the army as a pre-requisite condition for establishing a national Ukrainian armed forces.

Col. V. Martirosian (who made three speeches) spoke with marked fervor. He sharply attacked the USSR Defense Ministry leadership, as an "institution which does not want to deal with the social and legal problems of military personnel." He demanded the immediate resignation of all of the deputies to the minister of defense, and the replacement of chief commanders and district commanders—with their replacements to be appointed by the republic's Supreme Soviet. He also advocated the disbanding of the military-political organs, which strictly follow the will of the CPSU.

In no uncertain terms, his speech stated that all the "hot spots" in the country were instigated by the center, and that the next would be Ukraine if the army was not placed under the authority of the republic's Supreme Soviet.

An especially aggressive speech was made by a reserve colonel, Kuznetsov, whose identity is now being checked on.

At their core, the majority of the speeches took advantage of the problems of social and legal protection for military personnel and members of their families as a major factor that shows the center's inability to deal with those problems and the possibility for their complete resolution only by the Ukrainian Supreme Soviet.

The activities of the Congress, speeches by delegates, and the documents that were adopted purport to be organic and sincere and have as their main goal the torpedoing of the Union Treaty, and dividing up the army into national units.

Active-duty officers of combat units, [military] groups, [military] colleges, and the district military commissariats, as well as the veteran community all unequivocally oppose the Congress' resolutions and stand for a unified armed forces.

The Congress demonstrated that Rukh strictly follows its new tactics of transition from confrontation with the army to using the problems of military personnel to its advantage and drawing the army to its side.

Establishing the Committee of Officers of Ukraine as a public organization will allow Rukh to boost its activities on establishing a Ukrainian army and to render serious pressure on the Supreme Soviet to pass laws on the armed forces and military service in Ukraine.

The Congress demonstrated that within the past year forces advocating the establishment of a Ukrainian army have gained a significant number of supporters, including reserve officers.

The Congress materials have a distinct emotional [...]

Nr 19/129   B. [*sic*] Sharikov -

ТЕЛЕГРАММА=РАКЕТА=

АБРИКОС ВИТЯЗЬ РЯБИНА ГИТАРА ДЕСНА МЫС ДОЛИНА
НАЧАЛЬНИКАМ ВОЕННО-ПОЛИТИЧЕСКИХ ОРГАНОВ=

ЛЕГЕНДЫ 120 55 30 1204=

НАПРАВЛЕННОСТЬ, СВЯЗАННУЮ С ПРОБЛЕМАМИ СЛУЖБЫ И ЖИЗНИ ОФИЦЕРСКОГО
СОСТАВА И ПОЭТОМУ ТРЕБУЮТ НЕМАЛЫХ ДОПОЛНИТЕЛЬНЫХ УСИЛИЙ ПО
РАЗЪЯСНЕНИЮ ВСЕМ КАТЕГОРИЯМ ВОЕННОСЛУЖАЩИХ ЕГО ИСТИННОГО
ХАРАКТЕРА И НАЗНАЧЕНИЯ.
   В СВЯЗИ С ЭТИМ КОМАНДОВАНИЕ И ВОЕННО-ПОЛИТИЧЕСКОЕ УПРАВЛЕНИЕ
ОКРУГА ПРЕДПОЛАГАЕТ ПРОВЕСТИ РЯД МЕРОПРИЯТИЙ ПО РАЗЪЯСНЕНИЮ
СОДЕРЖАНИЯ СЪЕЗДА И НЕЙТРАЛИЗАЦИИ В СРЕДЕ ВОЕННОСЛУЖАЩИХ
ВОЗМОЖНЫХ ПОСЛЕДСТВИЙ ЕГО РЕШЕНИЙ=

НР 19/129   Б ШАРИКОВ-

[Translation from Russian; sheet 4, *conclusion*]

TELEGRAM = "ROCKET"=

Apricot, Knight, Ashberry, Guitar, Desna, Cape, Valley

To the Chief Officers of the Military-Political Organs

Legends 120 55 30 1204=

[…] character that is connected with the problems in the officer corps' service and in their [personal] lives. Because of this fact, it will require significant additional effort to [overcome the emotional appeal of the Congress in order to] reveal the true character and purpose of the Congress to all levels of military personnel.

Taking into consideration the above-mentioned facts, the District Command and Military-Political Department are planning to take a series of steps to clarify the Congress' content and to diminish possible results deriving from its resolutions among military personnel =

Nr 19/129   B. [*sic*] Sharikov -

3. *Decree of the Parliament (Verkhovna Rada) of Ukraine Regarding Military Formations in Ukraine (August 24, 1991)* [1 sheet]

П О С Т А Н О В А
ВЕРХОВНОЇ РАДИ УКРАЇНИ
~~Верховної Ради Української РСР~~

<u>Про військові формування на Україні</u>

Верховна Рада України   п о с т а н о в л я є:

1. Підпорядкувати всі військові формування, дислоковані на території республіки, Верховній Раді України.

2. Утворити Міністерство оборони України.

3. Урядові України приступити до створення Збройних Сил України, республіканської гвардії та підрозділу охорони Верховної Ради, Кабінету Міністрів і Національного банку України.

Голова Верховної Ради
України   Л.КРАВЧУК

м.К и ї в
24 серпня 1991 року
№ 1431-ХІІ

[Translation from Ukrainian]

(STATE EMBLEM OF THE UKRAINIAN S.S.R.)

DECREE
of the Parliament of Ukraine
[stricken out: Parliament of the Ukrainian SSR]

On Military Units in Ukraine

The Parliament of Ukraine hereby *decrees:*

1. To place all military units, stationed on the territory of the [Ukrainian] Republic under the authority of the Parliament of Ukraine.

2. To establish the Ministry of Defense of Ukraine.

3. That the Government of Ukraine should commence establishing a Ukrainian Armed Forces, National Guard, and a Security Detachment responsible for the protection of the Parliament, Cabinet of Ministers, and National Bank of Ukraine.

Chairperson,
the Parliament of Ukraine   L. KRAVCHUK

(SEAL)

City of Kyiv

August 24, 1991

No. 1431-XII

[signature] August 24, 1991   [signature] August 24, 1991

4. *Decree of the Parliament (Verkhovna Rada) of Ukraine Regarding the Minister of Defense of Ukraine (September 3, 1991)* [1 sheet]

ПОСТАНОВА

Верховної Ради України

Про Міністра оборони України

Верховна Рада України постановляє:

Призначити Міністром оборони України генерал-майора МОРОЗОВА Костянтина Петровича.

Голова Верховної Ради   Л.КРАВЧУК
        України

    м.К и ї в
3 вересня 1991 року
  № 1472-XII

[Translation from Ukrainian]

(STATE EMBLEM OF THE UKRAINIAN S.S.R.)

RESOLUTION
of the Parliament of Ukraine

On the Defense Minister of Ukraine

The Parliament of Ukraine hereby *decrees:*

That Major General Kostiantyn Petrovych MOROZOV be appointed the minister of defense of Ukraine.

Chairperson,
the Parliament of Ukraine   L. KRAVCHUK

(SEAL)

City of Kyiv

3 September 1991

No. 1472-XII

5. *Decree of the Cabinet of Ministers of Ukraine on the Question of the Ministry of Defense of Ukraine (September 24, 1991)* [1 sheet]

Міністерству оборони України

КАБІНЕТ МІНІСТРІВ УКРАЇНИ

ПОСТАНОВА

від 24 вересня 1991 р. № 224

Київ

Питання Міністерства оборони України

Кабінет Міністрів України ПОСТАНОВЛЯЄ:

I. У зв"язку із створенням Міністерства оборони України ліквідувати Державний комітет України з військових справ.

Міністерству оборони України забезпечити відповідно до чинного законодавства працевлаштування працівників зазначеного Комітету, маючи на увазі максимальне залучення їх до роботи в центральному апараті Міністерства.

2. Міністерству оборони України подати Кабінету Міністрів України до 15 жовтня ц.р. погоджений з Міністерством юстиції України проект Положення про Міністерство та пропозиції щодо структури та чисельності його центрального апарату.

3. Розмістити Міністерство оборони України за адресою: м. Київ, вул. Орджонікідзе, 6-8.

Прем'єр-міністр України   В.ФОКІН

Державний секретар
Кабінету Міністрів України   В.ПЄХОТА

Інд.29

236

[Translation from Ukrainian]

To the Defense Ministry of Ukraine.

(STAMPED:)   Entry # 665
           09-25-1991

(STATE EMBLEM OF THE UKRAINIAN S.S.R.)

CABINET OF MINISTERS OF UKRAINE

DECREE
No. 224 as of 24 September 1991

Kyiv

On a Ministry of Defense of Ukraine

The Cabinet of Ministers of Ukraine hereby *decrees:*

1. That the State Committee of Ukraine on Military Affairs be dissolved, in view of the establishment of the Ministry of Defense of Ukraine.

The Ministry of Defense of Ukraine is to provide, in accordance with existing law, employment to the employees of the above-mentioned Committee, and preferrably involving them as much as possible in the work of the Ministry at its central apparatus.

2. That the Ministry of Defense of Ukraine submit to the Cabinet of Ministers of Ukraine, by October 15 of this year and in accordance with [stipulations of] the Ministry of Justice, draft Ministry regulations and proposals regarding the structure and number of personnel of its central apparatus.

3. That the premises for the Defense Ministry of Ukraine be assigned at the following address: City of Kyiv, Ordzhonikidze Street, 6-8.

	Prime Minister of Ukraine	V. FOKIN
(SEAL)		
	State Secretary of the Cabinet of Ministers of Ukraine	V. PIEKHOTA

Ind. 29

6. *List of the Organizational Group for the Creation of the Ministry of Defense of Ukraine in 1991* [1 sheet]

С П И С О К

оргтруппы по созданию Министерства обороны
Украины в 1991 году
[сентябрь - декабрь] Добровольцы.

№№ пп	Воинское звание, фамилия, имя, отчество
1.	Генерал-лейтенант БИЖАН Иван Васильевич
2.	Генерал-лейтенант ЖИВИЦА Георгий Владимирович
3.	Генерал-майор ПАНКРАТОВ Георгий Александрович
4.	Генерал-майор ГРЕЧАНИНОВ Вадим Александрович
5.	Генерал-майор ПАЛАМАРЧУК Анатолий Васильевич
6.	Генерал-майор АВДЕЕВ Григорий Григорьевич
7.	Генерал-майор ШТОПЕНКО Иван Иванович
8.	Генерал-майор ПРОКОФЬЕВ Юрий Михайлович
9.	Полковник МУЛЯВА Владимир Саввович
10.	Полковник КОКОЙКО Иван Михайлович
11.	Полковник ЛАЗОРКИН Виталий Ильич
12.	Полковник ГУРА Виктор Иванович
13.	Полковник СКИПАЛЬСКИЙ Александр Александрович
14.	Полковник НИКОЛЬСКИЙ Александр Вадимович
15.	Полковник БРАГАР Павел Аникеевич
16.	Полковник ХАЛЕЦКИЙ Иван Павлович
17.	Полковник Матирка Василий Данилович
18.	Полковник ПИЛИПЧУК Валерий Леонидович
19.	Подполковник ИЩЕНКО Игорь Владимирович
20.	Подполковник КУЗНЕЦОВ Георгий Васильевич
21.	Майор КЛУБАНЬ Александр Михайлович
22.	Майор КАРАСЕНКОВ Геннадий Александрович
23.	Майор ИЛЬЮЩЕНКО Юрий Михайлович
24.	Майор БИЩУК Сергей Иванович
25.	Майор ФЕДОРЕНКО Александр Михайлович
26	Капитан 3-го ранг.ТЕНЮХ Игорь Иосифович
27.	Капитан УСТИНОВ Юрий Гаврилович
28.	Старший лейтенант АНУФРИЕВ Руслан Анатольевич
29.	Лейтенант ГАЙДАМАКА Александр Викторович
30.	Старший прапорщ. УТЕНИН Владимир Дмитриевич

238

[Translation from Russian; *Ukrainian forms of names are given in the index*]

[*Handwritten in Ukrainian:*] They were the first

L I S T of the
Organizational group for establishing the Defense Ministry of Ukraine in 1991

[*Handwritten in Russian:*] [September – December] Volunteers

##	Military Rank, Last Name, First Name, Patronimic Name	
1.	Lieutenant General	BIZHAN Ivan Vasilievich
2.	Lieutenant General	ZHIVITSA Georgii Vladimirovich
3.	Major General	PANKRATOV Georgii Aleksandrovich
4.	Major General	GRECHANINOV Vadim Aleksandrovich
5.	Major General	PALAMARCHUK Anatolii Vasilievich
6.	Major General	AVDEEV Grigorii Grigorievich
7.	Major General	SHTOPENKO Ivan Ivanovich
8.	Major General	PROKOFIEV Iurii Mikhailovich
9.	Colonel	-MULIAVA Vladimir Savvovich
10.	Colonel	KOKOIKO Ivan Mikhailovich
11.	Colonel	-LAZORKIN Viktor Ilich
12.	Colonel	GURA Viktor Ivanovich
13.	Colonel	-SKIPALSKII Aleksandr Aleksandrovich
14.	Colonel	NIKOLSKII Aleksandr Vadimovich
15.	Colonel	BRAGAR Pavel Anikeevich
16.	Colonel	KHALETSKII Ivan Pavlovich
17.	Colonel	Matirka Vasilii Danilovich
18.	Colonel	-PILIPCHUK Valerii Leonidovich
19.	Lieutenant Colonel	ISHCHENKO Igor Vladimirovich
20.	Lieutenant Colonel	KUZNETSOV Georgii Vasilievich
21.	Major	KLUBAN Aleksandr Mikhailovich
22.	Major	KARASENKOV Gennadii Aleksandrovich
23.	Major	ILIUSHCHENKO Iurii Mikhailovich
24.	Major	BISHCHUK Sergei Ivanovich
[*Handwritten in Russian:*] August—		
25.	Major	FEDORENKO Aleksandr Mikhailovich
26.	Captain 3rd Grade[*]	TENIUKH Igor Iosifovich
27.	Captain	USTINOV Iurii Gavrilovich
28.	Senior Lieutenant	ANUFRIEV Ruslan Anatolievich
29.	Lieutenant	GAIDAMAKA Aleksandr Viktorovich
30.	Chief Warrant Officer	UTENIN Vladimir Dmitrievich

[*Handwritten:*] MOROZOV

[* i.e., Lieutenant Commander, Navy]

7. *Decree of the Presidium of the Parliament (Verkhovna Rada) of Ukraine Regarding Placing Certain USSR Military Assets and Units under the Authority of Ukraine (October 7, 1991)* [2 sheets]

У К А З

Президії Верховної Ради України

Про підпорядкування Україні дислокованих на її
території військових частин і підрозділів залізничних військ СРСР, військ урядового зв"язку
КДБ СРСР і Цивільної оборони СРСР та військової
техніки і майна Міністерства оборони СРСР, пере-
даних безоплатно навчальним організаціям Товариства сприяння обороні України

Президія Верховної Ради України постановляє:

I. Відповідно до Постанови Верховної Ради України від 24
серпня 1991 року "Про військові формування на Україні" переве-
сти у відання України всі дислоковані на її території військові частини і підрозділи залізничних військ СРСР, військ урядового зв"язку КДБ СРСР і Цивільної оборони СРСР, їх органи
управління з озброєнням і матеріально-технічною базою та військову техніку і майно Міністерства оборони СРСР, передані
безоплатно навчальним організаціям Товариства сприяння обороні
України.

2. Підпорядкувати:

— Міністерству оборони України військові частини і підрозділи залізничних військ СРСР та військову техніку і майно
Міністерства оборони СРСР, передані безоплатно навчальним
організаціям Товариства сприяння обороні України;

— Службі урядового зв"язку, яка переведена у відання
Верховної Ради України, військові частини і підрозділи урядового зв"язку КДБ СРСР;

— Кабінету Міністрів України штаби та військові частини
і підрозділи військ Цивільної оборони СРСР.

240

[Translation from Ukrainian; sheet 1, *continues*]

(STATE EMBLEM OF THE UKRAINIAN S.S.R.)

DECREE
of the Parliament of Ukraine

On Placing the Military Units and Detachments of the USSR Railroad Troops, the USSR KGB Government Communication Signal Troops, the USSR Civil Defense [Civil Militia], stationed on the Ukrainian territory, and military matériel and property of the USSR Ministry of Defense, transferred without charge to the training organizations of the Society for the Defense of Ukraine, under the authority of Ukraine

The Presidium of the Parliament of Ukraine hereby *decrees:*

1. Pursuant to the Resolution of the Parliament of Ukraine "On Military Units in Ukraine" as of August 24, 1991, military units and detachments of the USSR Railroad Troops, the USSR KGB Government Communication Signal Troops, the USSR Civil Defense, stationed on the Ukrainian territory, with their command, armaments and military matériel, military equipment and property of the USSR Ministry of Defense that were transferred without charge to the training organizations of the Society for the Defense of Ukraine, are to be placed under the authority of Ukraine.

2. Assign the following:

- The Defense Ministry of Ukraine to be in charge of the military units and detachments of the USSR Railroad Troops, military equipment and property of the USSR Ministry of Defense that were transferred without charge to the training organizations of the Society for the Defense of Ukraine;

- The Government Communications Service, which has been subordinated to the Parliament of Ukraine, to be in charge of the military units and detachments of the USSR KGB Government Communication Signal Troops;

- The Cabinet of Ministers of Ukraine to be in charge of the staffs, military units and detachments of the USSR Civil Defense.

2

3. Кабінету Міністрів України провести переговори з Міністерством оборони СРСР, КДБ СРСР та командуванням залізничних військ СРСР і Цивільної оборони СРСР щодо вироблення та здійснення механізму реалізації цього Указу.

4. Кабінету Міністрів України забезпечити фінансування підготовки спеціалістів з числа призовників для потреб Міністерства оборони України, Республіканської гвардії України і прикордонних військ України в навчальних організаціях Товариства сприяння обороні України, безоплатне забезпечення їх військовою і спеціальною технікою та майном.

5. Указ набирає чинності з моменту прийняття.

Голова Верховної Ради
України

Л.КРАВЧУК

м.Київ
7 жовтня 1991 року
№ 1608-XII

[Translation from Ukrainian; sheet 2, *conclusion*]

3. The Cabinet of Ministers of Ukraine is to conduct negotiations with the USSR Ministry of Defense, the USSR KGB and the commands of the USSR Railroad Troops and the USSR Civil Defense, regarding the implementation of this Decree.

4. The Cabinet of Ministers of Ukraine is to provide funding for training specialists from among recruits in order to meet the needs of the Defense Ministry of Ukraine, the Republican [National] Guard of Ukraine, and the Border Guard of Ukraine within the training organizations of the Society for the Defense of Ukraine, as well as the provision, without charge, of military and special equipment and property.

5. This Decree becomes effective at the moment of its adoption.

Chairperson,
the Parliament of Ukraine   L. KRAVCHUK

(SEAL)

City of Kyiv

7 October 1991

No. 1608-XII

8. *Decree of the Parliament of Ukraine (Verkhovna Rada) on a Defense Concept and the Building of an Armed Forces of Ukraine (October 11, 1991)* [2 sheets]

ПОСТАНОВА
Верховної Ради України

Про Концепцію оборони та будівництва
Збройних Сил України

Верховна Рада України п о с т а н о в л я є :

1. Схвалити подану Кабінетом Міністрів України і Комісією Верховної Ради України з питань оборони і державної безпеки Концепцію оборони та будівництва Збройних Сил України.

2. Кабінету Міністрів України, Комісії Верховної Ради України з питань оборони і державної безпеки у місячний строк розробити воєнну доктрину України та внести на розгляд Верховної Ради України.

3. Президії Верховної Ради України утворити Державну комісію повноважних представників України для ведення переговорів з Міністерством оборони СРСР та підготовки міждержавних угод з усього комплексу питань, пов"язаних з створенням Збройних Сил України.

4. Доручити Президії Верховної Ради України призначити за поданням Кабінету Міністрів України повноважного представника України для роботи в Комітеті по підготовці і проведенню воєнної реформи при Державній Раді СРСР.

5. Надати газеті "Народна армія" /правоприємниця газети Київського військового округу "Ленинское знамя"/ статус центрального органу Міністерства оборони України.

6. Вважати за доцільне проекти законів України, які випливають з Концепції оборони та будівництва Збройних Сил України, про оборону України, про Збройні Сили України, про

244

[Translation from Ukrainian; sheet 1, *continues*]

(STAMPED:)   Entry # 1354
      10-21-1991

(STATE EMBLEM OF THE UKRAINIAN S.S.R.)

RESOLUTION
of the Parliament of Ukraine

On a Defense Concept and the Building of an Armed Forces of Ukraine

The Parliament of Ukraine hereby *decrees:*

1. To approve the Defense Concept and the Building of the Ukrainian Armed Forces, as submitted by the Cabinet of Ministers of Ukraine and the Commission of the Parliament of Ukraine on Issues of Defense and National Security.

2. The Cabinet of Ministers of Ukraine and the Commission of the Parliament of Ukraine on Issues of Defense and National Security are to elaborate a military doctrine of Ukraine within one month and submit it for review by the Parliament of Ukraine.

3. The Presidium of the Parliament of Ukraine is to establish the State Commission of Plenipotentiary Representatives of Ukraine to conduct negotiations with the USSR Ministry of Defense and prepare a package of inter-governmental agreements in conjunction with the creation of the Ukrainian Armed Forces.

4. To authorize the Presidium of the Parliament of Ukraine to appoint, upon recommendation of the Cabinet of Ministers of Ukraine, a plenipotentiary representative of Ukraine to work within the Committee on Preparation and Implementation of Military Reform under the State Soviet of the USSR.

5. To assign to the newspaper *Narodna Armiia* [The People's Army] (the successor of the newspaper of the Kyiv Military District *Leninskoe Znamia* [Lenin's Flag]) the status of the main publication of the Defense Ministry of Ukraine.

6. To publish in national and oblast newspapers and open for public discussion those Ukrainian draft acts that derive from the Concept of Defense and Building the Ukrainian Armed Forces, On the Defense of Ukraine, On the Ukrainian Armed Forces, [...]

2

Республіканську гвардію України, про державний кордон України,
про прикордонні війська України, про соціальний і правовий за-
хист військовослужбовців, які проходять службу на території
України, та членів їх сімей, про альтернативну /трудову/ службу
опублікувати в республіканських та обласних газетах для народного
обговорення.

Голова Верховної Ради
України

Л.КРАВЧУК

М. Київ

II жовтня 1991 року

№ 1658-XII

[Translation from Ukrainian; sheet 2, *conclusion*]

2

[...] On the National Guard of Ukraine, On the state border of Ukraine, On the Border Guards of Ukraine, On the social and juridical defense of military servicemen who serve on the territory of Ukraine, and members of their families, and on alternative (labor) service.

Chairperson,
the Parliament of Ukraine   L. KRAVCHUK

(SEAL)

City of Kyiv

11 October 1991

No. 1659-XII

9. *Speech of Minister of Defense Morozov at the Congress of the Union of Officers of Ukraine (November 2–3, 1991)* [*extract*, 3 sheets]

II з'їзд СОУ
2-3 листопада 1991 року

Тезисы
выступления Министра обороны
Украины на с"езде Союза
офицеров Украины

Уважаемые делегаты с"езда!

Уважаемые гости!

Мы имели честь в этот исторический период истории Украины быть причастными к свершению народа по созданию государства Украина, по созданию ее ВС.

24 октября этого года в Министерстве юстиции в торжественной обстановке состоялась регистрация новой общественной организации Союза офицеров Украины, с чем хочу поздравить всех присутствующих в этом зале.

Большая честь и заслуга офицеров, нам предстоит еще оправдать доверие народа создать условия для спокойного ... нар. в спец. ист-ие вершить свои преобразования. ...

Но ваша, еще не зарегистрированная организация, стала широко известной на Украине и за ее пределами добрыми делами многих ее членов.

Официальному признанию Союза офицеров Украины предшествовала самоотверженная теоретическая и организаторская работа в условиях тоталитарного режима многих основателей организации. В числе первых из них: Виталий Чечило, Валентин Пилипчук, Виталий Лазоркин, ныне состоящие в руководстве Союза офицеров Украины.

Несмотря на гонения, дискредитацию и увольнения активистов демократического движения в армии, была одержана значительная победа прогрессивных сил - проведение учредительного с"езда Союза офицеров - граждан Украины.

Всего три месяца прошло со дня открытия первого с"езда, казалось бы срок для иных времен небольшой, но в жизни народа

[Translation from Russian; sheet 1, *continues*]

[*Handwritten in Ukrainian:*]
II Congress of the UOU
2–3 November 1991

Theses
of the speech of the Ukrainian Defense Minister
at the Congress of the Union
of Officers of Ukraine

Dear Delegates of the Congress!
Dear Guests!

[*Handwritten:*]
We have the honor, at this period of Ukrainian history, of being part of the achievements of the people in creating the state of Ukraine, and establishing its armed forces.

It is to the great honor and credit of us officers that we continue to justify the people's trust in us to maintain stability in their lives. [We must] implement our changes responsibly.

[*Typed:*]
On October 24 of this year the registration of a new public organization, the Union of Officers of Ukraine, took place at the Ministry of Justice in a gala occasion. I would like to congratulate the audience in this assembly on that.

However, while unregistered, your organization still was widely known throughout Ukraine and beyond for the good deeds of its numerous members.

The official recognition of the Union of Officers of Ukraine followed dedicated theoretic and organizational work of the many founders of the organization—work that was conducted under a totalitarian regime Among the first to undertake this work were Vitalii Chechilo, Valentin Pilipchuk, and Vitalii Lazorkin, now leaders of the Union of Officers of Ukraine.

Despite the persecutions, defamation, and discharge from service of the democratic activists within the army, a significant victory of progressive forces was achieved—carrying out the Constituent Congress of the Union of Officers of Ukraine/Citizens of Ukraine.

Only three months have passed since the opening day of that first congress, seemingly a short period in other times, but in the lives of the people of [...]

249

2

Украины это поистине революционный период, в дни которого спресованы десятилетия пробуждения.

Одним из ударов набата, пробудившего Украину, стало создание Союза офицеров, вызвавшего переполох и замешательство в стане консерваторов. Учредительный с"езд явился катализатором в действиях сил, осуществивших государственный переворот. Августовские события наглядно показали, что Украина оказалась полностью беззащитной перед антиконституционными действиями лиц, направленных на насильственную смену государственного строя с использованием Вооруженных Сил, дислоцированных на территории Украины.

Руководство Украины не имело никакой информации о намерениях и действиях армии. Для суверенного государства это не нормальное явление.

Под влиянием смертельной опасности, нависшей над демократией, Верховный Совет Украины утвердил Акт провозглашения независимости Украины и принял ряд постановлений, предписывающих правительству развернуть работу по созданию собственных Вооруженных Сил Украины и Республиканской гвардии, выполнив, таким образом, одно из требований Союза офицеров, записанных в обращении учредительного с"езда к Верховному Совету Украины.

Отсутствие военного законодательства Украины потребовало привлечения к процессу создания проектов законов широкого круга творческих сил. В первую очередь для этой сложной и

[Translation from Russian; sheet 2, *continues*]

2

[…] Ukraine it has indeed been a revolutionary period, which has decades of [national] awakening compressed into it.

The establishment of the Union of Officers of Ukraine was the sounding of an alarm that awoke Ukraine and shook and confused the conservative camp. The Constituent Congress catalyzed the forces that attempted the coup. Those August events demonstrated that Ukraine was totally unprotected in the face of anti-constitutional actions that sought to violently change the government by using the armed forces stationed on the territory of Ukraine.

The Ukrainian leadership had no information regarding the intentions and actions of the army. There is something wrong when a sovereign state finds itself in such a situation.

Under the threat of mortal danger, with democracy in the balance, the Supreme Soviet of Ukraine adopted the Act of Independence of Ukraine and made a series of resolutions, directing the government to begin work toward establishing a Ukrainian national armed forces and national guard, fulfilling in that way one of the demands of the Officers' Union that was included in the Constituent Congress' address to the Parliament of Ukraine.

The absence of [previous republic-level] military legislation in Ukraine required drawing on a wide circle of creative forces while drafting such legislation. Representatives of the Union of Officers of Ukraine were the first to be invited to participate in that complicated and weighty work. […]

3

ответственной работы были приглашены представители Союза офицеров Украины.

Следует отметить, что эта группа офицеров с честью выполнила поставленную задачу, существенно повысив авторитет вашей организации на Украине. Это офицеры Говоруха, Козырь, Пилипчук, Мельник, Лазоркин, Костюк, Кузнецов, Скипальский и другие.

Был подготовлен пакет проектов основных законов военного строительства Украины, составляющий юридическую основу для создания Министерства обороны Украины и его дальнейшей работы по строительству Вооруженных Сил Украины и Республиканской гвардии. Хочу выразить благодарность Союзу офицеров за большую помощь в этом важном и ответственном деле.

Весь пакет проекта законов был принят Верховным Советом в первом чтении. Сейчас идет подготовка этих законов для окончательного рассмотрения и принятия.

Параллельно с законотворчеством идет процесс формирования Министерства обороны Украины. Правительство Украины делает все возможное, чтобы создание Вооруженных Сил проходило цивилизованным путем.

Однако этот процесс наталкивается на сопротивление консервативных сил бывшего Союза.

Из Москвы в войска идут распоряжения всячески тормозить создание на Украине собственных Вооруженных Сил.

[Translation from Russian; sheet 3, *conclusion*]

3

[…] We must remark on how this group of officers accomplished with honor what was necessary, significantly raising the authority of your organization in Ukraine. Those officers are: Govorukha, Kozyr, Pilipchuk, Melnik, Lazorkin, Kostiuk, Kuznetsov, Skipalskii, and others.

A package of basic laws on military building in Ukraine, which created the underlying basis for the establishment of the Ministry of Defense of Ukraine and its future work on building the Ukrainian Armed Forces and National Guard, was prepared. I would like to express my gratitude to the Union of Officers of Ukraine for its significant help in that important and responsible matter.

The entire package of draft laws was accepted by the Parliament in its first reading. Now, the package is being prepared for final review and a vote to make it law.

Parallel to the legislative process, the process of establishing the Ministry of Defense of Ukraine is now under way. The Government of Ukraine is doing everything possible to establish the Ministry of Defense of Ukraine in an orderly manner.

However, this process is running into resistance by the conservative forces of the former [*sic*] [Soviet] Union.

Moscow sends orders to the troops to hinder in every way the creation of the Ukrainian Armed Forces.

10. *Letter from Minister of Defense Morozov to President Leonid Kravchuk Proposing New Commanders for the Kyiv, Carpathian, and Odesa Military Districts (January 27, 1992)* [1 sheet]

ПРЕЗИДЕНТУ УКРАИНЫ

КРАВЧУКУ Л.М.

Уважаемый Леонид Макарович!

В соответствии с решением Совета обороны Украины от 23 января 1992 года об освобождении от обязанностей Командующих войсками военных округов генерал-полковников Чечеватова В.С., Морозова И.С., Скокова В.В.,

представляю к назначению на должности Командующих войсками Киевского военного округа генерал-лейтенанта Борискина В.Д., Одесского военного округа генерал-лейтенанта Радецкого В.Г., Прикарпатского военного округа генерал-лейтенанта Степанова В.М.

Кандидатуры рассмотрены на заседании Комиссии Верховного Совета Украины по вопросам обороны и государственной безопасности. Предложения поддержаны.

Министр обороны Украины
генерал-полковник

К.МОРОЗОВ

"27" января 1992 года

24.I.92г.

[Translation from Russian]

[*Handwritten*:] L. Kravchuk

TO THE PRESIDENT OF UKRAINE
L. M. KRAVCHUK

Esteemed Leonid Makarovych!

Pursuant to the Resolution of the Defense Council of Ukraine as of January 23, 1992, on relieving from their duties as military district Commanders Colonels General V. S. Chechevatov, I. S. Morozov, V. V. Skokov,

I hereby present for appointment as Kyiv Military District Commander Lieutenant General V. D. Boriskin, as Odesa Military District Commander Lieutenant General V. G. Radetskyi, as Carpathian Military District Commander Lieutenant General V. G. Stepanov.

These candidates were reviewed at the meeting of the Committee on National Security and Defense of the Ukrainian Parliament. They were approved.

Defense Minister of Ukraine
Colonel General   (Signed) K. MOROZOV

January 27, 1992

[*Handwritten*:]
V. Durdynets'
01-27-92

11. *Information Regarding the Progress of the Oath of Loyalty to the Ukrainian People (January 30, 1992)* [1 sheet]

СПРАВКА
о ходе принятия военной присяги на верность народу Украины
30 января 1992 г.

Категория и количество военнослужащих приведенных к присяге	Ш.и Упр. МО	Сухопутные войска			Объединения, соединения и части ВВС и ЗА войск				8 ОА ПВО	2 ... ПВС	Т	Соед.и части непоср. подчин. МО	Всего за Вооруженные Силы Украины
		КВО	ОдВО	ПрикВО	17 ВА	14 ВА	5 ВА	24 ВА					
Приняло военную присягу. ВСЕГО	259	54970	31167	70804	23807	9120	3401	8774	27305	9268	422	68356	310595
- в % запланированному		63%	68%	75%	75%	65%	63%	65%	66%	84%	-	92%	73%
в т.ч.-офицеров,пр-к, св.сл.,женщин	259	17971	12861	26540	12868	5654	2015	6643	11773	2119	246	29129	128893
- солдат, сержантов		36999	18286	44264	12939	3466	786	1871	16032	7649	176	39229	131687
Отказалось принять присягу. ВСЕГО		6184	8550	10270	2945	3315	1565	2494	7001	1949	-	9714	53987
- в % /процентах/		10%	27%	11%	11%	27%	32%	19%	20%	20%	-	12%	19%
в т.ч.-офицеров,пр-к, св.сл.,женщин		727	1229	1600	243	637	350	759	1632	279	-	1120	8626
- солдат, сержантов		5457	7321	8670	2702	2678	1215	1735	5319	1670	-	8594	45361
Спланировано принятие присяги, дата ВСЕГО:	3.2-16.2	3.2-16.2	3.2-4.3	3.2-15.2	3.2-4.3	3.02-10.2	3.02-12.2	10.2-15.2	3.02-12.2	10.2-15.2		10.2-20.2	3.2-4.3
в т.ч.-офицеров,пр-к, свсл., женщин	14208	727	2667	2535	395	261	121	793	971	1180		3740	3113
- солдат, сержантов	9449	4760	1145	1744	1379	142	140	502	342	80		270	13216
			1542	2159	1156	253			539	1100		1030	17900

Примечание: в графе соединения и части непосредственного подчинения МО включены - ВУЗы, военные кафедры, части и учреждения типа МО, военные строители.

И.О. НАЧАЛЬНИКА ГЛАВНОГО ШТАБА ВООРУЖЕННЫХ СИЛ УКРАИНЫ
ГЕНЕРАЛ-МАЙОР   Г.ЖИВИЦА

256

[Translation from Russian]

Information Regarding the Progress of the Oath of Loyalty to the Ukrainian People (January 30, 1992)

Category and Quantity of Soldiers Who Have Been Administered the Oath	General Staff, Direct. of Min. of Defense	Army Groups			Air Force, Air Defense Forces, and Railroad Forces Groups, Detachments, and Units						Black Sea Fleet	Detachments and Units subordinated to the Min. of Def.	*Total* for the Ukrainian Armed Forces
		Kyiv Mil. Dist.	Odesa Mil. Dist.	Carpathian Mil. Dist.	17th Air Army	14th Air Army	5th Air Army	24th Air Army	8th ADF Group	2nd RRF Group			
Those who have taken the oath. *Total*	259	54,970	31,167	70,804	25,807	9,120	3,401	8,714	27,805	9,768	422	68,358	310,595
as a % of the plan	—	68%	68%	75%	75%	65%	63%	65%	68%	84%	—	92%	73%
number of officers, warrant officers, active duty (cadre) officers, women	259	17,971	12,881	26,540	12,868	5,654	2,615	6,843	11,773	2,119	246	29,129	128,898
enlisted ranks and sergeants	—	36,999	18,286	44,264	12,939	3,466	786	1,871	16,032	7,649	176	39,229	181,697
Those who have refused the oath. *Total*	—	6,184	8,550	10,270	2,945	3,315	1,565	2,494	7,001	1,949	—	9,714	53,987
as a % of total number	—	10%	27%	11%	11%	27%	32%	19%	20%	20%	—	12%	19%
number of officers, warrant officers, active duty (cadre) officers, women	—	727	1,229	1,600	243	637	350	759	1,682	279	—	1,120	8,626
enlisted ranks and sergeants	—	5,457	7,321	8,670	2,702	2,678	1,215	1,735	5,319	1,670	—	8,594	45,361
Planned dates for future oath administration	—	Feb. 3 – Feb. 16	by March 1	by Feb. 15	by March 1	Feb. 3 – Feb. 10	Feb. 3 – Feb. 12	by Feb. 15	Feb. 3 – Feb. 12	by Feb. 15		Feb. 18 – Feb. 20	
TOTAL [to be administered]:		14,209	2,687	3,903	2,535	395	261	1,295	911	1,180		3,740	31,116
number of officers, warrant officers, active duty (cadre) officers, women		4,760	1,145	1,744	1,379	142	121	793	342	80		2,710	13,216
enlisted ranks and sergeants		9,449	1,542	2,159	1,156	253	140	502	569	1,100		1,030	17,900

Note: in the graph detachments and units that are directly subordinated to the Ministry of Defense include: Schools, Departments of Military Science in universities, units and institutions of the logistical command and Quartermaster of the MoD, and engineering brigades.

FOR THE HEAD OF THE GENERAL STAFF OF THE ARMED FORCES OF UKRAINE

MAJ. GEN. [Signature] G. Zhivitsa

12. *Decree of the President of Ukraine Regarding the Return to Ukraine for the Continuation of Their Service of Those Servicemen-Citizens of Ukraine from Military Units Located on the Territories of Azerbaijan, Armenia, and Moldova (March 24, 1992)* [1 sheet]

У К А З

Президента України

Про повернення в Україну для проходження служби
військовослужбовців - громадян України із військових
частин, дислокованих на території Азербайджану,
Вірменії та Молдови

На виконання Закону України "Про Збройні Сили України"
п о с т а н о в л я ю:

I. Кабінету Міністрів України:

а/ забезпечити повернення в Україну з Азербайджану, Вірменії та Молдови військовослужбовців - громадян України з урахуванням їх бажання служити на території своєї держави:

- військовослужбовців строкової служби - до 20 травня 1992 року;

- офіцерів і прапорщиків - протягом 1992-1993 років в індивідуальному порядку та за узгодженням між Головним управлінням кадрів Об"єднаних Збройних Сил держав Співдружності і Управлінням кадрів Міністерства оборони України;

б/ направити в Азербайджан, Вірменію та Молдову делегації за участю представників Міністерства оборони України, Комітету з питань соціального захисту військовослужбовців і Комітету солдатських матерів для проведення переговорів з керівниками урядів і командуванням Збройних Сил цих держав з питань повернення військовослужбовців в Україну.

2. Міністерству оборони України забезпечити перевезення в Україну військовослужбовців з місць дислокації їх частин в Азербайджані, Вірменії та Молдові, в тому числі й з використанням військово-транспортної авіації.

3. Указ набуває чинності з дня його підписання.

Президент України   Л.КРАВЧУК

м. Київ
24 березня 1992 року
№ 189

258

[Translation from Ukrainian]

DECREE
of the President of Ukraine

Regarding the Return to Ukraine for the Continuation of their Service
of Those Serviceman-Citizens of Ukraine from Military Units Located
on the Territories of Azerbaijan, Armenia, and Moldova

In order to execute the Act of Ukraine On the Ukrainian Armed Forces, I
hereby *decree:*

1. That the Cabinet of Ministers of Ukraine is charged with the following:

a) To secure the return of the military personnel who are citizens of Ukraine,
from Azerbaijan, Armenia, and Moldova, taking into consideration their desire to
serve on the territory of their country:

—enlisted personnel—by May 20, 1992;

—officers and warrant officers—during the years 1992–1993 on a case-by-case
basis, as well as in agreement with the Main Personnel Department of the Commonwealth of Independent States Unified Armed Forces and the Personnel Department of the Defense Ministry of Ukraine;

b) To dispatch delegations, consisting of the representatives of the Defense
Ministry of Ukraine, Committee on the Social Welfare of Military Personnel, and
Committee of Soldiers' Mothers to Azerbaijan, Armenia, and Moldova to conduct
negotiations with the leadership and the armed forces command of the respective
states on the issues of returning the military personnel to Ukraine.

2. The Defense Ministry of Ukraine is to secure transit of the military personnel
to Ukraine from their units, stationed/deployed in Azerbaijan, Armenia, and
Moldova, including engagement of the military cargo aviation/aircraft.

3. This Decree becomes effective on the date of is signing.

Chairperson,
the Parliament of Ukraine   L. KRAVCHUK

(SEAL)
City of Kyiv
March 24, 1992
No. 189

(STAMPED:)
Number of Pages: 1   Entry # 686/3
03/26/1992
Defense Ministry of Ukraine
Executive Office

13. *Decree of the President of Ukraine Regarding Urgent Measures Concerning the Establishment and Building of the Armed Forces of Ukraine (April 5, 1992)* [2 sheets]

У К А З

Президента Украины

О неотложных мерах по строительству Вооруженных Сил

Украины

Во исполнение Закона Украины "О Вооруженных Силах Украины" и постановления Верховного Совета Украины от 24 августа 1991 года "О воинских формированиях в Украине", а также в связи с вмешательством руководства Российской Федерации и Главного Командования Об"единенными Вооруженными Силами Содружества во внутренние дела Украины и обострением вследствие этого социально-политической обстановки в войсках, расположенных на территории Украины и не включенных в состав Вооруженных Сил Украины, отсутствием должного управления войсками п о с т а н о в л я ю:

I. Подчинить Министерству обороны Украины все воинские формирования, дислоцированные на территории Украины и не указанные в статье I Указа Президента Украины от I2 декабря 1991 года "О Вооруженных Силах Украины".

Стратегические ядерные силы, дислоцированные на территории Украины на период до их полного разукомплектования, передать в оперативное подчинение Командующему Стратегическими Силами Государств Содружества для обеспечения единого контроля над ядерным оружием, порядок осуществления которого регулируется специальным соглашением.

2. Сформировать Военно-Морские Силы Украины на базе сил Черноморского флота, дислоцируемых на территории Украины.

Министерству обороны Украины приступить к формированию органов управления Военно-Морскими Силами Украины, согласовав с Главнокомандующим Об"единенными Вооруженными Силами Государств Содружества перечень кораблей и частей Черноморского флота, которые временно передаются в оперативное подчинение командованию Стратегическими Силами Государств Содружества.

[Translation from Russian; sheet 1, *continues*]

DECREE
of the President of Ukraine

On Urgent Measures for Establishing and Building
the Ukrainian Armed Forces

Pursuant to the Law of Ukraine "On the Ukrainian Armed Forces" and the decree of the Supreme Soviet of Ukraine "On Military Formations in Ukraine" of August 24, 1991, as well as in connection with the interference of the Russian Federation leadership and the Commonwealth Unified Armed Forces Chief Command in Ukrainian internal affairs that has led to a heightened tension of the social and political situation among the troops stationed on the territory of Ukraine who are not included in the Commonwealth Unified Armed Forces, as well as the lack of proper control over said troops I hereby *decree:*

1. That all military units stationed on the territory of Ukraine and not included in Article 1 of the Presidential Decree as of December 12, 1991 "On the Ukrainian Armed Forces" be placed under the authority of the Defense Ministry of Ukraine.

Strategic nuclear forces stationed on the territory of Ukraine for the duration of their complete dismantling are to be transferred to the operational command of the Commonwealth of States Strategic Forces Commander to provide unitary control over the nuclear armament, the order of implementation of which is governed by a special agreement.

2. That a Ukrainian navy on the basis of the Black Sea Fleet forces be established and stationed on the territory of Ukraine.

The Ministry of Defense of Ukraine is to commence establishing command structures of the Navy of Ukraine, upon having confirmed with the Commonwealth of States Strategic Forces Commander the list of the Black Sea Fleet vessels and units that have been temporarily transferred to the operational command of the Commonwealth States' Strategic Forces Command. [...]

2

3. Министру обороны Украины организовать непосредственное /для Стратегических Сил — административное/ управление всеми войсками, дислоцированными на территории Украины, обеспечить их постоянную боевую готовность и поддержание воинской дис- циплины.

4. Указ довести до воинских частей, учреждений и об"явить всему личному составу.

5. Указ вступает в силу со дня его подписания.

 Президент України   Л.КРАВЧУК

г.К и е в

05 апреля 1992 года

№ 209

[Translation from Russian; sheet 2, *conclusion*]

2

3. The minister of defense of Ukraine is to organize direct (for the Strategic Forces—administrative) command over all the troops stationed on the territory of Ukraine, to provide for their permanent combat readiness, and to maintain military discipline.

4. This Decree is to be delivered to all military units, institutions, and announced to all personnel [in the Ukrainian Armed Forces].

5. This Decree becomes effective on the date it is signed.

President of Ukraine   L. KRAVCHUK

(SEAL)
City of Kyiv
April 5, 1992
No. 209

Editorial Notes

(*to page*)

1   Marshal of Aviation Yevgeny Ivanovich Shaposhnikov was the commander of the air force of the USSR. In August 1991 he supported Boris Yeltsin in the struggle against the State Committee for the State of Emergency (SCSE), that is those that had attempted a putsch to oust Mikhail Gorbachev. He went on to become the minister of defense of the USSR and later, when the Russian Federation declared its own armed forces, he became the commander of the Strategic Forces of the CIS.

2   Of course, Morozov and Shaposhnikov spoke in Russian and the latter used the Russian form of Morozov's name and patronymic. Russian was the lingua franca of the Soviet military.

5   For the periods from 1935 to 1958 and 1970 to 1990, Luhansk city was called Voroshylovhrad (*Rus.* Voroshilovgrad) after the Soviet Marshal Kliment Voroshilov, a native of the region and war hero during the Civil War and World War II. He was a staunch Stalinist, which explains the twelve-year interval when his name was dropped from the city during the Soviet period. Luhansk Oblast was formed in 1938 and underwent the same name changes.

18   The two Soviet higher military aviation schools in the Ukrainian SSR—commonly considered the best in the USSR for fighter pilot training—were located in Chernihiv and Kharkiv (the Chernihiv Higher Military Aviation School for Pilots, named for Lenin's Komsomol; and the Kharkiv Higher Military Aviation School for Pilots, named for S. I. Gritsevets). Others existed in the USSR, but the two schools in Ukraine were considered to be the best. There were other specialized higher military schools serving the air force, especially for pilots of transport planes, helicopters, and bombers. Sergei Ivanovich Gritsevets (1909–1939) was a fighter ace from the Brest region of Belarus. He had a total of thirty kills in the Spanish Civil War (the most of any pilot in combat there) and another twelve against the Japanese while in action in the Battle of Khalkin Gol in

(*to page*)

the Soviet Far East in 1939. He was the first person to receive the order of "Hero of the Soviet Union" twice. He was killed in action by Japanese forces in September, 1939.

27   Perestroika (*Ukr. perebudova*), literally "rebuilding," was a Communist Party-directed movement to allow greater social initiative in structuring economic relations in the USSR. Some elements of perestroika were reminiscent of Stalinist initiatives—for example, trying to motivate workers psychologically to achieve greater productivity, increasing volunteerism, and so forth. Other aspects of perestroika sought to loosen somewhat the central strictures of the Party-driven command economy. Mikhail Gorbachev, general secretary of the Communist Party of the USSR and initiator of perestroika, complemented it with a policy of greater social openness, called glasnost. In Gorbachev's conception, glasnost was to create the personal and social initiative that economic restructuring would need. He did not see glasnost as an end in itself.

37   Centered in Ashkhabad (Ashgabat), Turkmenistan, the 1948 earthquake killed almost 20,000 people. The 1966 earthquake left some 300,000 people homeless in Tashkent alone.

38   Under Russian domination since the late nineteenth century, Turkmenistan became a constituent republic of the Soviet Union in 1925. It declared its independence from the USSR on October 27, 1991, and became an independent state when the USSR was officially dissolved in December of that year. About ninety percent of the republic is desert and sparsely populated.

39   The Amu Darya River was known in ancient times as the Oxus River, which formed the southern border of Bactria. Alexander the Great conquered this region in 329 BC.

40   Sharaf R. Rashidov became first secretary of the Central Committee of the Communist Party of the Uzbek SSR in 1959. He reintroduced clan-based politics and maintained a notoriously corrupt power structure there. He was one of the early targets of the anti-corruption movement begun by Andropov in 1983 that focused on Central Asia. Soon after he was condemned and marked from removal from his Uzbek and USSR posts, he died, under mysterious circumstances in late 1983, of what was officially called a heart attack. In the post-

(to page)

independence period an official cult of Rashidov has been promoted, focusing on his ability to bilk the central Soviet government of several billion dollars for Uzbekistan and remaining faithful to the country's clan system during the Soviet period. Mukhamednazar Gapurov became first secretary of the Central Committee of the Communist Party of Turkmen SSR in 1969 and likewise was notoriously corrupt. He was forced to retire in December 1982.

61 One small step toward rectifying that situation was taken by holding a conference on the Ukrainian military tradition at Harvard University in 1994. The conference proceedings are included in the bibliography.

65 For a discussion of ethnicities in the military from the time of the Imperial army in World War I, see Teresa Rakowska-Harmstone, Christopher D. Jones, John Jaworsky, Ivan Sylvain, and Zoltan Barany, *Warsaw Pact: The Question of Cohesion*, vol. 3, pp. 13–30.

65 *Bahlai* is the Ukrainian form of a last name. *Baglaev* is its Russian counterpart.

66 In Soviet military parlance (in Russian), an *attestatsiia*, "attestation," roughly corresponds to a U.S. military promotion board. Many parts of the Soviet governmental structure used an annual *attestatsiia* as a means of making sure that an individual was "reliable." Party fidelity (*partiinost'*) was used as a means of controlling individuals threatened by the specter of the review and accreditation process. Conformity was thereby assured.

69 *Nomenklatura* refers to actual lists of positions in various parts of the Communist Party and societal life that were to be strictly controlled by the Party. Those that held such positions wielded greater authority and privilege than others. The term came to designate the part of the political apparatus that controlled society and its economic and security assets.

71 The bathhouse was a focal point in Soviet society, with each social level enjoying its own version of the luxury. It consisted of a sauna, baths, and areas for relaxation. By tradition, one takes a sauna, flagellates oneself with beech or oak branches, then plunges headlong into a tub of ice-cold water. Drinking good vodka and eating fine foods constitute a major part of the ritual. Quite ornate and well-appointed,

(*to page*)

the bathhouses for the upper nomenklatura are the social equivalents of private country clubs in the United States.

77 Dudayev strongly sympathized with the local drive for autonomy and independence. In 1989, he even allowed the Estonian national flag to be raised.

77 The situation was complicated. Chechnya was part of a larger administrative unit called the Chechen-Ingush Autonomous Republic. Doku Zavgayev was the last chairman of its supreme soviet in 1989. Also in 1989 the National Congress of the Chechen People (or Chechen All-National Congress), a popular front, met for the first time. Dudayev eventually became the leader of its Executive Committee and used that body to supplant the old administrative structures of the republic by the end of 1991, after what was effectively a coup in September of that year. He was elected president of the new Chechen Republic in elections in October 1991. Yeltsin tried to send in the troops, but was soundly repulsed by Dudayev's "National Guard." This further enhanced Dudayev's reputation in the general population. The split of Chechnya and Ingushetia was formalized by the federal government of the Russian Federation in 1992. Dudayev lead Chechen resistance forces successfully against Russian Federation troops in the war of 1994–1996. He was killed by Soviet forces in a missile attack in April 1996.

78 The word *samizdat* came into English from the Russian, where it means 'self published'; the Ukrainian term is *samvydav,* with the same meaning. It refers both to actual physical objects and a phenomenon of intellectual resistance to and dissent from the official order. Samizdat literature usually circulated in handwritten or mimeographed copies that were carefully hidden from authorities.

78 Most of western Ukraine was part of the Second Polish Republic before 1939. That year, the Soviet Union invaded under the terms of the Molotov-Ribbentrop Non-Aggression Pact between Stalin and Hitler. The Nazis attacked and took the region in 1941, when hostilities between the Nazis and Soviets broke out. The Soviets retook the area starting in 1944. All throughout this time there were various insurgencies, counter-insurgencies, and massive atrocities on all sides, compounded by the horrors of the Holocaust and Nazi slave

(*to page*)

labor drives. At the end of the war there were ethnic cleansing operations on both sides of the new Soviet-Polish frontier. Memories of the period are still raw among inhabitants of the region.

78   Drach actually played a rather ambiguous role during the 1970s. Maintaining his role as an "official" writer, he continued to be published in spite of his association with dissidents during the late 1960s and early 1970s. Pavlychko also was not part of the dissident movement, but a prominent figure within the official, state-sponsored writers' organization.

81   Petr Grigorenko (*Ukr.* Petro Hryhorenko) (1907–1987) was a Soviet major general (*Rus. general maior,* equivalent of a U.S. brigadier general). From the early 1960s, he championed various dissident causes, especially the cause of the deported Crimean Tatars, who demanded that they be allowed to return to their homeland following Stalin's death. He was committed to psychiatric prisons from 1964 to 1965 and again from 1969 to 1974. While in the United States for medical treatment, he was stripped of his Soviet citizenship, effectively exiling him. His memoirs appeared in several languages.

81   Sablin (1939–1977) ostensibly sought to defect from the USSR to Sweden, although it was rumored that he intended to sail to Leningrad as a sign of rebellion against the Soviet system. The mutiny was quelled, and Sablin was captured and court-martialed. Eventually he was executed by military authorities. The story of his mutiny inspired Tom Clancy to write *The Hunt for Red October.*

87   The Popular Movement of Ukraine (Narodnyi Rukh Ukraïny; called simply "Rukh"), began in 1989 as the Popular Movement for Perestroika in Ukraine, and was as much an intellectual and cultural movement as a political movement. Among its founders were Ivan Drach, Dmytro Pavlychko, Mykhailo Horyn, Viacheslav Chornovil, Yurii Kostenko, Ivan Zaiets, and Viacheslav Briukhovetskyi. The movement was instrumental in shaping politics in the early part of the 90s and advocated for the government to declare independence, maintain and independent standing army, adopt pro-Western, market-oriented policies, and to ensure the dominant role of the Ukrainian language and culture in a multi-ethnic, multi-confessional state. Originally it acted as an umbrella organization to support pro-de-

(*to page*)

mocracy political parties, but in 1992 it was transformed into a formal political party under Chornovil. The party lost popularity over the decade and has since split into two factions, one headed by Yurii Kostenko and the other by former foreign minister Hennadii Udovenko.

88 The Ukrainian Public Group to Promote the Implementation of the Helsinki Accords (called the "Ukrainian Helsinki Group") was formed on November 9, 1976. The group's aim was to ensure Soviet adherence to the Helsinki Accords that the USSR had signed in 1975. The group used the Accords' emphasis on human rights to publicize current and past Soviet violations of Ukrainians' human rights. The central government responded with massive reprisals against the Group's members. One of its founders, the poet Vasyl Stus, was sent to the GULag and was the last political prisoner during the Soviet period to die during his incarceration. The group became an important conduit for information and contacts between Ukraine and the West regarding human rights in the Ukrainian SSR.

91 The Novo-Ogarevo negotiations were conceived as a *process*, initiated on April 23, 1991 at a government dacha in Novo Ogarevo, near Moscow. Negotiations continued during the next few months as the parties attempted to work on the text of a new Union treaty. Gorbachev attempted to revive the Novo-Ogarevo process after the coup attempt, but failed. Representatives of nine of the fifteen republics attended (the Baltic republics and Georgia had already declared themselves independent states, and Armenia and Moldova boycotted the talks). In the negotiations Gorbachev made a number of concessions to the republics, much to the displeasure of conservative Communists.

94 Examples of the Committee's priorities, often expressed in its official statements or displayed, in a modified form, on placards at demonstrations, include:

- *Create a professional, depoliticized Ukrainian army.*
- *Recall all Ukrainians serving in "hot spots" of inter-ethnic conflict throughout the USSR (especially the Caucasus region).*
- *Ensure that Ukrainian citizens serve only in Ukraine.*

(*to page*)

- *Prosecute officers who tolerate or even encourage hooliganism, abusive hazing (Ukr.* didivshchyna, *Rus.* dedovshchina*), and other forms of mistreatment of conscripts.*
- *Reduce the term of service for conscripts.*
- *Improve living conditions and medical care facilities for officers and conscripts.*

For more information on the Committee, see Bohdan Pyskir, "Mothers for a Fatherland: Ukrainian Statehood, Motherhood and National Security."

96   There is no consistent information on suicides and other "non-combat" deaths within the Soviet armed forces. However, according to Odom (*The Collapse of the Soviet Military,* p. 293), in December, 1990, Marshal Yazov told a closed meeting of officers that about 500 conscripts had committed suicide in 1990, while 69 officers and 32 NCOs had been murdered. In June, 1990, the soldiers' mothers movement announced that some 15,000 soldiers had died over the preceding four or five years. Presumably the Committee of Soldiers' Mothers was not restricted to "mothers," but they were certainly the only activists within this organization. See Pyskir, "Mothers for a Fatherland."

98   According to Barylski, *The Soldier in Russian Politics,* p. 101, Aviation Day (he calls it Soviet Air Power Day) occurred on Sunday, August 18. However, the context of Morozov's description makes it clear that the observation of the holiday included the entire weekend.

98   Shaposhnikov had been promoted from colonel general to marshal of aviation when he was appointed commander in chief of the Soviet air force in 1989.

100   Marshal Dmitrii T. Yazov, the Soviet minister of defense at the time, was one of the coup leaders. He was not a charismatic figure, and was popularly described in the post-coup press as being either incapable of or unwilling to adapt to the changes in Soviet society under Gorbachev. He was arrested and dismissed on August 21, 1991.

115   The practice of broadcasting a ballet or concert at times of crisis, such as the death of the country's leader, was a standard Soviet tradition. The airwaves would be dominated by somber classical music to underline the gravity of the occasion.

(*to page*)

116   On August 18, 1991, the eight members of the State Committee for the State of Emergency declared that President Gorbachev could no longer fulfill his duties because of ill health. The leaders of the coup were: Gennadii Yanaev, vice president of the USSR; Valentin Pavlov, prime minister of the USSR; Oleg Baklanov, first deputy chairman of the Defense Council; Marshal Dmitrii Yazov, the minister of defense of the USSR; Boris Pugo, head of the Ministry of Internal Affairs; Vladimir Kriuchkov, chairman of the KGB; Aleksandr Tiziakov, president of the Association of State Industries; and Vasilii Starodubtsev, chairman of the Union of Peasants. For a discussion of military developments before, during, and after the coup attempt, see Odom, *The Collapse of the Soviet Military*, pp. 305–46, and Staar, *The New Military in Russia*, pp. 2–9.

116   These included an aviation-technical school at Vasylkiv, engineering schools in Kyiv and Kharkiv, flight schools in Chernihiv and Kharkiv, a radio electronics (aviation signal) school in Kharkiv, a navigation school in Luhansk, and a command and general staff school in Baherovo, Crimea. Of the twenty-six aviation-related military schools in the USSR, eight were in Ukraine.

123   Prior to the coup, Varennikov was one of the senior military officials responsible for maintaining "domestic order" within the boundaries of the USSR and putting down "nationalist" unrest in the Baltic states and the Caucasus region. During the coup Varennikov was deputy minister of defense and commander of Soviet ground forces. As a possible signal of the putsch to come, Varennikov had signed his name to a letter that was highly critical of Gorbachev (although not mentioning Gorbachev by name) in July 1991 in *Sovetskaia Rossiia*. He apparently behaved in a very rude fashion during his encounters with Gorbachev (August 18) and Kravchuk (August 19). After the coup he was retired as part of the post-coup purge of the military. In the mid-1990s he was active in the Communist Party of the Russian Federation, continuing to fight for a strong Russian state and for the economic and military reintegration of most of the former Soviet republics.

132   On August 24, Gorbachev resigned as general secretary of the Communist Party and dissolved its central committee.

(to page)

133 The figure most frequently mentioned is approximately 750,000 military personnel on Ukraine's territory in August, 1991, although other estimates range as high as one million. These discrepancies can be attributed, in part, to the fact that personnel in other military-type formations—border troops, internal security troops, railway troops, and the like—are not included in the lower estimate.

133 In his *Ukraine: Nuclear Weapons Capability Rising*, Lt. Com. Martin DeWing estimates a total of 1,768 nuclear warheads on Ukrainian soil at the time of independence. These included 1,240 warheads on MIRVed and non-MIRVed ICBMs, 21 Tu-95 "Bear H" strategic bombers carrying 16 AS-15s each, and 16 Tu-160 "Blackjack" bombers carrying 12 AS-15s each.

134 Following the parliamentary elections of March 4, 1990, over one hundred deputies (primarily those of a nationalist or national-democratic persuasion) formally organized themselves into a parliamentary opposition known as the Narodna Rada, or People's Council.

135 Muliava greatly helped Morozov during the fall of 1991 in preparing the groundwork for the establishment of the Ukrainian armed forces (UAF). From late 1991 to late 1993, he headed the controversial Social-Psychological Service of the UAF, and from October, 1992 until October, 1998, he was the controversial leader ("hetman") of the Ukrainian Cossack movement.

138 On August 24 the Presidium decided to confiscate the CPU's buildings and freeze its assets. On August 26, after more evidence of the CPU's complicity in the attempted coup emerged, the Presidium decided to "temporarily suspend the Party's activities."

139 Translation courtesy of *The Ukrainian Weekly* (Parsipanny, NJ). Reproduced with permission.

150 Vasyl V. Durdynets (1943–), was a Komsomol and Party activist, deputy and first deputy minister for internal affairs of Ukraine, an MP, head of the standing committee of the Parliament on state defense and security, vice-prime minister for state security and emergencies, and has stood on several anti-corruption committees. Yevhen K. Marchuk (1941–) rose through the ranks of the KGB of Ukraine and was the minister for defense, security, and emergenies

(*to page*)

from June 1991 to September 1991. From November 1991 through July 1994 he was the head of the State Security Service of Ukraine. He was prime minister of Ukraine from June 1995 through May 1996. He continues to be a leading opposition candidate in the country. Oleksandr I. Yemets (1959–), has been an MP, the head of the Parliamentary Committee on Juridical Affairs, a presidential advisor on law and politics, minister of Nationalities and Migration, and vice-prime minister for political-juridical affairs.

154 It is difficult to get an accurate count for the forces disposition in Ukraine at that time. During Ukrainian negotiations with the Ministry of Defense of the USSR, the Ukrainian side was not able to get exact figures for forces disposition. The Soviet side claimed that it did not maintain separate figures for Ukraine as a whole.

156 Ukraine's leaders have, over the years, debated what to do with the strategic air force matériel inherited from the Soviet Union. During the 90s, various schemes arose to transfer strategic assets to Russia in exchange for debt relief or compensation from a third party (the U.S. according to the "Trilateral" scheme.) Eleven bombers finally were transferred to Russia in 1999 for over $280 million in debt relief, but the scheduled transfer of more bombers in 2000 remains controversial and also has encountered American disapproval. Others were scheduled for destruction, but the Ukrainian government balked when it felt the compensation offered from Western sources was too low. Some strategic aircraft remain in use with a non-strategic mission.

156 The General Staff of the Soviet armed forces functioned as the largest constituent body of the Soviet High Command and was immediately subordinated to the Main Military Council, which in turn was subordinated to the Council of Defense. The General Staff consisted of three sections and ten directorates. It represented the centralization of military command in Moscow. For a good overview, see Scott and Scott, *The Armed Forces of the USSR*, 3rd ed.

156 The UOU was formally established during its first (founding) congress in late July, 1991. However, prior to this several "underground" meetings had been held to discuss the UOU's formation. The initiative to create the UOU came from Rukh and, to a certain extent,

(*to page*)

from the Narodna Rada faction in Ukraine's Parliament. The UOU's organizational committee was chaired by Volodymyr Muliava. Another individual associated with its formation included the prominent parliamentarian and government official Oleksandr Ivanovych Yemets.

157 Vilen Martyrosian, an ethnic Armenian (whose wife is Ukrainian), was a colonel commanding a communications regiment stationed in or near Rivne when he was elected to the All-Union Congress of People's Deputies. In early 1992, his regiment was the first to take the oath of loyalty to Ukraine.

158 Prior to December, 1991, Ukraine, which was not formally recognized as an independent state, could not (at least formally) be said to have its own citizens. Also note that toward the end of the Soviet period, the armed forces began to station increasing numbers of junior personnel near their places of residence in order to coup with the severe housing shortages that it was then facing. This was amplified in many republics by internal political pressure to keep military conscripts within their native republics. See also above, in the text, p. 176.

165 Ivan Vasylovych Bizhan, who was born in 1941, graduated from the Voroshilov General Staff Academy of the Armed Forces of the USSR in 1982. Between 1982 and 1991, he commanded increasingly larger and more complex military units ranging from a division to a corps to an entire army. In 1987–1989, he was placed at the disposal of the commander of the 10th Main Administration of the General Staff of the USSR armed forces, and in 1991 he was appointed a deputy to the commander of the Main Operational Administration of the General Staff of the USSR armed forces, and transferred to Ukraine in December, 1991.

167 Ukrainian authorities had no experience of organizing such transfers. Financial/budgetary planning in Ukraine's armed forces was chaotic during the early period of its existence. Kravchuk apparently tried to ensure that funds were made available to Morozov and the military when he was persuaded of the importance of such funding, but it was done on an ad hoc basis. Funding for military needs and decreased under Morozov's successors.

(*to page*)

167 Other estimates put the number of officers stationed outside of Ukraine (mostly in Russia) who returned to Ukraine in 1992 as high as 33,000.

168 Volodymyr Mykhailovych Antonets was born in 1945. He completed studies at the Voroshilov Academy of the General Staff of the Armed Forces of the USSR in 1991.

169 Mykola Mykolaiovych Horyn is the youngest of the three Horyn brothers from western Ukraine. Mykhailo and Bohdan Horyn played prominent roles in the dissident movement and served time as political prisoners. Mykola's main claim to fame was his term as head of the Lviv Oblast council. Stepan Antonovych Davymuka, was a Rukh member from 1989 on. In 1991, he was the first deputy chair of the Lviv Oblast executive committee, and between March, 1992 and July, 1994, he was the representative of the president of Ukraine for Lviv Oblast.

170 The usual figure one finds for the number of individuals who declined to take the oath of loyalty is 10,000 individuals. However, that number has been estimated as high as 13,000.

175 "First echelon" troops are military units expected to engage quickly in combat after a military engagement has begun. The Warsaw Pact units consisted of the Soviet troops stationed in the GDR and elsewhere in Warsaw Pact ally states, together with select units from those states. Ukraine played a crucial role as a staging ground for "second echelon" troops and their equipment, which were expected to move quickly into "first echelon" territory to supplement or replace those troops and equipment. At the same time, troops and equipment from outlying areas of the Soviet Union (for example, from Russia) were to move into Ukraine, where they would be transferred to the front. Such staging grounds are involved in quickly preparing large numbers of troops and military equipment for combat action. They are typically characterized by a heavy concentration of troops and a well-developed military infrastructure.

177 The three generals—Chechevatov, Skokov, and Ivan S. Morozov—were officially removed from their posts on January 27, 1992, after President Kravchuk issued the appropriate decree. Their removal

(*to page*)

was facilitated by the fact that at an important meeting on January 9, 1992 to discuss the challenges facing Ukraine's military, those three individuals failed to state their support clearly and unambiguously for Ukraine's independence and the formation of an independent Ukrainian military. General Skokov, who has remained in western Ukraine after his retirement, is a leading figure in the Russian community in Lviv. Admiral Mikhail Khronopulo of the Black Sea Fleet had been removed from his post much earlier—on September 17, 1991. Official sources in Moscow stated that he "retired" at his personal request and in connection with a deterioration of his health—the typical Soviet explanation. In truth, however, he was removed from his post because he was seen as playing an ambiguous role during the coup.

192 It is impossible to estimate the full cost of this assistance, but expenses were covered by the armed forces budget. In the case of military personnel who did not wish to take the oath of loyalty, Morozov personally drafted the memorandum to all military units in Ukraine directing them to provide whatever assistance was needed to help these people and their families leave Ukraine and return to their homelands.

197 Oleksandr Oleksandrovych Skipalskyi (1945–) was appointed to his position in the SBU in September, 1991. Prior to that appointment, he had served as a military counterintelligence officer in the Soviet armed forces. He resigned from the CPSU in October, 1990. Between October, 1992 and January, 1997 he was head of the Defense Ministry's main intelligence administration. He was also one of the first heads of the UOU. Hryhorii Omelianovych Omelchenko (1951–) was an officer in Soviet Ukraine's Ministry of Internal Affairs. A deputy in the current Parliament, he is well known as an anti-corruption activist.

References in the Notes and Suggestions for Further Reading

Barylski, Robert V. *The Soldier in Russian Politics: Duty, Dictatorship, and Democracy under Gorbachev and Yeltsin.* New Brunswick, NJ: Transaction, 1998.

Colton, Timothy J., and Thane Gustafson, eds. *Soldiers and the Soviet State: Civil-Military Relations from Brezhnev to Gorbachev.* Princeton: Princeton University Press, 1990.

DeWing, Martin. *Ukraine: Nuclear Weapons Capability Rising.* MA thesis, U.S. Naval Postgraduate School, Monterey, CA, 1993.

Hajda, Lubomyr, ed. *Ukraine in the World: Studies in the International Relations and Security Structure of a Newly Independent State.* Cambridge, MA: Harvard University Press for the Harvard Ukrainian Research Institute, 1998.

Garnett, Sherman W. *Keystone in the Arch: Ukraine in the Emerging Security Environment of Central and Eastern Europe.* Washington, DC: Carnegie Endowment for International Peace, 1997.

Morozov, Kostiantyn Petrovych, et al. *The Military Tradition in Ukraine: Its Role in the Construction of Ukraine's Armed Forces (Conference Proceedings, 12–13 May 1994).* Cambridge, MA: Harvard University Press for the Harvard Ukrainian Research Institute, 1995.

Odom, William E. *The Collapse of the Soviet Military.* New Haven: Yale University Press, 1998.

Pyskir, Bohdan. "Mothers for a Fatherland: Ukrainian Statehood, Motherhood and National Security." *The Journal of Slavic Military Studies* 7(1) March 1994: 50–66.

— . "The Silent Coup: The Building of Ukraine's Military." *European Security* 2(2) Spring 1993: 140–61.

Rakowska-Harmstone, Teresa, Christopher D. Jones, John Jaworsky, Ivan Sylvain, and Zoltan Barany. *Warsaw Pact: The Question of Cohesion.* 3 vols. Ottawa: Operational Research & Analysis Establishment, March, 1986.

Scott, Harriet Fast, and William F. Scott. *The Armed Forces of the USSR,* 3rd ed. Boulder, CO: Westview, 1984.

Staar, Richard F. *The New Military in Russia: Ten Myths that Shape the Image.* Annapolis: Naval Institute Press, 1996.

Szporluk, Roman. *Russia, Ukraine, and the Breakup of the Soviet Union.* Stanford: Hoover Institution Press, 2000.

Index*

---

*   In order to facilitate cross-referencing of Ukrainian and Russian personal names with other sources, the editors have included Cyrillic forms in those cases in which variant transliteration forms commonly exist in the literature. Transliterated forms that vary from the one given as the index head word are given after the Cyrillic forms. Numerals in italics indicate photographs or other illustrative material.

team-building activities, 164–72, 178–80

removing military commanders, 177, 248–49, 276–77

feeling of loneliness at the top, 181–83

blueprint for action, 183–88

Shaposhnikov attempts to pressure Ukrainian officials, 186–87

oath of allegiance, 188–93, 276

overcoming resistance of Ukrainian independence, 193–95

supporting Ukrainian independence and Ukrainian armed forces, 199–218

photographs:

age 18, after graduation from high school, *41*

cadet at Gritsevets Kharkiv Higher Military Aviation School (Fall 1963), *42*

first parachute jump, *42*

cadet, flying MiG-17 (1966), *43*

cadet, flying MiG-21 (1967), *44*

presenting sports award in Milovice, Czechoslovakia (1982), *47*

training exercise in Hungary (1983), *48*

conclusion of training exercise in Hungary (1983), *49*

in family portrait with wife and daughter (1986), *50*

standing with mother and wife (1987), *51*

commander of 17th Air Army (1990), *101*

with Shaposhnikov, taking part in a graduation ceremony (1991), *102*

reviewing a division, *103*

as Minister of Defense (1992), *104*

touring Pivdenmash factory

complex (1992), *105*

at Yavoriv Training Range (1992), *106*

near Chernivtsi in Carpathian Military District (1992), *107*

with Raisa near Konch Zaspa (1992), *108*

with General Shalikashvili of NATO (1992), *109*

Victory Day ceremonies (1993), *110*

with Commander of Ukrainian navy in Sevastopol (1993), *111*

checking plans for new uniforms with President Kravchuk (1993), *112*

with Secretary General Manfred Wörner of NATO (1992), *201*

with U.S. Secretary of Defense, Dick Cheney (1992), *202*

with wife and Major General Krawciw at Ukrainian-American community meeting, *203*

with wife and Roman Popadiuk, first U.S. Ambassador to Ukraine (1992), *204*

flying U.S. aircraft (1992), *205*

Ukrainian delegation at Nellis AFB (1992), *206*

at meeting to discuss Black Sea Fleet (1992), *207*

signing bilateral military accord with Poland (1993), *208*

at Pershotravneve missile complex (1993), *209*

signing bilateral military accord with Turkey (1993), *210*

observes the raising of Ukrainian flag at Norfolk Naval Base (1993), *211*

preparing memorandum of understanding with United States (1993), *212*

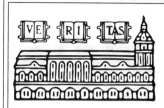

Ukrainian Research Institute
Harvard University
Selected Publications

The Military Tradition in Ukrainian History: Its Role in the Construction of Ukraine's Armed Forces. Kostiantyn P. Morozov, et al. Harvard Papers in Ukrainian Studies. Softcover, ISBN 0-916458-73-3.

Trophies of War and Empire: The Archival Heritage of Ukraine, World War II, and the International Politics of Restitution. Patricia Kennedy Grimsted. Harvard Papers in Ukrainian Studies. Softcover, ISBN 0-916458-76-8.

The Great Soviet Peasant War. Bolsheviks and Peasants, 1917–1933. Andrea Graziosi. Harvard Papers in Ukrainian Studies. Softcover, ISBN 0-916458-83-0.

Ukraine in the World: Studies in the International Relations and Security Structure of a Newly Independent State. Ed. Lubomyr A. Hajda. Harvard Papers in Ukrainian Studies. Softcover, ISBN 0-916458-83-0.

Cultures and Nations of Central and Eastern Europe: Essays in Honor of Roman Szporluk. Ed. Zvi Gitelman et al. HURI Publications. Softcover, ISBN 0-916458-93-8.

The Strategic Role of Ukraine: Diplomatic Addresses and Essays (1994–1997). Yuri Shcherbak. Harvard Papers in Ukrainian Studies. Softcover, ISBN 0-916458-85-7.

Carpatho-Ukraine in the Twentieth Century: A Political and Legal History. Vincent Shandor. HURI Publications. Clothbound, ISBN 0-916458-86-5.

Kistiakovsky: The Struggle for National and Constitutional Rights in the Last Years of Tsarism. Susan Heuman. Harvard Series in Ukrainian Studies. Clothbound, ISBN 0-916458-61-X.

To receive a free catalog of all Harvard Ukrainian Research Institute publications (including the journal *Harvard Ukrainian Studies*) please write, fax, or call to:

HURI Publications
1583 Massachusetts Avenue
Cambridge, MA 02138 USA
tel. 617-495-4053 *fax.* 617-495-8097
e-mail: huri@fas.harvard.edu
on-line catalog for HURI Publications: www.huri.harvard.edu

HURI Publications are distributed by Harvard University Press:
1-800-448-2242 (U.S. and Canada) 1-617-495-2242 (others)
e-mail: hup@harvard.edu
on-line catalog for HUP: www.hup.harvard.edu